Guide to

Disaster Recovery

Michael Erbschloe

THOMSON

™

COURSE TECHNOLOGY

Australia • Canada • Mexico • Singapore • Spain • United Kingdom • United States

THOMSON
™
COURSE TECHNOLOGY

Guide to Disaster Recovery
is published by Course Technology

Senior Editor:
William Pitkin III

Senior Editor:
Lisa Egan

Product Manager:
Amy M. Lyon

Developmental Editor:
Dan Seiter, The Software Resource

Production Editors:
Danielle Power, Brooke Booth

Technical Editor:
Randy Weaver

Manufacturing Coordinator:
Trevor Kallop

Product Marketing Manager:
Jason Sakos

Associate Product Managers:
Tim Gleeson, Nick Lombardi

Editorial Assistant:
Christy Urban

Cover Design:
Julie Malone

Text Designer:
GEX Publishing Services

Compositor:
GEX Publishing Services

Disclaimer
Course Technology reserves the right to revise this publication and make changes from time to time in its content without notice.

ISBN 0-619-13122-5

TABLE OF
Contents

Chapter 3

Chapter 6

Preface

This book shows students how to work through a step-by-step process to develop, implement, and manage a disaster recovery plan. Disaster recovery planning was once just good business sense, but it now has become a matter of national security as well. The terrorist attacks on the World Trade Center and the federal office building in Oklahoma City demonstrate how many organizations can be affected by a disaster, even if they aren't specifically targeted in an attack. In Oklahoma City, buildings for several blocks around the bombing were severely damaged. In New York City, at least 20 buildings were damaged badly enough that most occupants had to be relocated at least temporarily.

Since September 2001, the U.S. government has worked to establish the Department of Homeland Security. The FBI and other law enforcement and intelligence agencies warn of more attacks on the United States and its interests abroad. If these warnings prove true, the biggest disasters that organizations face in the future may be created by people, not forces of nature. The need for disaster recovery planning is accentuated by these circumstances, and is the reason this textbook was created.

To illustrate weaknesses in disaster recovery planning and perspectives, the book includes a survey of 254 planners and managers across 13 industries. The survey results were used to help emphasize critical aspects of disaster recovery planning that merit special attention. Survey respondents contended, for example, that documentation of disaster recovery plans and procedures needs to be improved in most organizations. Survey respondents also indicated that testing and rehearsing plans and procedures is a valuable process, but that not all organizations are emphasizing this aspect of planning.

The Intended Audience

This book is intended for students, managers, and staff in all types of organizations that need to prepare to respond to a disaster and restore normal operations afterward. Starting in Chapter 1, students have the opportunity to work through the material while developing a disaster recovery plan and procedures for the organization of their choice. Each chapter in this text includes Hands-on Projects that assign students various tasks based on the chapter topics. Each chapter also contains Case Projects that place readers in the roles of problem solvers, requiring them to apply concepts presented in the chapter to a real-life work environment.

Chapter Descriptions

Chapter 1, "Introduction to Disaster Recovery," discusses how an organization develops a disaster recovery philosophy as well as a disaster recovery plan. The process includes organizing a planning team, assessing risks, developing and documenting policies and procedures, selecting and training emergency response teams, and testing their effectiveness in live simulations.

Chapter 2, "Preparing to Develop the Disaster Recovery Plan," describes how to organize the disaster recovery planning team, which is the first step in developing a plan. The team must be a well-rounded group that represents all the functions of an organization.

Chapter 3, "Assessing Risks in the Enterprise," describes a fundamental building block of disaster recovery planning: working with key people inside and outside an organization to ensure that all risks are thoroughly reviewed and assessed.

Chapter 4, "Prioritizing Systems and Functions for Recovery," explains how representatives from all departments can determine which business activities are most critical to the organization. The planning team needs to develop procedures to restore these activities as quickly as possible in case of disaster.

Chapter 5, "Developing Plans and Procedures," explains how the disaster recovery planning team develops recovery procedures for each facility that the organization operates. Although some basic procedures need to be in place for all facilities, other procedures must be tailored to address special conditions and staffing patterns at a facility.

Chapter 6, "Organizational Relationships in Disaster Recovery," discusses various agencies an organization needs to work with to recover from a disaster, including law enforcement, emergency services, utilities, business partners, and suppliers. The organization must also communicate with customers, employees and their families, and the surrounding community.

Chapter 7, "Procedures for Responding to Attacks on Computers," describes disasters that can result from cyberattacks and hackers, rather than from natural occurrences or accidents. Procedures for dealing with such disasters require considerable data collection and analysis, as well as cooperation with law enforcement agencies.

Chapter 8, "Developing Procedures for Special Circumstances," provides tips for protecting special assets in the event of a disaster. These assets include hazardous materials, controlled substances, historic documents, and trade secrets.

Chapter 9, "Implementing Disaster Recovery Plans," explains how an organization puts its plan into effect. This process includes developing an implementation plan, assessing the value of mitigation steps, assigning responsibilities for implementation, establishing an implementation schedule, and training employees.

Chapter 10, "Testing and Rehearsal," explains how to develop testing scenarios to evaluate how well disaster recovery plans and procedures actually work. The planning team observes these rehearsals and then fine-tunes the plans accordingly.

Chapter 11, "Continued Assessment of Needs, Threats, and Solutions," describes how an organization can make the transition into maintenance mode after the disaster recovery planning team has developed, implemented, and tested recovery plans and procedures. The team should develop methods to monitor and manage the plan over a long period of time.

Chapter 12, "Living Through a Disaster," discusses how organizations can capture the knowledge and experience they gain during a disaster. Managers and planners must recognize that disasters can have long-term residual effects on individual employees and entire organizations.

Appendices A and B summarize results of the survey conducted for this book and list some of the best resources for disaster recovery on the World Wide Web, respectively.

Features

This book includes many features that are designed to enhance your learning experience.

- **Chapter Objectives.** Each chapter begins with a detailed list of the concepts to be mastered within that chapter. This list provides you with both a quick reference to the chapter's contents and a useful study aid.

- **Chapter Summaries.** Each chapter's text is followed by a summary of the concepts introduced in that chapter. These summaries provide a helpful way to recap and revisit the ideas covered in each chapter.

- **Key Terms.** All of the terms that are introduced with boldfaced text in the chapter are gathered in the Key Terms list at the end of the chapter. This list provides you with a method of checking your understanding of all the new terms.

- **Review Questions.** A list of review questions is included to reinforce the ideas introduced in each chapter. Answering these questions ensures that you have mastered the important concepts.

- **Hands-on Projects.** Each chapter offers numerous hands-on projects intended to provide you with practical experience and real-world solutions.

- **Case Projects.** The end of each chapter includes several case projects. To complete these exercises, you must draw on common sense as well as your knowledge of the topics covered to that point in the book. Your goal for each project is to develop answers to problems similar to those you will face as a disaster recovery planner.

Text and Graphic Conventions

Wherever appropriate, additional information and exercises have been added to this book to help you better understand the topic at hand. Icons throughout the text alert you to additional materials. The icons used in this textbook are described below.

The Note icon draws your attention to additional helpful material related to the subject being described.

Each hands-on activity in this book is preceded by the Hands-on icon and a description of the exercise that follows.

Tips based on the author's experience provide extra information about how to attack a problem or what to do in real-world situations.

The Caution icon warns you about potential mistakes or problems and explains how to avoid them.

The Case Project icon marks case projects, which are more involved, scenario-based assignments. In these extensive case examples, you are asked to implement independently what you have learned.

Instructor's Resources

The following supplemental materials are available when this book is used in a classroom setting. All of these supplements are provided to the instructor on a single CD-ROM.

Electronic Instructor's Manual. The Instructor's Manual that accompanies this textbook includes additional instructional material to assist in class preparation, including suggestions for classroom activities, discussion topics, and additional projects.

Solutions. Solutions are included for all end-of-chapter material, including the Review Questions, Hands-on Projects, and Case Projects.

ExamView®. This textbook is accompanied by ExamView, a powerful testing software package that allows instructors to create and administer printed, computer (LAN-based), and Internet exams. ExamView includes hundreds of questions that correspond to the topics covered in this text, enabling students to generate detailed study guides that include page references for further review. The computer-based and Internet testing components allow students to take exams at their computers, and also save the instructor time by grading each exam automatically.

PowerPoint presentations. This book comes with Microsoft PowerPoint slides for each chapter. These are included as a teaching aid for classroom presentation, to make available to students on the network for chapter review, or to be printed for classroom distribution. Instructors, please feel at liberty to add your own slides for additional topics you introduce to the class.

Figure files. All of the figures in the book are reproduced on the Instructor's Resources CD, in bitmapped format. Similar to the PowerPoint presentations, these figures are included as a teaching aid for classroom presentation, to make available to students for review, or to be printed for classroom distribution.

ACKNOWLEDGMENTS

I first need to acknowledge and thank my friends for encouraging and supporting me while I wrote this book. I also want to thank Amy Lyon, the Product Manager; Randy Weaver for his thoughtful technical editing and quality assurance work; Dan Seiter, the Developmental Editor; and Danielle Power and Brooke Booth, the Production Editors.

I am grateful to the reviewers who provided valuable input during the development of this book, including Barbara Belon of Norwalk Community College; Farbod Karimi of Heald College; Michael Nicholas of Davenport University; and Randy Nichols of George Washington University.

1

INTRODUCTION TO DISASTER RECOVERY

After reading this chapter, you will be able to:

- ◆ Develop a disaster recovery philosophy
- ◆ Describe the basic principles of disaster recovery planning
- ◆ Describe and establish a business continuity and disaster recovery function
- ◆ Understand the steps of disaster recovery planning
- ◆ Understand the role of IT and network management in disaster recovery

Disaster strikes often. Almost all parts of the world suffer turbulent weather, floods, earthquakes, landslides, political upheaval, terrorist attacks, or civil war. Everyday life is filled with incidents that can disrupt business, including power outages, broken water mains, fires, severed telecommunications lines, and train wrecks.

To successfully manage business continuity during a disaster and restore normal operations, organizations require a good disaster recovery plan. When disaster strikes, organizations must mobilize all the talent and resources needed to continue their operations and return to a normal state as soon as possible. Time is money, and in today's economy, an hour could be worth thousands of dollars. Every department in an organization has responsibilities during a disaster. Planning for a disaster and then dealing with it is a team effort by all parts of an organization.

If any part of this team does not have a good grasp of the whole plan, then the groups are merely working side by side, rather than together in an integrated fashion to solve a problem. It requires much more than a battalion of dedicated sandbaggers to survive most disasters. When the alarm sounds, the organizations that most successfully deal with disasters are the ones that run like proverbial well-oiled machines.

This chapter discusses how an organization develops a disaster recovery philosophy as well as a disaster plan. The process begins by organizing a planning team, then assessing risks, developing and documenting policies and procedures, selecting and training emergency response teams, and testing their effectiveness in live simulations. These measures are designed to assure that the impact of a disaster is mitigated, that business continues, and that normal operations are restored as quickly as possible.

DEVELOPING A DISASTER RECOVERY PHILOSOPHY

The underlying philosophy of disaster recovery needs to be rooted in an organization's desire to protect and preserve its positive public image, as well as its physical assets and the lives of employees. This image includes the high levels of customer satisfaction and the faith of stockholders and other stakeholders that an organization has worked so hard to develop.

Many organizations have suffered through a disaster, and the ones that haven't should be well aware that they are not immune. More than 250 organizations were surveyed for this book to determine trends and problems in disaster recovery planning and preparation. As shown in Figure 1-1, three of every 10 organizations surveyed for this book have been through a disaster.

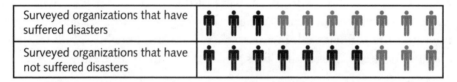

| Surveyed organizations that have suffered disasters | |
| Surveyed organizations that have not suffered disasters | |

Figure 1-1   Organizations that have suffered disasters

Disaster recovery planning is the process of assessing risks that an organization faces, then developing, documenting, implementing, testing, and maintaining procedures that help the organization quickly return to normal operations and minimize losses after a disaster. In the survey conducted for this book, nearly three of every four organizations reported having a disaster recovery plan in place. However, disaster recovery planning is still a new process in many organizations. Figure 1-2 shows the status of disaster recovery plans in the more than 250 organizations surveyed.

Organizations that do not have a plan in place	
Organizations with plans in development	
Organizations that have had plans in place for less than one year	
Organizations that have had plans in place for two to five years	
Organizations that have had plans in place for six to 10 years	
Organizations that have had plans in place for more than 10 years	

Figure 1-2   Status of disaster recovery plans in surveyed organizations

Far too many people consider disaster recovery planning a merely mechanical process. There are certainly tedious and laborious aspects to developing a plan. However, organizations have cultures, spirits, and images that permeate relationships within the organization, as well as relationships with customers, business partners, and the public at large. These relationships should drive an organization's disaster recovery planning. Several examples can help explain this point.

In recent years it has become apparent that a customer's view of an organization is crucial to the organization's success. All marketing managers dream that customers will view their products as having high quality and good value. Marketers and product planners have also learned a great deal about the economics of customer acquisition during the last decade. A basic lesson they've learned is that new customers are difficult and costly to gain; it is less costly to keep current customers satisfied and maintain them as repeat customers. Once customers are lost, it is nearly impossible to get them back or regain their trust. Customer satisfaction has also become a prime marketing tool, because customers report their experiences to their associates and friends.

An organization cannot achieve excellent customer service merely by sending memos that encourage employees to be nice to customers. The desire for customer satisfaction runs from top to bottom in an organization, and the process is not mechanical—it is spiritual. Perpetuating this spirit begins when employees are hired and trained. People should be hired if their demeanor and attitude match the spirit of the organization, and if their drive to satisfy customers is constant.

Programs designed to improve and maintain an organization's positive public image are similar to customer satisfaction programs. A good public image is an asset that takes years to achieve and considerable diligence to maintain. As a result, organizations of all types have created offices of social responsibility or community relations units that are dedicated to polishing public image. The economics of public image are similar to those of customer satisfaction. It requires less effort and costs less money to maintain a positive public image than to repair an image damaged by a lack of diligence.

Another major effort of publicly traded companies is stockholder and investor relations. Major stockholders often receive "red–carpet" information services from a good investor relations specialist, because maintaining investor faith is extremely important. If a major institutional investor becomes disenchanted, then ceases to invest or starts selling off stock, the actions may be interpreted as a sign of trouble within the company. Therefore, considerable effort is exerted to develop the faith and trust of investors. Again, efforts that help maintain faith are far less expensive than those required to regain lost faith.

All of these efforts are designed to achieve a common goal—organizations want to be viewed in the most positive light possible. The attitudes and philosophies inherent in an organization's culture should be the foundation of its disaster recovery philosophy. The nuts and bolts of disaster recovery, including backup computers, emergency networks, and temporary quarters, are only tools.

An example that lives in many people's minds is the disaster response of organizations in the World Trade Center during the terrorist attacks on September 11, 2001. Many organizations were able to respond quickly, suffered few or no casualties, and resumed critical operations in less than 24 hours. Others, we learned sadly, were not as well-prepared or as fortunate.

Disaster recovery planning has intensified since September 2001. As shown in Figure 1-3, three of every 10 organizations surveyed for this book report that their spending for disaster recovery planning has increased. One of every 10 organizations reports that spending has increased dramatically.

Organizations that say their spending for disaster recovery planning has stayed the same	👤 👤 👤 👤 👤 👤 👤 👤 👤 👤
Organizations that say their spending for disaster recovery planning has increased slightly	👤 👤 👤 👤 👤 👤 👤 👤 👤 👤
Organizations that report spending dramatically more for disaster recovery planning	👤 👤 👤 👤 👤 👤 👤 👤 👤 👤
Organizations that report spending dramatically less for disaster recovery planning	👤 👤 👤 👤 👤 👤 👤 👤 👤 👤
Organizations that would not answer this question	👤 👤 👤 👤 👤 👤 👤 👤 👤 👤

Figure 1-3 Spending for disaster recovery planning after September 2001

THE BASIC PRINCIPLES OF DISASTER RECOVERY PLANNING

No off-the-shelf disaster recovery plan can possibly meet the needs of all organizations. Instead, an effective plan recognizes an organization's size and other defining characteristics. For example, plans must account for an organization's dependence on automation, the location of its facilities, available resources, number of employees, breadth and depth of the disaster, and legal requirements for operations.

This book provides a step-by-step process for determining which elements belong in a disaster recovery plan, and how to implement, test, and manage this plan over a long period of time. The following principles provide a foundation for understanding disaster recovery planning. They can help guide the people in an organization who need to develop the plan.

- Developing a solid disaster recovery plan requires the support and participation of upper-level managers, all business unit managers, legal counsel, and directors of all functional departments such as Human Resources, Facilities Management, IT, and Corporate Security.

- Assessing an organization's risks requires time-consuming, detailed analysis based on a realistic understanding of the environmental, economic, social, and political conditions in which the organization, its suppliers, and its customers operate.

- All policies and procedures in the disaster recovery plan must support the critical needs of business operations, comply with all relevant laws and regulations, be understood by the parties responsible for implementing them, and be approved by upper management.

- The disaster recovery plan must clearly delineate and document the chain of command of the managers responsible for declaring, responding to, and recovering from a disaster. The plan must also document the role of each department and outside support organization in a disaster.

- The disaster recovery system must facilitate and allow control of communications among decision-makers, managers, and staff, as well as with external support organizations, law enforcement, emergency services, and media.

- All policies and procedures in the disaster recovery plan must be documented clearly so that all participating employees can understand and implement them.

- Disaster recovery policies and procedures must be available to all departments, managers, and staff at all times during disaster response and recovery.

- All employees involved in disaster response and recovery must be trained to implement documented procedures and to address unanticipated problems.

- Disaster recovery procedures must be tested and rehearsed. Planners should evaluate each test and rehearsal to determine weaknesses in the plan, and use the results of these evaluations to modify the plan, procedures, or training.

- Planners must continually evaluate new threats and business conditions as they develop, and then update disaster recovery plans and procedures accordingly.

- During disaster response and recovery, the organization must evaluate the effectiveness of its procedures and monitor the physical safety and mental health of employees at all times. The results of these evaluations should be used to improve the organization's disaster recovery abilities.

Understanding the basic principles of disaster recovery planning can keep team members from getting lost in the long process of developing a solid plan for their organization. As the team is assembled, all members should be briefed on the basic planning principles and the eight steps of developing a plan, as discussed later in this chapter. This information helps team members understand how the pieces fit together to form an integrated, comprehensive plan.

Understanding the Processes of Disaster Recovery Planning

The first essential principle of a solid disaster recovery plan is the support and participation of upper-level managers, all business unit managers, legal counsel, and directors of all functional departments such as Human Resources, Facilities Management, IT, and Corporate Security.

This principle has several implications. First, implementing the plan and responding to disaster is an organization-wide effort. Second, plan development requires many types of knowledge and skills. Third, every organization-wide effort is laden with social and political obstacles that need to be addressed during planning.

Disaster recovery planning can be broken down into eight major steps. Each step is interrelated and builds upon the others. The **disaster recovery planning team** is responsible for developing the plan. Every member of the team needs to be familiar with the following steps and how they relate to each other. These steps are described in more detail later in this chapter and covered in depth in subsequent chapters:

- Step One: Organizing the team

- Step Two: Assessing risks in the enterprise

- Step Three: Establishing roles across departments and organizations

- Step Four: Developing policies and procedures

- Step Five: Documenting disaster recovery procedures

- Step Six: Preparing to handle disasters

- Step Seven: Training, testing, and rehearsal

- Step Eight: Ongoing management

These basic steps provide a guide for project managers to organize and plan their efforts over a long period of time. The steps also serve as important milestones for the planning team. Building a solid disaster recovery plan can take many months and, in some cases, years. When team members understand where they are in the planning stages, they become less frustrated by what many people consider a long and tedious process.

Team members also need to know that the plan requires ongoing evaluation and maintenance once it is developed. To be effective, the plan must be updated to ensure that business operations are sustainable over long periods of time.

ESTABLISHING CONTINUITY AND RECOVERY FUNCTION

The **disaster recovery function** consists of the people, departments, and support organizations that implement the plan and facilitate disaster recovery. How this function is organized depends on the geographical dispersal of facilities within an organization, the type of facilities occupied, the number of employees, and other factors. In general, three major groups staff an organization's disaster recovery function:

- A centralized authority or group coordinates the development of disaster recovery plans and plays a role in disaster response and recovery. A centralized group is more important in large organizations because disaster response and coordinated recovery efforts are more complex. In smaller organizations, disaster response and recovery might be assigned to the chief executive officer (CEO) or business manager.

- Managers and staff in functional departments such as Human Resources, Facilities Management, IT, and Corporate Security have enterprise-wide roles in disaster response and recovery. The larger an organization is, the more specialized its departments must be to manage day-to-day functions. Organizations with thousands of employees usually have several administrative departments, including Human Resources, Facilities Management, Security, Purchasing, and Shipping and Receiving. Smaller organizations often have few administrative departments, and tend to cluster these responsibilities under one operations or business manager.

- Department managers and representatives from business units have roles in disaster response and recovery to ensure the continued function of their business units. When an organization's products or services are diverse or widely distributed geographically, more business unit or product managers are required to oversee business operations. Smaller organizations, as well as those with simple business operations, usually have fewer business unit or product managers.

Disaster recovery planners must work within the structure of the organization for which the plan is being developed. In an organization with 100 or fewer employees, a centralized office of disaster recovery is probably not necessary. The disaster recovery function may work best if it is part of a centralized administrative office and is supported by staff in other parts of the organization that have specialized knowledge or skills. Very large organizations probably require a specialized office of disaster recovery planning and response.

Regardless of how the disaster recovery function fits into an organization, the basic principles of disaster recovery planning still apply. Each organization must address these principles to meet its own specific needs.

UNDERSTANDING THE STEPS OF DISASTER RECOVERY PLANNING

Disaster recovery planning consists of eight major steps. Smaller organizations may be able to develop and document a plan in a few months. In larger organizations, initial planning can take many months and sometimes years.

Management and all other members of the planning team need to understand the steps involved in developing a plan, and how these steps build upon each other and fit together as a whole. The following sections introduce each of the eight steps. Subsequent chapters cover the steps in greater detail.

Step One: Organizing the Disaster Recovery Planning Team

Organizing the planning team is the first step in developing a disaster recovery plan. The team must be a well-rounded group that represents all the functions of an organization. This representation ensures that essential business processes are not overlooked during plan development.

Disaster recovery planning also requires a high-level manager as a champion. Ideally, the champion should be the CEO or a high-level manager designated by the CEO. The champion's role is to publicly support and endorse the plan, as well as eliminate obstacles that hinder its development.

The team must also have a designated leader, or even better, two people who act as co-leaders. This helps to maintain momentum and continuity if one co-leader is unavailable.

Each participating department should assign a primary representative and an alternate to the team. The alternate can provide continuity if the primary representative is unavailable.

The team should be trained in disaster recovery planning, either by attending outside training or an in-house session taught by a knowledgeable instructor. If an outside consultant trains the team or works with it during plan development, the team champion or leader must thoroughly check the consultant's references.

Once the team is in place, it should establish a schedule of activities, including meeting times and dates for completing the eight steps of planning. The schedule can always be modified as necessary, but its presence is important. When teams work without schedules or deadlines, projects tend to flounder or not receive the attention they need.

The team should begin an awareness campaign about disaster recovery planning within the organization. The high-level manager who champions the project should lead this campaign, and all employees should be made aware that a plan is under way.

Step Two: Assessing Risks in the Enterprise

Assessing the risk that an enterprise faces is the next step in disaster recovery planning. A **business impact analysis** is a method of assessing risks and determining the potential economic loss that could occur as a result of these risks.

All business processes must be identified and analyzed during a business impact analysis. Then, these business processes are ranked as critical, essential, necessary, and desirable. Each process is evaluated to determine the potential loss that would be incurred in the event of disruption. The analysis also determines the likelihood of disruptions by reviewing the types of threats an organization faces.

As a part of this analysis, the planning team should review legal and contractual requirements to determine the consequences of business disruption. The team should also review disaster-related insurance to determine what coverage may be available, and the requirements for eligibility.

The results of the business impact analysis help guide disaster recovery planning and help the team develop procedures for recovering from various types of incidents. Many organizations conduct a return-on-investment analysis to determine what types of backup systems and disaster recovery processes they need to mitigate damage.

The type of disaster that managers fear most varies by the location of their facilities and the nature of their business. For example, managers in three of every 10 organizations surveyed for this book think the worst disaster would involve outages of IT services and loss of customer data. Figure 1-4 shows which types of disasters would most severely affect organizations, in the opinions of the surveyed managers.

The worst disaster would affect national infrastructure	👤 👤 👤 👤 👤 👤 👤 👤 👤 👤
The worst disaster would be fire-related	👤 👤 👤 👤 👤 👤 👤 👤 👤 👤
The worst disaster would involve outages of IT services and loss of customer data	👤 👤 👤 👤 👤 👤 👤 👤 👤 👤
The worst disaster would be regional, including earthquakes, floods, and windstorms	👤 👤 👤 👤 👤 👤 👤 👤 👤 👤
The worst disaster would destroy buildings and facilities	👤 👤 👤 👤 👤 👤 👤 👤 👤 👤

Figure 1-4 Worst disaster fears of surveyed managers

Step Three: Establishing Roles Across Departments and Organizations

The third step in disaster recovery planning is establishing the roles that each department, business partner, and outside service organization plays in disaster recovery. The planning team determines the contribution that each department can make to the plan and disaster recovery. This step helps to assure that all necessary resources and expertise are mobilized in a disaster. The team should create a chart that shows which people in each department have responsibilities for disaster recovery.

When an organization has multiple locations, it must identify local departments and employees who can participate in disaster recovery planning. In some cases, operations at different locations are supported by centralized functions such as IT and network management, human resources, and corporate security.

The planning team also determines the role that other organizations should play in the plan. These organizations could include business partners, local emergency services, law enforcement agencies, public utilities, telecommunications providers, and IT and network service providers.

Step Four: Developing Policies and Procedures

Developing actual disaster recovery policies and procedures is the next step in plan development. **Disaster recovery policies** are the guidelines that govern the development of disaster recovery procedures. **Disaster recovery procedures** are step-by-step methods designed to restore an organizational function or business process.

Developing policies and procedures to recover from disasters requires attention to detail and thorough analysis. Procedures must be established for each step of disaster recovery and response, starting with determining the extent of the disaster, declaring a disaster, mobilizing resources, and implementing emergency procedures. The planning team must also establish procedures for communicating with employees, the media, law enforcement, and emergency services.

One difficulty in developing policies and procedures is that many people just do their jobs, and are never confronted with the need to evaluate or explain what they do. Effective policies and procedures require detailed analysis of each business process; disaster recovery procedures must be thought out in great detail. The managers and other employees who are responsible for implementing these procedures must review and thoroughly understand them.

Another essential part of developing policies and procedures is determining the interdependency of each department and organization involved in implementing each procedure. This can be a complicated puzzle to put together, because team members cannot assume that all participants have common knowledge about each other or the procedures. Flow charts and work flow analysis are often required to illustrate the interdependency of organizations and procedures.

When procedures require action from more than one department, organization, or location, staff from each entity must help develop and analyze the procedures.

Step Five: Documenting Disaster Recovery Procedures

The fifth step of the disaster recovery plan is to document the policies and procedures developed in the previous step. Part of this documentation is done in conjunction with drafting, reviewing, and approving policies and procedures. The approved documentation is included in the actual disaster recovery plan.

Proper and thorough documentation of policies and procedures is essential to the plan's success. Each policy and procedure must be drafted, reviewed, and approved by management and all of the departments and organizations responsible for its implementation. Documentation must be clearly written so that employees can quickly refer to it and understand their responsibilities during disaster response and recovery. The disaster recovery plan must also be available at all times during testing phases, and especially during disaster response.

A group must be established to manage documentation and the cycles of reviews, approvals, and updates. Disaster recovery plans must be self-contained and include all contact organizations, names, telephone numbers, and other information necessary to enable disaster response.

Step Six: Preparing to Handle Disasters

Implementing the disaster recovery plan is the next step in the process. During this step the final plan is distributed to all of the departments, organizations, and employees involved in disaster response and recovery.

During this step the planning team begins to intensify the internal and external awareness programs to ensure that all parties know about the plan. Executives are briefed on the plan and their roles in disaster response and recovery. Staffs in all departments are trained on general procedures and the ones for which their department is directly responsible.

If outside services or new equipment are required to implement the plan, it is usually purchased or contracted for during the implementation phase.

Step Seven: Training, Testing, and Rehearsal

The next step of the disaster recovery plan is to test and rehearse parts of it, and eventually to run a live simulation of a disaster. A **disaster recovery rehearsal** is a live simulation in which all departments and support organizations run through the entire disaster recovery process, just as they would during an actual disaster. Managers in eight of every 10 organizations surveyed for this book think that testing and rehearsing disaster recovery plans is beneficial.

During the rehearsal, observers monitor and evaluate response to determine how well procedures are implemented. A full-scale rehearsal is the best way to determine weaknesses in the plan, adjust procedures, and modify the roles and responsibilities of departments, support organizations, and employees. Figure 1-5 shows the status of disaster recovery plan testing and rehearsal in the organizations surveyed for this book.

Surveyed organizations that do not test or rehearse disaster recovery plans	👤👤👤👤👤👤👤👤👤👤
Surveyed organizations that only test or rehearse parts of their plan	👤👤👤👤👤👤👤👤👤👤
Surveyed organizations that rehearse their entire plan	👤👤👤👤👤👤👤👤👤👤
Not applicable	👤👤👤👤👤👤👤👤👤👤

Figure 1-5 Status of disaster recovery plan testing and rehearsal

Step Eight: Ongoing Management

The final step in disaster recovery planning is often called the maintenance phase. Once the plan is developed and tested, the planning team must continually assess the emergence of new threats, adjust for changes in organizational structure, and determine the impact of new technology on recovery procedures.

In many industries, planning teams may also need to monitor changes in laws and regulations that may affect their disaster recovery requirements. Organizations that have a multinational structure need to stay aware of changes in legal requirements, social conditions, and the political climate in countries where they operate.

When procedures are changed and documentation is updated, training requirements and staff skills must be updated as well. Regular reviews help to keep procedures current, and ongoing training ensures that new staff are trained and that all staff are trained on new or modified procedures. Figure 1-6 shows the frequency of disaster recovery plan updates among the organizations surveyed for this book.

Organizations that update their disaster recovery plans quarterly	👤👤👤👤👤👤👤👤👤👤
Organizations that update their plans annually	👤👤👤👤👤👤👤👤👤👤
Organizations that update their plans as needed	👤👤👤👤👤👤👤👤👤👤
Not applicable, or respondent was unsure of the update schedule	👤👤👤👤👤👤👤👤👤👤

Figure 1-6 Frequency of disaster recovery plan updates

THE ROLE OF IT AND NETWORK MANAGEMENT IN DISASTER RECOVERY

Most organizations rely heavily on their computer systems and communications networks. Thus, the IT and network management in every organization have essential roles in disaster recovery planning and response. IT and network management staff not only play a leadership role in the overall planning effort, they are involved in each of the eight disaster recovery planning steps.

As the planning team is organized, knowledgeable representatives from IT and network management need to be assigned to the team. The mix of IT architecture and software applications helps determine how many IT staff need to be on the team, and their level of expertise. In general, at least one representative is needed for each of the following functions: data center operations, network management, desktop computing, and voice communications. Also, at least one person is needed for each major IT application, including financial management support, supply chain systems, enterprise resource planning (ERP), and human resources support.

During risk assessment and business impact analysis, IT and network managers need to help the team answer critical questions about the potential consequences of system downtime. These managers also assist in developing and documenting procedures for end-user departments and the IT departments that facilitate disaster response and recovery.

IT and network managers help develop and deliver training to department managers and employees who will assist in recovery procedures for computer systems and networks. These managers and employees will also help test and rehearse procedures to ensure that their organization can effectively recover from a disaster.

Finally, IT and network managers have a key role in supporting and managing the ongoing disaster recovery plan. As computer systems and networks evolve and new technology is added, plans and procedures must be updated. IT and network managers must determine how each new upgrade or additional application affects these plans and procedures, then inform the staff who maintain disaster recovery documents of the necessary changes to keep the plan current. In addition, it may be necessary to develop new training materials and refresher courses for managers and employees.

CHAPTER SUMMARY

❏ Disaster recovery planning is the process of assessing risks that an organization faces, then developing procedures that enable it to return to normal operations as quickly as possible and minimize economic loss after a disaster.

❏ No off-the-shelf disaster recovery plan can possibly meet the needs of all organizations. An effective plan must account for an organization's size and other defining characteristics.

❏ Understanding the basic principles of disaster recovery planning can keep team members from getting lost in the long process of developing a solid plan for their organization. As the team is assembled, all members should be briefed on the basic planning principles and the eight steps of developing a plan.

❏ The disaster recovery function consists of the people, departments, and support organizations that implement the disaster recovery plan and facilitate recovery. How the function is organized depends on the geographical dispersal of facilities, the type of facilities occupied, the number of employees, and other factors.

❏ The first step in developing a disaster recovery plan is to establish a well-rounded team that represents all the functions of an organization. Next, the organization develops a business impact analysis to assess its risks, then establishes roles that each department, business partner, and outside service agency play in the plan. The organization then develops and documents disaster recovery policies and procedures.

❏ After documenting policies and procedures, the organization implements its disaster recovery plan. During this step the final plan is distributed to all departments, organizations, and employees involved in disaster response and recovery. Next, the plan must be tested and rehearsed, and eventually the organization should run a live simulation of a disaster.

❏ The final step in disaster recovery planning is the maintenance phase, which includes continual assessment of new threats, adjustments for organizational changes, and determining the impact of new technology on recovery procedures.

❏ Most organizations rely heavily on their computer systems and communications networks. Thus, the IT and network management staff have essential roles in disaster recovery planning and response.

KEY TERMS

business impact analysis — The assessment of risks that an enterprise faces and the potential economic losses that could occur as a result of these risks.

disaster recovery function — The people, departments, and support organizations that implement the disaster recovery plan and facilitate disaster recovery.

disaster recovery planning — The process of assessing risks that an organization faces, then developing procedures that enable it to return to normal operations as quickly as possible to minimize economic loss after a disaster.

disaster recovery planning team — The designated group responsible for developing a disaster recovery plan.

disaster recovery policies — The guidelines that govern the development of disaster recovery procedures.

disaster recovery procedures — Step-by-step methods designed to restore an organizational function or business process.

disaster recovery rehearsal — A live simulation in which all departments and support organizations go through the entire disaster recovery plan, just as they would during an actual disaster.

REVIEW QUESTIONS

1. Developing a solid disaster recovery plan requires the support and participation of which of the following groups? (Choose all that apply.)

   a. upper-level managers

   b. directors of all functional departments

   c. corporate security

   d. managers of all business units

2. All policies and procedures in the disaster recovery plan must be designed to do which of the following? (Choose all that apply.)

   a. Support the critical needs of business operations.

   b. Comply with all relevant laws and regulations.

   c. Be understood by parties responsible for implementing them.

   d. Be approved by the U.S. government.

3. The disaster recovery function includes which of the following groups?

   a. the people, departments, and support organizations that implement the disaster recovery plan and facilitate disaster recovery

   b. only staff in the Networking and IT departments

   c. the Corporate Security and IT departments

   d. corporate security staff and upper-level managers

4. During a business impact analysis, business processes are ranked _____.

   a as critical, essential, necessary, and desirable

   b from the bosses' favorites to their least favorite

   c from the least expensive to fix to the most expensive to fix

   d none of the above; only critical business processes are considered

5. How many basic steps are there in developing a disaster recovery plan?

   a. 16

   b. 12

   c. 8

   d 4

6. When an organization's products or services are diverse or widely distributed geographically, which of the following statements is true?

   a. More business unit or product managers are required to oversee business operations.

   b. Fewer business unit or product managers are required to oversee business operations.

   c. Diversity in products and services does not affect the need for managers.

   d The product or service mix affects only certain types of organizations.

7. Assessing an organization's risks requires time-consuming, detailed analysis based on a realistic understanding of all the environmental, economic, social, and political conditions in which the organization, its suppliers, and its customers operate. True or False?

8. The chain of command of managers responsible for declaring, responding to, and recovering from a disaster must be clearly delineated and documented in the disaster recovery plan. True or False?

9. Very large organizations most likely require a specialized office of disaster recovery planning and response. True or False?

10. The steps involved in developing a disaster recovery plan are not interrelated and do not build upon each other. True or False?

11. The role of each department and outside support organization does not need to be delineated or documented in the disaster recovery plan. True or False?

12. The disaster recovery system must facilitate and allow control of communications among decision-makers, managers, and staff, as well as with external support organizations, law enforcement, emergency services, and media. True or False?

13. Disaster recovery policies and procedures do not need to be available to departments, managers, and staff at all times during disaster response and recovery. True or False?

14. Two people should act as co-leaders so the disaster recovery planning team can maintain momentum and continuity in case one of the leaders is unavailable. True or False?

15. Not all employees involved in disaster response and recovery need training to implement documented procedures or address unanticipated problems. True or False?

16. Disaster recovery procedures must be tested and rehearsed to determine their weaknesses, and the results of these evaluations should be used to modify the procedures. True or False?

17. Disaster recovery plans and procedures do not need to be updated because conditions usually do not change enough to affect the plan. True or False?

18. During disaster response and recovery, the mental health of employees is not an important consideration. True or False?

19. Building a solid disaster recovery plan for an average-sized organization takes less than a month. True or False?

20. When an organization has multiple locations, it must identify local departments and employees who can participate in disaster recovery planning. True or False?

21. Why is it helpful for management and all members of the disaster recovery planning team to understand the steps for developing a plan, including how the steps build upon each other and fit together as a whole?

22. Why should the disaster recovery team establish a schedule of activities?

23. What is the difference between disaster recovery policies and disaster recovery procedures?

24. What is the purpose of a disaster recovery rehearsal?

25. Why do the IT and Network Management departments play a key role in disaster recovery planning?

HANDS-ON PROJECTS

For these projects, form teams in your class and then work with them for the entire term.

Project 1-1

Develop and document various parts of a disaster recovery plan for an organization. You can choose an organization where a team member works, an organization with which a team member is familiar, or an organization assigned by the instructor.

1. Review the eight steps of developing a disaster recovery plan and assign initial tasks to team members.

2. Write a description of the organization for which you will develop a plan. The description should include the organization's name, location(s), primary business activity, number of employees, and the types of computer systems, networks, and computer applications it uses.

3. Develop an initial schedule for completing each of the eight steps of a disaster recovery plan. (Note that you will probably not be able to simulate a disaster.)

4. Submit the organization description and initial schedule to your instructor.

HANDS-ON PROJECTS

Project 1-2

Write a mission statement for your team's disaster recovery planning project. The mission statement should identify the following elements:

■ The purpose of the plan

■ Where the directive to develop the plan originated (for example, the board of directors or the CEO)

■ The highest-level manager in the organization who is overseeing plan development

When you finish, submit the mission statement to your instructor for review.

HANDS-ON PROJECTS

Project 1-3

Write a memorandum that describes the purpose and goals of the disaster recovery planning project. Write the memo to be suitable for distribution to all employees in the organization. The memo should include the following items:

■ The purpose of the disaster recovery planning project

■ The name and title of the person who is directing plan development

■ Contact information for the person(s) that employees should call if they have questions about plan development

When you finish, submit the memo to your instructor for review.

CASE PROJECTS

CASE PROJECTS

Case Project: Harris and Heartfield Manufacturing

The Harris and Heartfield Manufacturing Company is a family-owned business that fabricates specialized metal parts. Matthew Harris and Henry Heartfield founded the company in 1942 to provide parts for defense contractors. The company has an excellent reputation for manufacturing high-quality parts and delivering orders on schedule. Brandon L. Harris and Tonya Heartfield, the grandchildren of the founders, now run the company.

Although the U.S. defense industry has consolidated and now spends less money on defense products, the company still receives about 60% of its revenue from defense contractors. Another 25% of revenue comes from manufacturing specialized metal parts for heavy-equipment manufacturers in North America. The remaining revenue is derived from orders for replacement parts that the company has manufactured in the past, and from custom orders for parts used to develop prototypes of equipment.

Harris and Heartfield has 200 employees at its only location in Carlsbad, California. The Administrative Department has 20 employees, all of whom have desktop computers connected to a local area network (LAN). The Research and Design Department has 15 engineers, all of whom use Sun Microsystems workstations that are connected to the company's LAN. There are three servers for administrative functions and six servers that support design and manufacturing. The shop floor has a variety of machining equipment, about half of which is computerized.

Management is concerned about the company's ability to remain competitive over the next several decades, and especially concerned about their ability to fulfill orders if some unexpected event hindered their manufacturing capabilities. The board of directors is relatively business-savvy, but does not invest money unless they think the investment can provide a positive return.

Harris and Heartfield has hired you as a consultant to create a rationale for developing a disaster recovery plan. Your first assignment is to make a brief presentation to the board that demonstrates how the company could benefit from having a plan in place. You have been asked to develop a list of 10 key points that convey the importance of disaster recovery planning to the board. These 10 points must be tied directly to business conditions and business practices at Harris and Heartfield.

OPTIONAL TEAM CASE PROJECTS

OPTIONAL CASE PROJECTS

Team Case One

Your boss has asked you to prepare a three- to five-minute presentation that explains the steps required to develop a disaster recovery plan. The presentation is for a meeting of department managers. The goal of the presentation is to build awareness among department managers about disaster recovery planning. Your assignment is to develop and rehearse the presentation. You may create a one-page handout, but you cannot use an overhead projector or a PowerPoint presentation.

OPTIONAL
CASE
PROJECTS

Team Case Two

Your boss has asked you to research Internet resources for help with your disaster recovery planning efforts. These resources can include professional organizations, government agencies that provide information about planning, Web portals that cover related topics, or tutorials that could help train staff. Your assignment is to find 10 possible resources and write a one-paragraph description of each resource. The description should include the name of the resource, how it can help your planning team, and the URL of the Web site where you found the information.

CHAPTER

2

PREPARING TO DEVELOP THE DISASTER RECOVERY PLAN

After reading this chapter, you will be able to:

- Understand the need for executive support of disaster recovery planning
- Establish leadership for disaster recovery planning
- Organize a disaster recovery planning team
- Create an inventory of planning team skills
- Help train the disaster recovery planning team
- Start an awareness campaign for disaster recovery planning
- Establish a budget for disaster recovery planning and management
- Cope with standards and regulatory bodies
- Assess progress of the plan and move ahead

Organizing the disaster recovery planning team is the first step in developing a plan. The team must be a well-rounded group that represents all the functions of an organization. This representation ensures that essential business processes are not overlooked during plan development.

Disaster recovery planners must work within the structure of the organization for which the plan is being developed. The disaster recovery function may work best if it is part of a centralized administrative office, and is supported by staff in other parts of the organization that have specialized knowledge or skills.

Regardless of where the disaster recovery function fits into an organization, the basic principles of disaster recovery planning still apply. Each organization must address these principles to meet its own specific needs.

THE NEED FOR EXECUTIVE SUPPORT

Successfully changing an organization or implementing an enterprise-wide initiative is easier when top managers support the effort. Executives are ultimately responsible for leading the development of disaster recovery plans in their organizations. However, executives will probably not continue to provide support if they do not receive support in return. They need training in disaster recovery planning and regular briefings on the progress of the plan.

One of the greatest frustrations for disaster recovery planners is the difficulty of gaining and maintaining support from upper-level managers. The author surveyed more than 250 organizations to determine trends and problems in disaster recovery planning. Figure 2-1 shows that four of every 10 managers surveyed for this book think the upper-level managers in their organizations do not take disaster recovery planning seriously enough.

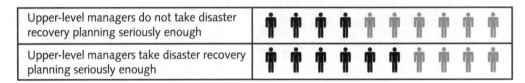

| Upper-level managers do not take disaster recovery planning seriously enough | |
| Upper-level managers take disaster recovery planning seriously enough | |

Figure 2-1 Survey of whether managers think upper-level managers take disaster recovery planning seriously enough

Although middle-level managers perform the detailed, day-to-day work to analyze disaster recovery needs and develop policies and procedures, executives play an essential role in developing disaster recovery plans that no other person can perform. They are high-level emissaries to boards of directors, investors, business partners, the general public, and the media.

Executive preparation is the process of training executives to articulate the organization's philosophy for disaster recovery planning. In many ways executives are the embodiment of their enterprise; they represent their organizations in a way that other employees cannot. Due to their status within the organization, executives need to serve as emissaries by attending a variety of public events and representing the organization in a positive light to each of their audiences. Table 2-1 shows the actions required to prepare executives to discuss disaster recovery planning in their organization.

Table 2-1 Preparing executives to discuss disaster recovery planning

Step	Executive preparation
Step 1	Establish a briefing process for upper-level managers on the ongoing development of disaster recovery plans
Step 2	Develop appropriate statements on the organization's disaster recovery planning for executives to deliver to the board of directors, investors, the media, business partners, and the general public
Step 3	Determine appropriate contacts in the organization to answer detailed questions regarding disaster recovery planning. Ensure that executives know where to refer outside parties for answers to these questions

The coordinator of the disaster recovery planning team should be responsible for briefing executives on the planning effort. In addition, planning team leaders from various departments should attend these briefings and answer specific questions to help executives understand how planning may affect business practices.

Key public relations personnel and legal counsel should also attend the briefings to make sure that executives know the types of issues they should address when discussing disaster recovery planning with the board of directors, investors, the media, business partners, and the general public.

Executives should receive a **disaster planning support list** of people with whom they can discuss planning issues. This support team can help executives prepare to address specific audiences about disaster recovery planning issues. If the audience is potentially hostile, the executive should be accompanied by the planning team coordinator or the lead staff person for privacy management. A trained public relations representative might need to attend as well.

The primary goal of having executives involved in planning is ensuring that they provide messages of consistent content and support. A good way to maintain this consistency and keep executives interested is to inform them of all positive developments in planning. These include achieving major milestones in the process, minimizing political squabbles during planning, and maintaining a positive atmosphere in planning meetings.

ESTABLISHING LEADERSHIP FOR DISASTER RECOVERY PLANNING

The highest levels of management, including the chief executive officer (**CEO**), chief operating officer (**COO**), chief financial officer (**CFO**), and chief information officer (**CIO**), need to support disaster recovery planning across the enterprise. Such support will underscore the importance of the plan, although chief officers will probably not participate in its day-to-day management. In smaller organizations that do not have a full executive staff, the CEO or COO may be the only executive manager who can support disaster recovery planning. However, the support of middle managers in smaller organizations is sufficient for the planning process.

The organization faces a major challenge in establishing effective leadership for the disaster recovery planning team. Good leaders must have political clout within the organization, as well as the motivation to stick with the time-consuming task of developing a plan.

As shown in Figure 2-2, five of every 10 organizations surveyed for this book have established some type of centralized disaster recovery planning.

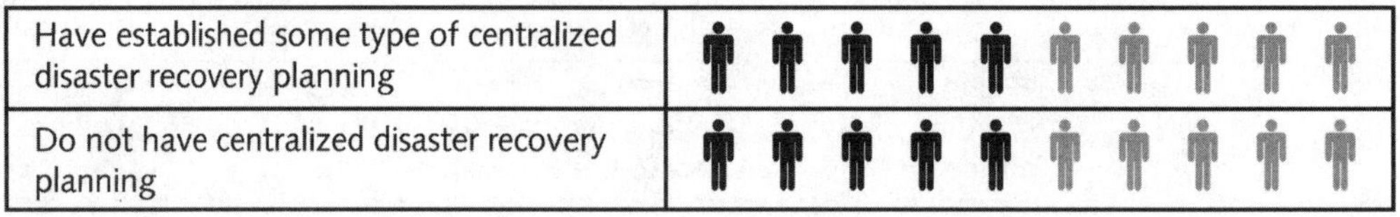

Figure 2-2   Survey of whether organizations have established centralized disaster recovery planning functions

The **disaster recovery planning coordinator** is responsible for project management and day-to-day leadership of the planning team. A mid-level manager should be assigned the coordinating role in developing a disaster recovery plan. As shown in Figure 2-3, seven of every 10 organizations surveyed have only one person assigned to planning. In five of every 10 organizations, the coordinator did not work full-time on the plan.

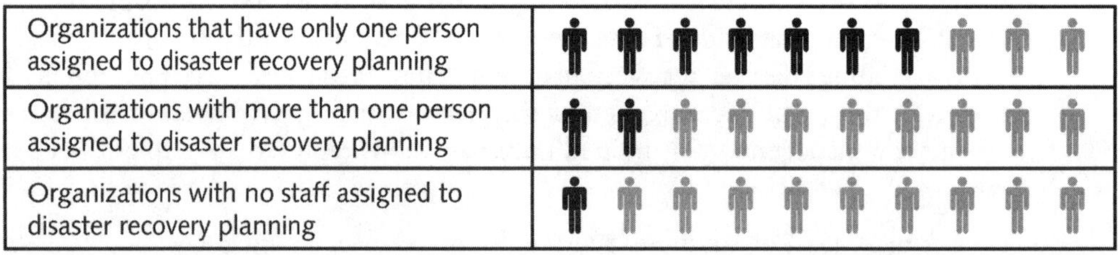

Figure 2-3   Survey of whether organizations have only one person assigned to disaster recovery planning

The person assigned to be the planning coordinator must dedicate considerable time to the process. The coordinator needs to be able to give the plan full attention when necessary, be detail-oriented without getting lost in the process, and be able to work diplomatically with all departments and external resources.

The disaster recovery planning coordinator should represent all corporate concerns for the plan and balance various department perspectives. Table 2-2 lists the coordinator's responsibilities.

Table 2-2 Responsibilities of a disaster recovery planning coordinator

Coordinator tasks
Reporting progress to upper-level managers
Developing a budget for disaster recovery planning
Maintaining the files of the disaster recovery planning team
Scheduling team meetings
Presiding at team meetings
Documenting disaster recovery policies and procedures
Handling correspondence with outside service providers for disaster recovery support
Overseeing the work of interdepartmental teams and subcommittees
Scheduling tests and rehearsals
Managing the maintenance of the disaster recovery plan
Updating plan documentation as necessary

All disaster recovery planning coordinators must have project management skills and experience to balance multiple tasks, track the different aspects of planning, and manage the work of the team. Coordinators also need solid communication skills to handle all the interaction and correspondence required to develop a good plan.

A fundamental rule of good project management is ensuring that all aspects of the project are sufficiently documented. If necessary, a new project manager must be able to step in and take over the project without disrupting its momentum. Thus, the disaster recovery planning coordinator must maintain orderly files of important planning documents. Table 2–3 shows the types of files the plan coordinator should maintain.

As shown in Figure 2-4, managers in five of every 10 organizations surveyed for this book think that disaster recovery procedures in their organization are not adequately documented. In addition, three of every 10 surveyed managers think their disaster recovery procedures are not easy to read, and that the employees responsible for implementing them do not understand them.

Table 2-3 Files that a disaster recovery coordinator should maintain

File type	Contents of file
Correspondence	Memos and letters from upper-level managers
	Memos from and between department managers
	Letters, proposals, and bids from outside contractors
	Letters to and from business partners
	Letters to and from customers
Meeting minutes and documents	Minutes from disaster recovery planning meetings
	Minutes and reports from planning team subcommittee meetings
Disaster recovery policies	Drafts of disaster recovery policies
	Final versions of policies
Disaster recovery procedures	Drafts of disaster recovery procedures
	Final versions of procedures
Contact lists	Contacts for disaster recovery planning resources
	Contacts to place in the final disaster recovery plan
Awareness campaign materials	Material used in internal awareness programs
	Material used in external awareness programs

Managers who think disaster recovery procedures in their organization are not adequately documented	👤👤👤👤👤 👤👤👤👤👤
Managers who think disaster recovery procedures in their organization are adequately documented	👤👤👤👤👤 👤👤👤👤👤
Managers who are undecided on the question	👤👤👤👤👤 👤👤👤👤👤

Figure 2-4 Survey of whether managers think disaster recovery procedures are adequately documented in their organization

In addition to the documents the planning coordinator keeps, a team member needs to keep current logs of disaster recovery planning activities. An **activity log** is a list of important events or accomplishments, the dates they occurred, and which departments or subcommittees participated. An example of an activity log is shown in Table 2-4. The activity log tracks events and works as a reference tool for new and incumbent planning staff, department representatives, and department planning groups.

Table 2-4 Example disaster recovery planning activity log

Date	Event	Departments/Subcommittees
1/15/04	First meeting of disaster recovery planning team	Corporate Security, Customer Support, Facilities Management, HR, IT, Investor Relations, legal counsel, mail room, Manufacturing, Marketing, Network Management, PR, R&D, Sales, Shipping and Receiving, Telecommunications, and Training
1/23/04	Launched internal awareness campaign	PR, HR
1/25/04	Started skills inventory subcommittee	Same as 1/15/04 meeting
1/30/04	Formed subcommittee for selecting outside consultant	Corporate Security, Facilities Management, IT, legal counsel, Manufacturing, Network Management, Telecommunications
2/1/04	Reviewed outside consultant's credentials	Consultant selection subcommittee
2/5/04	Second meeting of disaster recovery planning team	Same as 1/15/04 meeting
2/8/04	Reviewed planning team skills inventory	Disaster recovery planning team skills subcommittee

ORGANIZING THE DISASTER RECOVERY PLANNING TEAM

Forming the disaster recovery planning team is the next essential activity in organizing planning efforts. Every department in the enterprise needs to be represented, and each department should have two representatives—a primary and an alternate. The **primary department representative** is a full member of the planning team, and the **alternate department representative** is a secondary member. The primary and alternate representatives are also co-leaders of their department's internal disaster recovery planning efforts.

Appointing two representatives from each department increases the chances of maintaining team continuity and decreases the difficulty in scheduling meetings. These department representatives need to be managers with a complete understanding of their department's operations and the authority to make decisions and implement plans. They must also make time to keep each other updated on all planning issues and department issues.

The big challenge in forming the team is getting the time and attention of busy managers throughout the organization. All managers already have a long list of goals, and achieving them often means more income for them. Thus, some executive clout is needed behind the disaster recovery team. The executive champion should ensure that the team gets the resources, participation, and cooperation needed to create a successful plan.

The executive champion's role is symbolic and supportive, and must convey the importance of the disaster recovery planning team across the organization. If managers know their efforts on the planning team will be recognized by an executive champion, they are much more likely to push for progress at both the corporate and department levels. To encourage adherence to the plan within departments, team members are expected to coordinate activities between the corporate planning group and the appointed groups within their own departments.

The team must also understand the responsibilities of each department in disaster recovery planning. Organizations can have many different structures and departments because of their size, location, and primary activities; these factors also affect the responsibilities of the planning team. Table 2-5 shows how departmental responsibilities are typically distributed within the planning team of a large organization.

Table 2-5   Departmental responsibilities in disaster recovery planning

Department/Function	Responsibility
Corporate Security	Advise on security issues and develop security-specific disaster recovery policies and procedures
Customer Support	Develop procedures that provide continuity in customer support
Facilities Management	Develop procedures to maintain damaged facilities, acquire new or temporary facilities, and provide logistical support to move staff and equipment
Human Resources	Develop procedures to communicate with employees during a disaster
Information Technology	Help assess business functions and the technology required to support them, including procedures to switch to backup computer systems
Investor Relations	Communicate disaster recovery planning efforts to investors and develop procedures to communicate with investors during a disaster
Legal counsel	Review and advise on all regulatory and contractual requirements for disaster recovery
Mail room	Develop procedures for a backup, alternate mail room
Manufacturing and Production	Develop procedures for alternate manufacturing processes or locations
Marketing	Determine how to leverage disaster recovery planning as a marketing tool
Network Management	Help assess business functions and the technology required to support them, including procedures to switch to backup networks
Public Relations	Facilitate awareness programs and develop procedures for communicating with external entities during a disaster

Department/Function	Responsibility
Research and Development	Develop procedures for alternate research and development processes or locations
Sales	Develop procedures for alternate sales processes or locations
Shipping and Receiving	Develop procedures for backup shipping and receiving support and facilities
Telecommunications (voice)	Help assess business functions and the technology required to support them, including procedures to switch to backup voice telecommunications systems
Training	Develop training programs for disaster recovery procedures

The Role of IT Staff and Network Managers on the Team

The IT and Network Management departments are represented on the disaster recovery planning team like any other department. However, the IT and Network Management departments probably require more representatives on the team than most other departments, and more of a role in planning.

IT and network managers on the team must address enterprise issues as well as specific department and business application issues. The mix of IT architecture and software applications helps determine how many IT staff need to be on the team, and their level of expertise.

In general, at least one representative each is needed for data center operations, network management, desktop computing, and each of the major IT applications, including financial management support, supply-chain systems, enterprise resource planning (ERP), and human resources support. Table 2-6 shows the planning areas in which IT and network managers need to be involved.

Table 2-6 Areas in which IT and network management assist the enterprise-wide disaster recovery planning team

Type of Staff	Technology support areas
Network management staff	Wide area network access
	Local area network access
	E-mail access
	Data backup and restoring data
	Access for telecommuters
	Access for mobile workers
Data center operations staff	Functioning of enterprise applications
	Functioning of department-specific applications
IT security staff	Maintenance of systems security
E-commerce staff	Functioning e-commerce applications, including Web servers, EDI applications, and supply-chain systems

Creating Interdepartmental Subcommittees

A **disaster recovery planning subcommittee** is a group of planning team members and technical experts from various departments that is formed to solve specific problems or explore special planning issues. These subcommittees typically address problems that do not need the full attention of the planning team, and require expertise that all team members may not possess.

For example, selecting outside consultants to assist in disaster recovery planning is a specialized task that not all team members need to address. Representatives from departments that perform more critical actions during disaster response and recovery may be better suited to assess and interview potential consultants. Because of their departments' activities and specific expertise, team members from corporate security, facilities management, IT, legal counsel, manufacturing, network management, and telecommunications may be better equipped to screen these consultants.

Organizing the Team at the Departmental Level

Each department should have its own disaster recovery planning group. These groups should conduct specific departmental research to help establish the corporate plan, help evaluate the plan as it is drafted by the enterprise team, and implement the plan at the department level once it is developed.

The size and membership of departmental teams vary depending on the department's diversity of activities. The teams should include a mix of supervisory personnel and technical experts for areas in which the department has enterprise responsibilities.

The major obstacle in forming well-rounded department planning groups is getting the time and interest of necessary supervisors and technical experts. As you recall, organizations encounter similar problems in establishing the enterprise planning team. Employees are already busy and focused on departmental performance goals that may affect their own compensation.

In addition, employees may feel threatened by the entire process of disaster recovery planning. Department managers are responsible for assembling a well-rounded team and motivating it to participate fully. One way to overcome resistance and objections is to establish a bonus program for department team members. Bonuses for working on special projects could range from $1000 to 5% of a team member's annual salary.

How IT Staff and Network Managers Should Work with Department Teams

IT staff and network managers should be prepared to work with departmental disaster recovery planning groups. Many departments may have specialized applications or systems, and IT and network managers can help department planning groups protect these systems in a crisis. They can also help departments overcome the technology challenges of operating in temporary quarters and completely recovering their operations.

Depending on how management is structured, some IT and network managers may work for a particular department or business unit or be assigned to support it full-time. These managers need to receive technical support or documentation about installed networks from the centralized IT and network management.

If IT and network managers are not assigned to particular departments or business units, the centralized management may need to provide technical support to department planning groups and advise them on the costs of disaster recovery alternatives.

CREATING AN INVENTORY OF PLANNING TEAM SKILLS

To help determine the skills of planning team members, the coordinator should compile an inventory of their background and training. A **skills inventory** includes a list of corporate team members and those in department planning groups, along with an assessment of each team member's skills. The inventory should point out which employee skills are most helpful in disaster recovery planning, and which team members have prior experience in managing such plans. This information should be available to everyone on the team.

Disaster recovery planners should also determine whether their team lacks any important skills, and then fill the gaps as necessary. This may require contracting with an outside consultant or seeking outside legal advice. Table 2-7 is an example of a skills inventory for the planning team.

Table 2-7   Skills inventory for disaster recovery planning team

Skill area	Assessment of skill base
Disaster recovery planning	None in-house, need outside help
Project management	Disaster recovery planning coordinator has managed large projects in the past and has a certificate in project management
Enterprise-wide planning	Representatives from facilities management and IT have worked on enterprise-wide planning projects
Written communications	Most members of the disaster recovery planning team have fairly good communication skills
Verbal communications	Most members of the disaster recovery planning team have made numerous presentations
Policy development types	Representatives from HR, security, and IT have developed other types of policies
Procedure development and writing	Representatives from HR, facilities management, and IT have developed and written many types of procedures
Manual/plan creation and writing	Representatives from HR and IT have created and written many manuals

In addition, all planning team members need to conduct initial assessments of their own departments to determine if any staff have experience with disaster recovery planning. Departmental team members with related experience need to be noted as potential resources to help other departments assess their planning needs, and to help implement the enterprise plan. Table 2-8 is an example of an **individual skill inventory** that may be helpful in disaster recovery planning.

The major obstacle to conducting this skills inventory is time. The planning team may need a full-time employee who can conduct the inventory and follow up with people who have not completed their skills assessments by the deadline. In addition, the skills inventories need to be catalogued after they have been assessed, which also takes time.

Some employees may resist participating in the skills inventory, because they may not be working with the departmental groups by choice. The department's planning team representative is clearly the key person in overcoming such resistance.

Once the disaster recovery planning team understands the skills of its own members and the individual department teams, it can begin training members to make up for the deficiencies identified during the skill assessments.

Table 2-8 Individual skill inventory form

Employee skill inventory report	
Employee name: _____	Department: _____
Job title: _____	Work location: _____
Job function: _____	Telephone: _____
Job duties: _____	E-mail: _____
Areas of expertise	**Comments**
Disaster recovery planning experience: Yes No	
Project management experience: Yes No	
Diagramming software experience: Yes No	
Written communications experience: Yes No	
Verbal communications experience: Yes No	
Business process analysis experience: Yes No	
Technical writing experience: Yes No	
Manual writing experience: Yes No	
Manual editing experience: Yes No	
Policy writing experience: Yes No	
Procedure writing experience: Yes No	
Procedure testing experience: Yes No	
Other (explain):	

TRAINING THE DISASTER RECOVERY PLANNING TEAM

The planning team needs training to understand what it is trying to do, as well as understand the issues and basic concepts of disaster recovery planning. Each team member should research disaster recovery issues that affect their disciplines or departments. This research includes case studies of what other organizations have done, professional papers from their disciplines, or government regulations that individual departments need to observe in their business processes. The departmental planning groups should do much of this research; each department representative should report back to the enterprise planning team with the results.

The biggest obstacle to disaster recovery training is getting all the team members together at one time and getting them to focus on the topic. Formal training sessions should be conducted away from organization facilities. Hotels and meeting centers are readily available and are not expensive. Of course, the basic rules of meeting etiquette apply during training—participants should turn off cell phones and beepers and wear "business casual" attire.

Training benefits everyone on the planning team and helps make the organization more effective in developing a successful plan. However, training the staff probably cannot develop all the skills the planning team requires. For skills that are not taught internally, organizations should recruit outside assistance.

Selecting Outside Help

Many organizations need outside help at some stage of disaster recovery planning. Once they have inventoried the skills of the planning team and members have undergone initial training, organizations are more likely to know what outside support they need. Most often, for example, organizations do not have in-house legal counsel. In other cases, they need trained policy and procedure writers. Organizations should identify the skills they need to contract for and recruit appropriate people early in disaster recovery planning. This helps maintain momentum as planning proceeds.

As shown in Figure 2-5, two of every 10 organizations surveyed for this book have hired outside consultants for disaster recovery planning. This trend has a good side and a bad side. It's always good to be able to contract outside talent when organizations need help, but it may be difficult to determine the consultant's quality and level of expertise.

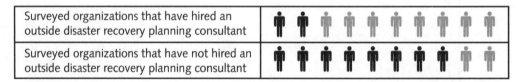

| Surveyed organizations that have hired an outside disaster recovery planning consultant | |
| Surveyed organizations that have not hired an outside disaster recovery planning consultant | |

Figure 2-5 Survey of whether organizations have hired an outside disaster recovery planning consultant

The consulting market is often flooded with new offerings when trends shift in business and technology. During the late 1990s, for example, organizations scurried to make sure their computer and communications technology would not fail because of Y2K problems. Managers were barraged by offers from consultants who claimed they could help solve the problem. Many of these consultants were talented and did excellent work. Unfortunately, many others were not, which caused considerable frustration and wasted plenty of time and money.

The disaster recovery and security markets boomed after the terrorist attacks of September 11, 2001, and as a result many entrepreneurs marketed their expertise in these areas. Many managers interviewed for this book find the situation reminiscent of the Y2K consulting boom, and are concerned about the quality of outside consultants. The major obstacle to finding outside assistance for disaster recovery planning is determining just what expertise is needed and then locating the appropriate people. Organizations should be cautioned not to rely too heavily on outside experts to develop disaster recovery plans.

Setting the Planning Team's Schedule

Organizations should establish an agenda for their disaster recovery planning team and set a schedule for accomplishing goals immediately after the team has been formed. The first step is to set a regular meeting schedule. Weekly meetings are recommended for the first several weeks. The planning team coordinator should oversee the scheduling of these meetings to ensure that all involved parties attend.

During these initial meetings, the team needs to establish a communications process, and if a company so chooses, form subcommittees, identify responsibilities, and assign interdepartmental tasks. The departmental planning groups should meet as often as necessary to keep their tasks on schedule and support the enterprise-wide planning team.

The major problem in setting a schedule is that the disaster recovery planning team does not know how complex its planning might become. After the team is established, an organization should assume that its team needs at least one year to implement the plan. Of course, this time varies depending on the organization's size, geographic distribution, and business processes, and how many people can dedicate time to the plan. In addition, organizations with a highly centralized and structured Information Management Department may be able to move through the planning process at a faster pace. Table 2-9 shows a sample disaster recovery planning schedule.

Table 2-9 Sample disaster recovery planning schedule

Duration	Activity
One month	Establishing the organization's disaster recovery planning team
Three months	Conducting risk assessment and business impact analysis
Three months	Drafting policies and procedures
Two months	Finishing and documenting policies and procedures
One month	Implementing changes and training staff on policies and procedures
One month	Testing and rehearsing parts of the disaster recovery plan, and eventually rehearsing the total plan
Indefinite	Ongoing plan maintenance and documentation

STARTING AN AWARENESS CAMPAIGN

To successfully implement a disaster recovery plan, an organization needs the support of all its employees. As shown in Figure 2-6, five of every 10 managers surveyed for this book think that employees in their organization do not take planning efforts seriously enough. Organizations must therefore start building awareness of their planning efforts early in the process.

The goal of an awareness campaign is to inform all the employees in an enterprise about the disaster recovery planning effort. In-house media campaigns are helpful in achieving this goal, as is enterprise-wide training. Media campaigns can include articles in employee newsletters, postings on enterprise intranets, and posters on bulletin boards. Public relations staff should be asked to help develop these campaigns.

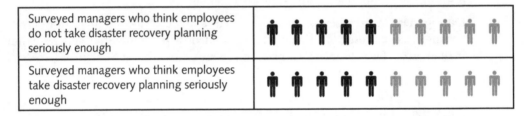

Surveyed managers who think employees do not take disaster recovery planning seriously enough	
Surveyed managers who think employees take disaster recovery planning seriously enough	

Figure 2-6 Survey of whether managers think employees in their organization take disaster recovery planning seriously enough

In addition to awareness campaigns, an organization should start training new employees and existing staff on the disaster recovery plan and planning topics in general. Because it can take a long time to get such campaigns rolling, awareness building should start during the early stages of planning.

The biggest obstacles to an effective awareness campaign are adequate funding and a lack of experienced communications staff. Of course, the amount of funding required for a successful campaign depends on the organization's size and geographical characteristics.

If an organization already has communications such as newsletters, annual or quarterly meetings, and intranets, the awareness campaign is less expensive to launch. If these communications do not exist, special efforts and more money are needed to publicize the campaign.

Many smaller enterprises do not have communications staffs, and need to contract with outside organizations to manage the awareness campaign. Regardless of whether in-house staff or external staff work on the campaign, they must have experience in such efforts. If an organization uses in-house staff, they should be trained in awareness building. If the organization uses outside agencies, they must demonstrate their experience in awareness building before being hired.

The Message Upper Management Should Convey to the Outside

As executives interact with their counterparts in other organizations, they should convey a consistent and uniform message about their disaster recovery planning efforts. The substance of these messages can surely be reinforced during training, but it is prudent to develop statements even earlier if possible.

In general, any executive statements regarding the organization's disaster recovery planning should be relatively short and to the point. These statements should be formulated in coordination with the planning team, the public relations staff, and even the legal counsel, depending on the circumstances. Only the well-versed executive should go into greater detail when discussing disaster recovery planning.

Also, executives should not comment on pending legislation or government regulations. Usually these laws and regulations are open to interpretation; they often take time to clarify and are sometimes overturned in court.

If asked about legislative issues, the executive should have a comment prepared, such as: "We have established a process in which our disaster recovery planning team reviews new laws with counsel and establishes appropriate procedures." Further comments are not advisable; if necessary, the inquirer should be referred to the planning team coordinator.

What Upper Management Should Tell the Board and Investors

Executives are responsible for briefing the board of directors on the organization's disaster recovery planning. These briefings should be precise reports on the plan's progress and obstacles.

As the team begins to implement the disaster recovery plan, the board may want a copy of the plan. If the board is not interested in the details, the planning team coordinator should prepare a five- to 10-minute presentation for the board that covers the plan's high points and its implementation.

The investor relations staff can work with executives to prepare a brief overview of the plan and post it on the corporate Web page. If investor meetings occur on a scheduled basis, the investor relations staff should work with executives to determine how much plan information should be distributed to attendees.

Executives and the investor relations staff should prepare a brief statement that captures the organization's basic philosophy of disaster recovery planning. The statement should inform investors that the organization is putting considerable effort into developing the plan.

Investors should also receive a telephone number to call if they have further inquiries about disaster recovery planning. Executives should avoid giving investors too many details about planning procedures. Instead, investors should be referred to the investor relations staff, who can work with the planning team to make sure investors receive consistent answers.

The Message to take to the Media and the General Public

Executives are constantly confronted with questions from the media, and sometimes from the general public at various functions and meetings. Their responses to questions about disaster recovery planning should be short and to the point, just like their responses to boards of directors, investors, and business partners. Executives should refer detailed questions to the public relations staff and the disaster recovery planning team.

The purpose of this approach is not to obfuscate or deceive, but to avoid putting executives in the awkward position of explaining details they may not know off the top of their heads. Besides helping the executives, this approach helps to ensure that the media and public receive consistent answers to questions.

If an organization decides to take a high profile with its disaster recovery planning efforts, it can hold a general press conference or analysts briefing. However, executives must script and refine all comments before the briefing, and have them reviewed by the planning team, the Public Relations Department, and legal counsel.

During such briefings, the planning team director should be present to address specific questions. The planning team, public relations staff, and legal counsel should try to anticipate questions beforehand, then agree which ones the executive should address at the briefing and which ones should be answered in a follow-up session or conversation.

BUDGETING FOR DISASTER RECOVERY PLANNING AND MANAGEMENT

Organizations use one of two major models to establish a disaster recovery function: a centralized office or a part-time coordinator. Four of every 10 organizations surveyed for this book use a centralized office, while the other six have placed the function in another department. As you might imagine, a centralized office requires a larger budget than a part-time planning coordinator. Regardless of the office structure, salaries are usually the most expensive item in a disaster recovery planning budget.

This section lists salaries for full-time planning staff, along with budget models for the two major structures of disaster recovery planning. As shown in Figure 2-7, five of every 10 organizations surveyed for this book had disaster recovery planning coordinators who did not work full-time on planning.

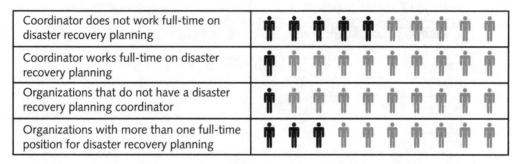

Coordinator does not work full-time on disaster recovery planning	
Coordinator works full-time on disaster recovery planning	
Organizations that do not have a disaster recovery planning coordinator	
Organizations with more than one full-time position for disaster recovery planning	

Figure 2-7 Survey of whether disaster recovery planning coordinators work full-time on planning

Salaries for Disaster Recovery Planning Staff

Salaries for full-time disaster recovery planners are influenced by location, years of experience, and related certifications. Tables 2-10, 2-11, and 2-12 show salary levels for full-time planners by region, by city, and by industry, respectively. Data for the salary surveys in this book was collected from a variety of resources, including recruiters, job postings, and disaster recovery planning coordinators. The data represents salary trends in more than 200 organizations.

Table 2-10 Average salaries for full-time disaster recovery planning staff, by region

Region	Noncertified	Certified
East	$79,000	$87,000
Midwest	$62,000	$69,000
Mountain	$60,000	$68,000
Pacific	$72,000	$81,000

Salary levels for IT professionals, security personnel, and disaster recovery planners tend to fluctuate wildly. For example, starting salaries for network engineers soared during the last decade, then leveled off and actually declined in many locations. Programmers with various levels of expertise have seen similar salary shifts. These shifts are usually tied to the classic laws of supply and demand. As demand goes up, salaries for new employees go up temporarily. As the supply of talent grows, or new technologies are brought to market to displace the need for talent, salaries tend to level off or decline.

The salaries presented in Tables 2-10, 2-11, and 2-12 are based on an analysis of trends after the terrorist attacks of September 11, 2001. These salaries are considerably higher than salaries offered in the late 1990s. Salaries for disaster recovery planners should continue to increase at a higher rate than those of other business and IT analysts until 2005. At that point, the wave of disaster recovery planning inspired by the terrorist attacks will probably be over. After 2005, salaries for disaster recovery planners will most likely level off, initial salary offers for new employees will decline, and most organizations will shift to a mainten-

Table 2-11 Average salaries for full-time disaster recovery planning staff, by city

City	Noncertified	Certified
Atlanta	$62,000	$69,000
Boston	$78,000	$87,000
Chicago	$60,000	$68,000
Dallas/Fort Worth	$58,000	$65,000
Denver	$56,000	$62,000
Los Angeles	$75,000	$85,000
Minneapolis	$58,000	$64,000
New York	$77,000	$86,000
San Francisco	$79,000	$86,000
San Jose	$75,000	$83,000
Seattle	$62,000	$68,000
Washington, D.C.	$67,000	$73,000

Table 2-12 Average salaries for full-time disaster recovery planning staff, by industry

Industry	Noncertified	Certified
Banking/finance	$68,000	$75,000
Education	$51,000	$54,000
Government	$55,000	$58,000
Insurance	$56,000	$62,000
Manufacturing	$72,000	$79,000
Professional services	$74,000	$82,000
Retail/wholesale distribution	$60,000	$66,000
Transportation	$78,000	$85,000

ance mode of disaster recovery planning. However, organizations will still need additional disaster recovery planners to update existing plans, and to develop plans for new operations or facilities.

Budget Structure for a Centralized Office of Disaster Recovery Planning

A centralized office of disaster recovery planning is probably necessary in large organizations. Each organization can place the office within a reporting structure that makes the most sense; this placement varies by organization. A centralized planning office requires several budget items, as shown in Table 2-13.

Table 2-13 Budget structure for a centralized office of disaster recovery planning

Budget item	Cost factors
Salary and benefits for coordinator or director, for documentation specialist, for administrative assistant, and for other staff	Salaries and benefit costs depend on the organization's location and industry activity; salaries are higher for certified staff
Office space	Many organizations charge their departments for office space; charges are usually calculated annually according to square footage
Computer systems, network connectivity, and software	Many organizations charge for network connectivity; the costs of desktop PCs, notebook computers, and peripherals usually come out of the department budget. In addition, specialized software for project management or department-specific tasks is charged directly to the department.
Telephone	Many organizations charge their departments for telephone service and long-distance calls; charges are usually calculated on an annual or monthly basis
Office equipment	Can include photocopiers, digital projectors, digital cameras, etc.
Outside services and consultants	Can include specialized consultants for disaster recovery planning or contracts for emergency services
Training programs	Can include training for the disaster recovery planning staff, enterprise planning team, or specialized training of managers or employees in the disaster recovery plan
Disaster response technology	Can include emergency radio communications systems or other technology that can be used during disaster response
Disaster response expenses	Can include emergency housing or office space needed during disaster response
Travel	Can include expenses for disaster recovery staff to attend training, conferences, or meetings at other corporate locations

Budget Structure for a Part-Time Disaster Recovery Coordinator

When centralized offices of disaster recovery planning are not necessary, the budget structure is considerably different. For example, a part-time disaster recovery coordinator usually requires fewer staff and less overhead. In addition, part-time coordinators have other responsibilities, so they usually have an office, computer, and telephone already in place. Table 2-14 shows a sample budget structure for a part-time disaster recovery coordinator.

Table 2-14 Budget structure for a part-time disaster recovery coordinator

Budget item	Cost factors
Salary and benefits for coordinator or director	Salaries and benefits costs depend on the organization's location and industry activity. Salaries are higher for certified staff. If the coordinator is part-time, only the salary paid for time spent on disaster recovery is charged to the disaster recovery budget.
Office space, computer systems, network connectivity, software, telephones, and office equipment	Part-time disaster recovery coordinators usually have an office, computer, and telephone to perform their other tasks. If charges to the disaster recovery budget are necessary, they can be prorated based on the amount of time spent on the activity. If specialized software is required, it is charged to the disaster recovery budget.
Outside services and consultants	Can include specialized consultants for disaster recovery planning or contracts for emergency services
Training programs	Can include training for the disaster recovery planning staff, enterprise planning team, or specialized training of managers or employees in the disaster recovery plan
Disaster response technology	Can include emergency radio communications systems or other technology that can be used during disaster response
Disaster response expenses	Can include emergency housing or office space needed during disaster response
Travel	Can include expenses for disaster recovery staff to attend training, conferences, or meetings at other corporate locations

COPING WITH STANDARDS AND REGULATORY BODIES

When developing a disaster recovery plan, the team must recognize that organizations in many industries are required by law to have specific procedures in place. Managers often have trouble interpreting what action or standard a regulation requires, so an organization's legal counsel must research and interpret these requirements. Disaster recovery planners need the same type of legal assistance.

Depending on the country where an organization operates, nongovernmental standards bodies and professional organizations might set standards for business operations, including disaster recovery planning.

Many professional business and technology-related organizations offer certification programs for employees, which can provide a level of confidence and security both to employers and the certified professionals. There has been considerable debate about the value and necessity of certified employees. Many employers err on the side of caution, considering it safer to hire people with certificates instead of relying on the experience that unknown applicants claim on their resumes. However, many successful people in various walks of life have not been certified.

For disaster recovery planners, certifications and extensive knowledge of the discipline do not compensate for strong project management and communication skills. Employers should balance the need for these skills when hiring disaster recovery planners and consultants.

ASSESSING PROGRESS AND PREPARING TO MOVE AHEAD

As an organization establishes a disaster recovery planning team and works to develop a plan, the upper-level managers, department managers, and team members are confronted with massive amounts of new material and a long list of challenges. It is wise for them to take time to absorb the new information and contemplate the challenges ahead.

It is easy to become overwhelmed by large projects, and the challenge of developing an enterprise-wide disaster recovery plan can seem endless during the early steps. Managers should evaluate progress as the process moves from one step to the next. For example, Table 2-15 shows a **disaster recovery planning checklist** . Once the planning team has completed all the items on the list, the team and department groups should be ready to move to Step Two of the plan—assessing risks in the enterprise. Chapter 3 describes this step in detail; it is far less ceremonial than Step One, but it requires thoroughness and great attention to detail.

Table 2-15   Checklist for organizing the disaster recovery plan

Activity	Status
An executive-level champion has been identified to uphold the organization's disaster recovery planning philosophy	(for example, complete, pending, or not applicable)
A disaster recovery planning coordinator has been appointed to manage the day-to-day efforts of the planning team; the coordinator has been provided resources to successfully develop the plan	
The disaster recovery planning team is in place and functioning	
Departments have formed their own disaster recovery planning groups	
The skills of the enterprise-wide planning team and department groups have been assessed	
Training has been conducted to round out the skills of the disaster recovery planning team	
If outside help is necessary, a consultant has been identified and selected	
A schedule has been developed for the work of the planning team	
An internal awareness program has begun	

CHAPTER SUMMARY

- One of the greatest frustrations for disaster recovery planners is the difficulty of gaining and maintaining support from upper-level managers. Executives need to be trained in disaster recovery planning and regularly briefed on the progress of the plan.

- The disaster recovery planning coordinator should represent all corporate concerns for the plan and balance various department perspectives. The coordinator needs to be detail-oriented without getting lost in the process, and be able to work diplomatically with all departments and external resources. In addition to the documents the planning coordinator keeps, a team member needs to keep current logs of disaster recovery planning activities.

- Every department in the organization needs to be represented on the disaster recovery planning team. Each department should have two representatives—a primary and an alternate. The primary department representative is a full member of the planning team, and the alternate department representative is a secondary member. The primary and alternate representatives are also co-leaders of their department's internal disaster recovery planning efforts.

- To help determine the skills of planning team members, the coordinator should compile an inventory of their background and training. A skills inventory includes a list of corporate team members and those in departmental planning groups, along with an assessment of each team member's skills. The inventory should point out which employee skills are most helpful in disaster recovery planning, and which team members have prior experience in managing such plans. This information should be available to everyone on the team.

- The major obstacle to disaster recovery training is getting all the team members together at one time and getting them to focus on the topic. Formal training sessions should be conducted away from organization facilities. Hotels and meeting centers are readily available and are not expensive.

- The goal of an awareness campaign is to inform all the employees in an enterprise about the disaster recovery planning effort. The biggest obstacles to an effective awareness campaign are adequate funding and experienced communications staff to work on the campaign. Of course, the funding required for a successful campaign depends on the organization's size and geographical characteristics.

- Organizations use one of two major models to establish a disaster recovery function: a centralized office or a part-time coordinator. Some organizations use a centralized office of disaster recovery planning, while others place the function in another department. The centralized office model requires a higher budget than a part-time planning coordinator. Regardless of the office structure for disaster recovery planning, salaries are usually the most expensive item in the budget.

- When developing a disaster recovery plan, the team must recognize that organizations in many industries are required by law to have specific procedures in place. Managers often have trouble interpreting what action or standard a regulation requires, so an organization's legal counsel must research and interpret these requirements. Disaster recovery planners need the same type of legal assistance.

❒ Once the planning team has completed all the tasks for organizing its disaster recovery plan, it should be ready to move to Step Two of the plan—assessing risks in the enterprise.

KEY TERMS

activity log — A list of important events or accomplishments, the dates they occurred, which departments participated, and how the events relate to other disaster recovery planning activities.

alternate department representative — An employee who serves as a secondary member of the enterprise disaster recovery planning team and a co-leader of a department's internal planning efforts.

CEO — Chief executive officer.

CFO — Chief financial officer.

CIO — Chief information officer.

COO — Chief operating officer.

disaster planning support list — A list of people with whom executives can discuss issues in preparation for addressing audiences about disaster recovery planning.

disaster recovery planning checklist — A checklist of tasks to accomplish in Step One of disaster recovery planning.

disaster recovery planning subcommittee — A group of planning team members and technical experts from various departments that is formed to solve specific problems or explore special planning issues.

executive preparation — Training executives to articulate an organization's philosophy for disaster recovery planning.

individual skill inventory — A form that lists skills of individual planning team members. This inventory may be helpful in disaster recovery planning.

primary department representative — A full member of the enterprise disaster recovery planning team and a co-leader of a department's internal disaster planning.

skills inventory — A skills assessment of each person on the disaster recovery planning team and departmental planning groups. These assessments can help determine how team members may be most useful in disaster recovery planning.

REVIEW QUESTIONS

1. What steps make it easier to successfully change an organization or implement an enterprise-wide initiative?

2. Who should brief executives on the disaster recovery planning effort?

3. How will executive support for disaster recovery planning affect the planning effort?

4. Every department in the enterprise needs to be represented on the disaster recovery planning team. True or False?

5. Departmental disaster recovery planners should not work with their corporate planning team, but carry out an independent effort. True or False?

6. Disaster recovery planners should determine if their team is missing any important skills, and then fill the gaps as necessary. True or False?

7. All members of the disaster recovery planning team should take responsibility for researching planning issues that directly affect their own departments. True or False?

8. Very few organizations need outside help at any stage of their disaster recovery planning. True or False?

9. An organization does not need to build awareness of its disaster recovery planning efforts early in the process, because it can always be done later. True or False?

10. How can an organization's size, geographic distribution, and business processes affect the disaster recovery planning effort?

11. Any statement that an executive makes regarding an organization's disaster recovery planning should be _____.

   a. detailed enough to convey meaning

   b. relatively short and to the point

   c. accompanied by supporting documents

   d. none of the above

12. Within an organization, who is responsible for briefing the board of directors about disaster recovery planning?

13. Explain why disaster recovery planners must work within the structure of the organization for which the plan is being developed.

14. What role should the Public Relations Department have during the early stages of disaster recovery planning?

15. Why should key public relations personnel and legal counsel work with executives before the executives make statements about disaster recovery planning?

16. Explain how to keep executive champions interested in disaster recovery planning.

17. Organizations need which of the following to successfully implement a disaster recovery plan?

 a. the support of all the employees in an organization

 b. the support of the employees' families

 c. approval of the U.S. government

 d. a certified disaster recovery planner

18. The major obstacle to training a disaster recovery planning team is _____. (Choose all that apply.)

 a. getting all of the team members together at one time

 b. getting all of the team members to focus on the topic

 c. having too many topics to cover

 d. finding a secluded place to hold training so team members are not distracted by day-to-day tasks

19. Explain two important skills that a disaster recovery planning coordinator should have. Explain how these skills will help the coordinator and the team accomplish their goals.

20. Explain the purpose of an activity log.

21. Explain the benefits of forming interdepartmental subcommittees for disaster recovery planning.

22. Explain how the central IT and network management functions can help departmental planning groups achieve their goals for disaster recovery planning.

23. What factors influence the salaries of full-time disaster recovery planners?

24. Explain why the budget structure for centralized offices of disaster recovery planning differs from that of part-time coordinators.

25. What major activities should the planning team accomplish during Step One of disaster recovery planning?

HANDS-ON PROJECTS

HANDS-ON PROJECTS

Project 2–1

Write a memorandum that informs all department heads how to prepare for the first meeting of the disaster recovery planning team. The memo should include the following items:

- Instructions to appoint a representative from their department to the organization's planning team

- Information on this representative's role at the enterprise planning level and the department level

- A notice that the team will conduct a skills inventory to determine which employees can best contribute to disaster recovery planning

- A notice that department heads will receive an agenda for the first meeting two weeks before the meeting

When you finish, submit the memo to your instructor for review.

Project 2–2

Develop an agenda for the first meeting of the enterprise disaster recovery planning team. Write the agenda to be appropriate for distribution to all department heads or appointed departmental representatives. The agenda should include the following items:

- The time and place of the meeting

- The purpose of the meeting

- The expected duration of the meeting

- What attendees can do to prepare for the meeting

When you finish, submit the agenda to your instructor for review.

Project 2–3

Develop a draft budget document for a disaster recovery planning team. Include as many budget items as you think are necessary. If you cannot estimate the expense for a specific item, develop a list of research questions that can help you determine its cost. The draft budget document should also include:

- The period of time covered by the disaster recovery planning budget

- A brief rationale for each budget item

- A description of how the budget will be evaluated when it is time to extend funding for disaster recovery planning

- A brief description of how major expenditures will be justified

When you finish, submit the document to your instructor for review.

CASE PROJECTS

**CASE
PROJECTS**

Case Project: Harris and Heartfield Manufacturing

The Harris and Heartfield Manufacturing Company is a family-owned business that fabricates specialized metal parts. Matthew Harris and Henry Heartfield founded the company in 1942 to provide parts for defense contractors. The company has an excellent reputation for manufacturing high-quality parts and delivering orders on schedule. Brandon L. Harris and Tonya Heartfield, the grandchildren of the founders, now run the company.

Although the U.S. defense industry has consolidated and now spends less money on defense products, the company still receives about 60% of its revenue from defense contractors. Another 25% of revenue comes from producing specialized metal parts for manufacturers of heavy equipment in North America. The remaining revenue is derived from orders for replacement parts that the company has manufactured in the past, and from custom orders for parts used to develop prototypes of equipment.

Harris and Heartfield has 200 employees at its only location in Carlsbad, California. The Administrative Department has 20 employees, all of whom have desktop computers connected to a local area network (LAN). The Research and Design Department has 15 engineers, all of whom use Sun Microsystems workstations that are connected to the company's LAN. There are three servers for administrative functions and six servers that support design and manufacturing. The shop floor has a variety of machining equipment, about half of which is computerized.

Management is concerned about the company's ability to remain competitive over the next several decades, and especially concerned about their ability to fulfill orders if some unexpected event hindered their manufacturing capabilities. The board of directors is relatively business savvy, but does not invest money unless they think the investment can provide a positive return.

Previously the company hired you as a consultant to create a list of 10 key points that conveyed the importance of disaster recovery planning to the board. The board has now directed you to compile a more detailed proposal for developing a plan.

Your assignment is to prepare for a discussion with company executives about the project. The discussion will focus on how the company should organize and prepare for developing a disaster recovery plan. Develop a list of 10 primary discussion points and the purpose of each point.

OPTIONAL TEAM CASE PROJECTS

Team Case One

Your boss has asked you to identify sources for training the disaster recovery planning team, including professional training organizations, colleges, and universities. Your assignment is to find five possible sources of training for the planning team and write a one-paragraph description of each. The description should include the name of the training organization and how it can help your planning team. If you use the Internet, identify the URL of the Web site where you found the information.

Team Case Two

Your boss has asked you to identify potential certifications for disaster recovery planning coordinators. Your assignment is to find such certifications in the United States and the European Union, and then write a one-paragraph description of each. Briefly describe each certification process, the cost of obtaining the certification, and the name of the certifying organization. If you use the Internet, identify the URL of the Web site where you found the information.

3

ASSESSING RISKS IN THE ENTERPRISE

After reading this chapter, you will be able to:

♦ Collect risk assessment data

♦ Inventory and document business processes

♦ Identify and categorize threats and vulnerabilities

♦ Measure and quantify threats

♦ Compile risk assessment reports

Assessing the risks that an organization faces is a complicated process. Disaster recovery planners need to work with many people in an organization to ensure that risks are thoroughly reviewed. Planners must also examine the conditions and potential risks of related communities, business partners, suppliers, and customers, which may ultimately affect the enterprise.

Next, the organization must reasonably quantify and qualify the potential business losses that could occur as a result of these risks. This requires an in-depth analysis of the importance of each business process to the organization's operations, revenue, legal responsibilities, and contractual obligations.

Risks and potential losses are delicately balanced against each other when determining how to approach disaster recovery planning. If national laws or regulations apply, planners must account for them. Some organizations need disaster recovery plans that require restored operations at some level within minutes or hours. Other organizations may be able to recover at a slower pace.

Regardless of the potential consequences an organization faces, the risk assessment step is critical. Risk assessment is the fundamental building block of disaster recovery planning; future steps in the planning process and successful disaster recovery depend on it.

COLLECTING RISK ASSESSMENT DATA

Risks are the potential consequences of events or conditions that can adversely affect an organization's operations and revenues, as well as its relationships with communities, business partners, suppliers, and customers. Before analyzing risks, the disaster recovery planning team must first determine the likelihood of an event's occurrence and their organization's related operating conditions.

To understand the possible impact of adverse events and related conditions, the disaster recovery planning team must inventory its exposure to such events. An **exposure inventory** is an annotated list of all facilities, processes, systems, and resources that an organization uses to maintain operations and sustain revenue. The scope of the exposure inventory depends on the organization's size, number of employees, number of locations, and numerous other factors. The exposure inventory should be conducted for each facility that an organization owns or operates; this inventory should include, but not necessarily be limited to, the following areas:

- Physical facilities

- Personnel

- Heavy equipment and light equipment

- Installed systems

- Information technology

- Office equipment

- Products or parts

Many organizations have asset inventory systems in place that provide considerable information for exposure inventory. If an organization has a Facilities Management Department or director, this information may have been compiled already. However, the records of the facilities manager probably do not contain all the necessary information. For example, a facilities manager seldom has up-to-date information for LANs or telephone systems. Before the disaster recovery planning team begins an exposure inventory, team members should check to determine what data might be available.

Depending on the level of centralization in network and telecommunications management, some of the information needed to inventory exposure may be available from the Information Technology (IT) Department. However, experience shows that assets often grow faster than the ability to track new items coming into an organization. Computers, servers, and LAN equipment have a way of multiplying rapidly. Thus, once the exposure inventory is completed, it should be kept up to date.

An organization should maintain a set of exposure inventory sheets for each facility. These forms can be printed and maintained on paper, but organizations can save considerable time and effort by maintaining the forms in a popular database or spreadsheet program, and by publishing the forms on an internal Web site for company-wide access.

Exposure inventory sheets are numbered in a series, as shown in Table 3-1.

3

Table 3-1 Numbering scheme for exposure inventory sheets

Form number	Sheet name
FEIOS01	Facility exposure inventory overview sheet
PFEIS01	Physical facilities exposure inventory sheet
PEIS01	Personnel exposure inventory sheet
HEEIS01	Heavy equipment exposure inventory sheet
LEEIS01	Light equipment exposure inventory sheet
ISEIS01	Installed systems exposure inventory sheet
ITEIS01	Information technology exposure inventory sheet
OEEIS01	Office equipment exposure inventory sheet
PPEIS01	Products/parts exposure inventory sheet

The first necessary sheet is the **facility exposure inventory overview sheet** (Table 3-2). Its purpose is to keep track of the more detailed exposure inventories needed for each facility. The overview sheet shows the name and address of the facility, as well as its main telephone number, fax number, e-mail address, and disaster recovery contact. In addition, there are spaces to indicate which detailed exposure inventories are attached, when the exposure inventories were last updated, and when the next update is scheduled. The bottom of the sheet includes a space to explain which business processes are performed at the facility.

As the overview sheet shows, there are individual **exposure inventory sheets** for physical facilities, personnel, heavy equipment, light equipment, installed systems, information technology, office equipment, and products or parts. The exposure inventory sheets provide details for assets at the facility identified by the inventory overview sheet.

If a specific exposure inventory sheet is not needed for the facility, you can circle N/A on the overview sheet to indicate that the sheet is not applicable. In some cases, for example, a facility may not have heavy equipment, so this exposure inventory sheet is unnecessary.

All of these inventory sheets are shown in the "Compiling Risk Assessment Reports" section later in this chapter, and briefly explained in the following list. Many of the inventory sheets include spaces for listing alternate facilities where equipment can be duplicated in case of disaster. The inventory sheets should also include a four-digit facility number and a building number to identify the buildings being inventoried. The building number combines the facility number with a unique, three-digit number.

Table 3-2 Facility exposure inventory overview sheet

<table>
<tr><td colspan="4" align="center">Facility Exposure Inventory Overview Sheet
(Form number FEIOS01)</td></tr>
<tr><td colspan="2">Facility number: 1000</td><td colspan="2">Number of buildings: 3
Number of employees:</td></tr>
<tr><td colspan="2">Facility name and location:
Name:
Address:

Main telephone:
Main fax number:
Main e-mail:</td><td colspan="2">Disaster recovery contact:
Name:
Address:

Telephone:
Fax number:
E-mail:</td></tr>
<tr><td>Exposure inventories attached:</td><td align="center">Status
(Circle one)</td><td align="center">Last Updated</td><td align="center">Next Update</td></tr>
<tr><td>Physical facilities</td><td>Yes No N/A</td><td></td><td></td></tr>
<tr><td>Personnel</td><td>Yes No N/A</td><td></td><td></td></tr>
<tr><td>Heavy equipment</td><td>Yes No N/A</td><td></td><td></td></tr>
<tr><td>Light equipment</td><td>Yes No N/A</td><td></td><td></td></tr>
<tr><td>Installed systems</td><td>Yes No N/A</td><td></td><td></td></tr>
<tr><td>Information technology</td><td>Yes No N/A</td><td></td><td></td></tr>
<tr><td>Office equipment</td><td>Yes No N/A</td><td></td><td></td></tr>
<tr><td>Products or parts</td><td>Yes No N/A</td><td></td><td></td></tr>
<tr><td colspan="4">Business processes performed at facility:</td></tr>
</table>

Disaster recovery planners should use additional inventory sheets if a single sheet cannot accommodate all the necessary data. Planners should number these sheets in the space provided directly under the form number.

- The facility exposure inventory overview sheet is described earlier in this section.

- Fill out a **physical facilities exposure inventory sheet** to describe every building at a facility. Physical facilities include manufacturing and processing plants, warehouses, offices, and shipping and receiving installations. This inventory sheet shows the square footage of the building, the number of employees who work in it, the business processes supported in it, and the dates of construction, renovation, and last safety inspections.

- Complete a **personnel exposure inventory sheet** for all employees in each building. The sheet lists the department(s) in the building, the number of employees in each department, and the business processes performed by each department in the building.

- The **heavy equipment exposure inventory sheet** lists all of the heavy equipment in each building. Heavy equipment includes manufacturing, transportation, and industrial plant equipment.

- The **light equipment exposure inventory sheet** lists all of the light equipment in each building, including tools, cleaning and maintenance equipment, and emergency equipment.

- The **installed systems exposure inventory sheet** lists all computer networks, telephone systems, fire prevention systems, and premises security systems in each building.

- The **information technology exposure inventory sheet** lists all of the information technology in each building, including large systems, servers, workstations, desktop computers, notebooks, PDAs, and related peripherals.

- The **office equipment exposure inventory sheet** lists all of the office equipment in each building, including furniture, built-in cabinetry, copiers, fax machines, and special lighting.

- The **products/parts exposure inventory sheet** lists all the products and parts in each building, including all finished products created by an organization and parts or raw material used to manufacture products.

DOCUMENTING BUSINESS PROCESSES

Once the disaster recovery planning team has completed an inventory of exposure, it should know which business processes are supported at every facility and by every department. At this point, the team needs to evaluate which business processes and facilities are most critical to the organization's operations and revenues, and to its relationships with communities, business partners, suppliers, and customers.

There are two primary types of organizations. A **product-focused organization** creates or distributes physical goods. A **service-focused organization** provides a specific service for a customer. Table 3-3 shows the five key goals for typical product-focused and service-focused organizations.

Table 3-3 Key organization goals

Product-focused organization	Service-focused organization
Revenue collection — The process of collecting money from customers	**Revenue collection** — The process of collecting money from customers
Product sales — The process of selling products to existing and new customers	**Service sales** — The process of selling services to existing and new customers
Product distribution — The delivery of products to distributors or customers	**Service delivery** — The provision of services to customers
Product manufacturing — The process and equipment required to create products	**Service platform** — The facility or equipment necessary to deliver services
Material, parts, and supplies procurement — The raw materials, parts, and supplies required to support operations	**Material, parts, and supplies procurement** — The raw materials, parts, and supplies required to support operations

Under normal conditions, organizations try to maintain a full level of functionality and achieve their key goals. However, when a disaster occurs, business processes can be completely or partially disabled. Disaster recovery planners need to examine the processes that make their organization successful. Before they can begin classifying the organization's systems and functions, planners must fully understand the organization's nature, mission, and goals. In addition, upper management must agree with the classification of systems and functions. Several key tests can be applied to help in this process.

Test one: Do any legal requirements affect the classification of systems and functions?

Depending on the industry and the geographical locations in which an organization operates, it may need to address legal requirements or government regulations. The legal counsel representative on the disaster recovery planning team must advise upper management and team members about these legal and regulatory requirements.

Test two: Do contractual requirements affect the classification of systems and functions?

Some organizations may have contractual arrangements with customers or suppliers that require certain functions or activities to be maintained at a specific level. If parts or finished goods must be delivered on schedule according to a contract, for example, then the organization has a contractual requirement to perform. Again, legal counsel must explain the meaning of these requirements to upper management and the planning team.

Test three: Do labor requirements affect the classification of systems and functions?

Some organizations may have labor union contracts in place. These contracts may specify working conditions that must be established before work can continue after a disaster. Again, legal counsel must explain the meaning of these requirements to upper management and the planning team.

Test four: Do competitive pressures affect the classification of systems and functions?

Almost all organizations face some level of competitive pressure. Representatives from the Marketing and Sales departments may be the best source of information about the magnitude of these pressures. These departments should advise upper management and the planning team accordingly.

Test five: Do financial pressures affect the classification of systems and functions?

Many organizations do not have sufficient cash reserves to absorb the cost or the potential loss caused by business disruptions. The chief financial officer (CFO) must advise upper management and the disaster recovery planning team about the financial consequences of disruptions.

Test six: Do humanitarian or social expectations affect the classification of systems and functions?

Some organizations face great humanitarian and social pressures that may affect their need to recover smoothly and quickly from a disaster. The Public Relations Department or the office of Social Responsibility must advise upper management and the planning team on the potential impact of these pressures on disaster recovery priorities and timelines.

Test seven: Do management requirements affect the classification of systems and functions?

Some organizations also face management or stockholder mandates regarding operations and the speed of disaster recovery. The Investor Relations Department and upper management must ensure that the planning team understands these mandates when formulating disaster recovery priorities and procedures.

Creating a Business Process Inventory

Understanding and documenting business processes is far more complicated than conducting an exposure inventory. The exposure inventory can easily be related to physical facilities and property. However, business processes can often span departments, buildings, and facilities that may not be located in the same geographical area.

A **business process inventory** is an annotated list of the key business processes needed to maintain operations, including revenue collection, sales, distribution and delivery, manufacturing, and procurement. A business process inventory illustrates:

- How a process works

- The facilities and buildings in which the process occurs

- The departments that perform the process

- The personnel who work in the departments

- The equipment used by the departments

- The installed systems on which the departments rely

- The information technology that the departments have in place

- The parts and supplies that the departments need to accomplish their work

Developing a business process inventory requires the assistance of all departments involved in a business process. Each department is represented on the disaster recovery planning team. When a business process spans more than one department, planning team representatives from each department must collaborate to create the business process inventory.

When developing a business process inventory, department representatives must use their own expertise and the information provided in the exposure inventory sheets described in the previous section. Staff from the Facilities Management, IT, Telecommunications, and Security departments can also assist department representatives in developing a business process inventory.

As with the exposure inventory, the business process inventory can be organized using a series of forms or computer-based records. Organizations should maintain **business process inventory sheets** for each facility or each group of related facilities in their business process. These inventory sheets provide details on the process, including which facilities, buildings, and departments support it, as well as the resources required to accomplish the process.

Table 3-4 shows a numbering scheme for business process inventory sheets. The processes shown in the table are common to many organizations. However, note that organizations may have unique business processes that need to be inventoried; the disaster recovery planning team must adjust the inventory scheme to fit its own organization.

These inventory sheets can be printed and maintained on paper, but organizations can save considerable time and effort by maintaining the forms in a popular database or spreadsheet program, and by publishing the forms on an internal Web site for company-wide access.

Table 3-4   Numbering schemes for business process inventories and support requirements sheets

Business process inventory form number	Business process support requirements form number	What the forms cover
BPIOS01	N/A	Business process inventory overview
RCIS01	RCSR01	Revenue collection
SIS01	SSR01	Sales
PDIS01	PDSR01	Product distribution
SDIS01	SDSR01	Service delivery
PMIS01	PMSR01	Product manufacturing
PIS01	PSR01	Procurement
Number accordingly	Number accordingly	Other business processes

The first necessary sheet is the **business process inventory overview sheet** (Table 3-5). Its purpose is to keep track of the more detailed business process inventories needed for each facility.

As you can see, there are specific business process inventory sheets for revenue collection, sales, product distribution, service delivery, product manufacturing, and procurement. Each inventory sheet provides detailed information for a specific division, product line, or location in an organization.

Note that the inventory sheets shown in the table may vary, depending on the nature of an organization. If a specific inventory sheet is not needed, you can circle N/A on the form to indicate that the sheet is not applicable to a facility.

Each inventory sheet also has a related **business process support requirements sheet**, which details the resources needed to support each process, including physical facilities, personnel, heavy equipment, light equipment, installed systems, information technology, and office equipment.

For the most part, data for the requirements analysis comes from the exposure inventory sheets for each facility. These processes need examination from more than one perspective. For example, the exposure inventory sheets provide a bottom-up data collection process, and should cover most requirements. However, disaster recovery planners must also look at the process from the top down. This view provides insight into the process as a whole; planners often find that items were overlooked during the exposure inventory.

Table 3-5 Business process inventory overview sheet

Business Process Inventory Overview Sheet (Form number BPIOS01)			
Facility name(s) and location(s): Name: Address: Main telephone: Main fax number: Main e-mail:		Disaster recovery contact(s): Name: Address: Telephone: Fax number: E-mail:	
Process inventories attached:	Status (Circle one)	Last Updated	Next Update
Revenue Collection	Yes No N/A		
Sales	Yes No N/A		
Product Distribution	Yes No N/A		
Service Delivery	Yes No N/A		
Product Manufacturing	Yes No N/A		
Procurement	Yes No N/A		
Other	Yes No N/A		
Comments:			

All of these inventory sheets and requirement sheets are shown in the "Compiling Risk Assessment Reports" section later in this chapter, and briefly explained in the following list. Each of these documents helps the disaster recovery planning team develop procedures later in the planning process.

Planners can use additional inventory sheets if a single sheet cannot accommodate all the necessary data. Planners should number these sheets in the space directly under the form number. There is also space for the entity name covered by the sheet, a business process number, a facility number, and a building number.

Each process inventoried in the following forms should be assigned a number to facilitate record keeping and orderly analysis. Complex organizations may have several unrelated points of revenue collection, sales, product distribution, service delivery, product manufacturing, and procurement. If so, each of these unrelated points requires its own inventory sheet and support requirements sheet.

- The **revenue collection inventory sheet** provides detailed information about revenue collection.

- The **revenue collection support requirements sheet** details the resources needed to support revenue collection.

- Each **sales inventory sheet** provides detailed information about product or service sales.

- The **sales support requirements sheet** details the resources needed to support sales.

- The **product distribution inventory sheet** provides detailed information about product distribution.

- The **distribution support requirements sheet** details the resources needed to support distribution.

- The **service delivery inventory sheet** provides detailed information about service delivery.

- The **service delivery support requirements sheet** details the resources needed to support service delivery.

- The **product manufacturing inventory sheet** provides detailed information about manufacturing.

- The **product manufacturing support requirements sheet** details the resources needed to support manufacturing.

- The **procurement inventory sheet** provides detailed information about procurement.

- The **procurement support requirements sheet** details the resources needed to support procurement.

IDENTIFYING THREATS AND VULNERABILITIES

After completing an exposure inventory and a business process inventory, disaster recovery planners need to determine which threats could adversely affect their organization's assets and operations. Planners should use a two-pronged approach—first they must inventory threats against their facilities, and then they must inventory threats against business processes.

The key to identifying threats is thoroughness. A good place to start is to study records of historic events that have affected a facility or its surrounding communities and regions. This study is especially important in the case of **recurring natural disasters**, such as severe storms, lightning strikes, earthquakes, floods, landslides, and fires. Assessing past natural disasters is a good way to project their potential for recurrence.

Other threats to consider are accidental events that may damage a facility and its operations. **Accidents** include train derailments, motor vehicle collisions, construction mishaps, plane crashes, equipment fires, stored material explosions or fires, building collapses, and bridge outages. Such accidents can result in loss of utility services, loss of access to facilities, or loss of telecommunications and network services. To determine what types of accidents may affect operations at a specific facility, the planning team must assess the areas surrounding a facility and its proximity to public thoroughfares and utility right-of-ways.

A third type of threat to consider is **destructive or disruptive deliberate actions** against a facility and its operations. These actions can include arson, bombings, terrorist attacks, riots, looting, and sabotage of buildings or equipment. By assessing the social and political conditions in the areas surrounding a facility, the planning team can gain insight into the possibility of deliberate actions. The team must also examine groups that may have a political or social animosity toward a facility or organization. This animosity could be directed toward an organization's products or services, its business practices, or political and social positions taken by stockholders or managers.

Four forms can help disaster recovery planners record the details of potential threats to their facilities, as well as details of actions and systems that can mitigate these threats. Each form provides space for information on the business entity, facility and building numbers, and contact information for the facility and its disaster recovery staff. These forms are briefly described below and shown in the "Compiling Risk Assessment Reports" section later in this chapter.

- The **facility threat inventory sheet** details the potential threats to an entire facility, as well as specific potential threats to personnel, heavy equipment, light equipment, installed systems, information technology, office equipment, and products or parts. Even though documentation may be lacking, a facility probably does not face many unknown threats. Natural disasters or accidents have probably occurred in the past. In addition, safety measures may have been implemented to ensure compliance with local, state, or federal laws. Thus, some actions probably have been taken to mitigate the impact of potential events.

- The **facility threat mitigation sheet** details the actions taken or the systems in place to reduce the impact of the threats described in the facility threat inventory sheet.

- The **business process threat inventory sheet** details the potential threats to a business process, as well as specific potential threats to personnel, equipment, installed systems, and information technology. This inventory sheet is even more important if a business process spans more than one department or facility. In these cases, a facility threat inventory sheet may not be adequate to address the many ways that business can be disrupted.

- The **business process threat mitigation sheet** details the actions taken or the systems in place to reduce the impact of the threats described in the business process threat inventory sheet.

MEASURING AND QUANTIFYING THREATS

Once an organization has determined the threats to its facilities and business processes, it needs to quantify these threats in support of disaster recovery planning. The organization also needs to quantify the likelihood of each potential threat being realized, as well as the level of disruption or damage to its operations, revenues, and relationships with its communities, business partners, suppliers, and customers.

The approach to quantifying this information depends on the type of threat being analyzed. The key to successfully measuring the likelihood of threats being realized is to obtain data from as many sources as possible.

Data on natural disasters, for example, is relatively easy to obtain from historical records. If severe storms happen every spring near an organization's facility, it is logical to expect them to continue in the future. In the "Tornado Belt," severe storms spawn tornados frequently enough each spring to be considered a threat. Disaster recovery planners can obtain sufficient data from local sources or the National Weather Service to document the frequency of severe storms and tornados at a specific facility.

Accidents, on the other hand, may be more difficult to quantify. Some locations certainly have a greater number of transportation-related accidents than others, depending on road conditions and weather patterns. Data on the frequency of such accidents is often available from police or public safety departments. Other data on the frequency of power outages may be readily available from facility maintenance staff.

The third type of threat, destructive or disruptive deliberate actions against a facility and its operations, can be extremely difficult to quantify. After the terrorist attacks on the World Trade Center and Pentagon on September 11, 2001, public officials repeatedly said they could not possibly have known that terrorists would fly passenger jets into the buildings. The same element of surprise was present in the bombing of the federal office building in Oklahoma City.

There has been considerable research on the frequency and severity of malicious hacking attacks. However, because this research is in its infancy, it is often difficult to determine threats to a specific organization. For more than a decade, information security professionals and law enforcement officials have been well aware that only a small percentage of computer crimes are reported. This underreporting also hinders attempts to measure the threat of computer hacking to a specific organization.

Table 3-6 provides examples of how an organization can research and quantify various threats.

Table 3-6 Threat evaluation and quantification methods

Type of threat	How to quantify
Severe rainstorm, tornado, hurricane, earthquake, wilderness fire, or flood	Collect data on frequency, severity, and proximity to facilities. Evaluate the past quality and speed of local and regional emergency response systems to determine if they helped minimize loss.
Train derailment, auto/truck accident, toxic air pollution caused by accident, or plane crash	Collect data on the proximity of railroads, highways, and airports to facilities. Evaluate the construction quality of these transportation systems and the rate of serious accidents on each system.
Building explosion or fire	Collect data on the frequency and severity of past incidents. Evaluate local emergency response to determine its effectiveness.
Militant group attacking facilities, riot or civil unrest	Collect data on the political stability of the region where facilities are located. Compile and evaluate a list of groups that may have specific political or social issues with the organization.
Computer hack (external) or computer fraud (internal)	Examine data on the frequency and severity of past incidents. Evaluate the effectiveness of existing computer security measures.

COMPILING RISK ASSESSMENT REPORTS

The extensive data collection and business analysis described in this chapter are all designed to support the development of risk assessment reports. A **risk assessment report** describes an asset or business process that is exposed to risk, the risks themselves, and the effectiveness of existing systems designed to mitigate these risks. The report ends by recommending which types of procedures an organization should include in its disaster recovery plan.

The format and length of a risk assessment report vary based on the complexity of the components described in the previous paragraph. The disaster recovery planning team uses this report as a decision-making tool and as a starting point in developing disaster recovery procedures. Upper-level managers may also review the report. When compiling a risk assessment report, use the following guidelines to make it a more valuable tool:

- The report should be easy to read by people with different knowledge and skill levels.

- The executive summary should be brief and to the point.

- The table of contents should be complete, and should list all sections and exhibits in the report.

- The narrative sections should clearly identify which sheets, forms, or reports were used to provide support.

- If photocopies are used in the exhibits, the copies should be clear and readable.

A risk assessment report may include proprietary information on business processes, market conditions and positions, manufacturing procedures, and IT security. Therefore, the reports and the material used to compile them should be treated as confidential. These reports should not be circulated outside the organization unless outside parties sign nondisclosure documents.

A sample outline of a risk assessment report is shown in Table 3-7.

Table 3-7   Risk assessment report outline

Report section	Form number
Title page (with facility name, location or business process description, date, and contact information for report compilers)	
Executive summary	
Table of contents	
Type of disaster recovery procedures recommended	
Description of facility or business process	
Description of support requirements for business process	
Description of risks	
Description of risk mitigation steps already taken	
Exhibits (as applicable to the specific report)	
Exposure inventory sheets	
Facility exposure inventory overview sheet	FEIOS01
Physical facilities exposure inventory sheet	PFEIS01
Personnel exposure inventory sheet	PEIS01
Heavy equipment exposure inventory sheet	HEEIS01
Light equipment exposure inventory sheet	LEEIS01
Installed systems exposure inventory sheet	ISEIS01
Information technology exposure inventory sheet	ITEIS01
Office equipment exposure inventory sheet	OEEIS01
Products/parts exposure inventory sheet	PPEIS01

Report section	Form number
Business process inventory sheets	
Business process inventory overview sheet	BPIOS01
Revenue collection inventory sheet	RCIS01
Sales inventory sheet	SIS01
Product distribution inventory sheet	PDIS01
Service delivery inventory sheet	SDIS01
Product manufacturing inventory sheet	PMIS01
Procurement inventory sheet	PIS01
Other business process inventory sheets	Number accordingly
Business process support requirements sheets	
Revenue collection support requirements sheet	RCSR01
Sales support requirements sheet	SSR01
Product distribution support requirements sheet	PDSR01
Service delivery support requirements sheet	SDSR01
Product manufacturing support requirements sheet	PMSR01
Procurement support requirements sheet	PSR01
Other support requirements sheets	Number accordingly
Threat inventory sheets	
Facility threat inventory sheet	FTIS01
Business process threat inventory sheet	BPTIS01
Threat mitigation sheets	
Facility threat mitigation sheet	FTMS01
Business process threat mitigation sheet	BPTMS01
Other items	
Risk measurement and quantification summary	
Risk measurement and quantification data	
Correspondence related to risk measurement and quantification data	
Reports from government agencies, consultants, or other parties about risks	

Examples of the inventory sheets and other forms that belong in the risk assessment report are shown in the following tables.

Table 3-8 Facility exposure inventory overview sheet

Facility Exposure Inventory Overview Sheet (Form number FEIOS01)			
Facility number: 1000		Number of buildings: 3 Number of employees:	
Facility name and location: Name: Address: Main telephone: Main fax number: Main e-mail:		Disaster recovery contact: Name: Address: Telephone: Fax number: E-mail:	
Exposure inventories attached:	Status (Circle one)	Last Updated	Next Update
Physical facilities	Yes No N/A		
Personnel	Yes No N/A		
Heavy equipment	Yes No N/A		
Light equipment	Yes No N/A		
Installed systems	Yes No N/A		
Information technology	Yes No N/A		
Office equipment	Yes No N/A		
Products or parts	Yes No N/A		
Business processes performed at facility:			

3

Table 3-9 Physical facilities exposure inventory sheet

Physical Facilities Exposure Inventory Sheet (Form number PFEIS01) Sheet _____ of _____ Date: _____			
Facility number: 1000		Building number: 1000-001	
Date constructed		Size of building (square feet)	
1st renovation date		Number of employees working in building	
2nd renovation date		Date of last fire safety inspection	
3rd renovation date		Date of last structural inspection	
Building description:			
Business processes performed at this building:			
Comments:			

Table 3-10   Personnel exposure inventory sheet

Personnel Exposure Inventory Sheet (Form number PEIS01) Sheet _____ of _____ Date: _____		
Facility number: 1000		Building number: 1000-001
Department name (list all)	Number of employees	Business processes performed by department
Comments:		

Table 3-11 Heavy equipment exposure inventory sheet

Heavy Equipment Exposure Inventory Sheet (Form number HEEIS01) Sheet _____ of _____ Date: _____			
Facility number: 1000		Building number: 1000-001	
Equipment type	Quantity	Purpose	Alternate facility where equipment can be duplicated in case of disaster
Comments:			

Table 3-12 Light equipment exposure inventory sheet

3

Light Equipment Exposure Inventory Sheet (Form number LEEIS01) Sheet _____ of _____ Date: _____			
Facility number: 1000		Building number: 1000-001	
Equipment type	Quantity	Purpose	Alternate facility where equipment can be duplicated in case of disaster
Comments:			

Table 3-13 Installed systems exposure inventory sheet

Installed Systems Exposure Inventory Sheet (Form number ISEIS01) Sheet _____ of _____ Date: _____			
Facility number: 1000		Building number: 1000-001	
System type	Quantity	Purpose	Alternate facility where equipment can be duplicated in case of disaster
Comments:			

Table 3-14 Information technology exposure inventory sheet

Information Technology Exposure Inventory Sheet (Form number ITEIS01) Sheet _____ of _____ Date: _____			
Facility number: 1000		Building number: 1000-001	
Equipment type	Quantity	Purpose	Alternate facility where equipment can be duplicated in case of disaster
Comments:			

3

Table 3-15 Office equipment exposure inventory sheet

Office Equipment Exposure Inventory Sheet (Form number OEEIS01) Sheet _____ of _____ Date: _____			
Facility number: 1000		Building number: 1000-001	
Equipment type	Quantity	Purpose	Alternate facility where equipment can be duplicated in case of disaster
Comments:			

Table 3-16   Products/parts exposure inventory sheet

Products/Parts Exposure Inventory Sheet (Form number PPEIS01) Sheet ____ of ____ Date: _____			
Facility number: 1000		Building number: 1000-001	
System type	Quantity	Purpose	Alternate facility where equipment can be duplicated in case of disaster
Comments:			

Table 3-17 Business process inventory overview sheet

Business Process Inventory Overview Sheet (Form number BPIOS01)			
Facility name(s) and location(s): Name: Address: Main telephone: Main fax number: Main e-mail:		Disaster recovery contact(s): Name: Address: Telephone: Fax number: E-mail:	
Process inventories attached:	Status (Circle one)	Last Updated	Next Update
Revenue Collection	Yes No N/A		
Sales	Yes No N/A		
Product Distribution	Yes No N/A		
Service Delivery	Yes No N/A		
Product Manufacturing	Yes No N/A		
Procurement	Yes No N/A		
Other	Yes No N/A		
Comments:			

3

Table 3-18 Revenue collection inventory sheet

Revenue Collection Inventory Sheet (Form number RCIS01) Sheet ____ of ____ Date: _____	
Entity:_____ Department:_____ Business process number: RCP-0001	Facility number(s): 1000 Building number(s): 1000-001
Department location(s): Name: Address: Main telephone: Main fax number: Main e-mail:	Disaster recovery contact(s): Name: Address: Telephone: Fax number: E-mail:

Requirements	Explanation:
Legal/regulatory	
Contractual	
Labor union contract	
Competitive pressures	
Financial pressures	
Humanitarian or social expectations	
Management	
Other	
Other	
Description of the business process:	

Table 3-19 Sales inventory sheet

Sales Inventory Sheet (Form number SIS01) Sheet _____ of _____ Date: _____	
Entity: _____ Department: _____ Business process number: SP-0001	Facility number(s): 1000 Building number(s): 1000-001
Department location(s): Name: Address: Main telephone: Main fax number: Main e-mail:	Disaster recovery contact(s): Name: Address: Telephone: Fax number: E-mail:

Requirements	Explanation:
Legal/regulatory	
Contractual	
Labor union contract	
Competitive pressures	
Financial pressures	
Humanitarian or social expectations	
Management	
Other	
Other	
Description of the business process:	

Table 3-20   Product distribution inventory sheet

Product Distribution Inventory Sheet (Form number PDIS01) Sheet _____ of _____ Date: _____	
Entity:_____ Department:_____ Business process number: PD-0001	Facility number(s): 1000 Building number(s): 1000-001
Department location(s): Name: Address: Main telephone: Main fax number: Main e-mail:	Disaster recovery contact(s): Name: Address: Telephone: Fax number: E-mail:

Requirements	Explanation:
Legal/regulatory	
Contractual	
Labor union contract	
Competitive pressures	
Financial pressures	
Humanitarian or social expectations	
Management	
Other	
Other	
Description of the business process:	

Table 3-21 Service delivery inventory sheet

Service Delivery Inventory Sheet (Form number SDIS01) Sheet _____ of _____ Date: _____	
Entity:_____ Department:_____ Business process number: SD-0001	Facility number(s): 1000 Building number(s): 1000-001
Department location(s): Name: Address: Main telephone: Main fax number: Main e-mail:	Disaster recovery contact(s): Name: Address: Telephone: Fax number: E-mail:

Requirements	Explanation:
Legal/regulatory	
Contractual	
Labor union contract	
Competitive pressures	
Financial pressures	
Humanitarian or social expectations	
Management	
Other	
Other	
Description of the business process:	

Table 3-22   Product manufacturing inventory sheet

Product Manufacturing Inventory Sheet (Form number PMIS01) Sheet ____ of ____ Date: _____	

Entity:_____ Department:_____ Business process number: PM-0001	Facility number(s): 1000 Building number(s): 1000-001
Department location(s): Name: Address: Main telephone: Main fax number: Main e-mail:	Disaster recovery contact(s): Name: Address: Telephone: Fax number: E-mail:

Requirements	Explanation:
Legal/regulatory	
Contractual	
Labor union contract	
Competitive pressures	
Financial pressures	
Humanitarian or social expectations	
Management	
Other	
Other	
Description of the business process:	

Table 3-23   Procurement inventory sheet

Procurement Inventory Sheet (Form number PIS01) Sheet ____ of ____ Date: _____	
Entity: _____ Department: _____ Business process number: PP-0001	Facility number(s): 1000 Building number(s): 1000-001
Department location(s): Name: Address: Main telephone: Main fax number: Main e-mail:	Disaster recovery contact(s): Name: Address: Telephone: Fax number: E-mail:

Requirements	Explanation:
Legal/regulatory	
Contractual	
Labor union contract	
Competitive pressures	
Financial pressures	
Humanitarian or social expectations	
Management	
Other	
Other	
Description of the business process:	

Table 3-24 Revenue collection support requirements sheet

<table>
<tr><td colspan="2" align="center">**Revenue Collection Support Requirements**
(Form number RCSR01)
Sheet _____ of _____ Date: _____</td></tr>
<tr><td>Entity: _____
Department: _____
Business process number: RCP-0001</td><td>Facility number(s): 1000
Building number(s): 1000-001</td></tr>
<tr><td>Department location(s):
Name:
Address:

Main telephone:
Main fax number:
Main e-mail:</td><td>Disaster recovery contact(s):
Name:
Address:

Telephone:
Fax number:
E-mail:</td></tr>
<tr><td>Support Requirements</td><td>Explanation:</td></tr>
<tr><td>Physical facilities</td><td></td></tr>
<tr><td>Personnel</td><td></td></tr>
<tr><td>Heavy equipment</td><td></td></tr>
<tr><td>Light equipment</td><td></td></tr>
<tr><td>Installed systems</td><td></td></tr>
<tr><td>Information technology</td><td></td></tr>
<tr><td>Office equipment</td><td></td></tr>
<tr><td>Other</td><td></td></tr>
<tr><td>Other</td><td></td></tr>
<tr><td colspan="2">Comments:</td></tr>
</table>

3

Table 3-25 Sales support requirements sheet

Sales Support Requirements (Form number SSR01) Sheet _____ of _____ Date: _____		
Entity: _____ Department: _____ Business process number: SP-0001		Facility number(s): 1000 Building number(s): 1000-001
Department location(s): Name: Address: Main telephone: Main fax number: Main e-mail:		Disaster recovery contact(s): Name: Address: Telephone: Fax number: E-mail:
Support Requirements	Explanation:	
Physical facilities		
Personnel		
Heavy equipment		
Light equipment		
Installed systems		
Information technology		
Office equipment		
Other		
Other		
Comments:		

Table 3-26 Product distribution support requirements sheet

<table>
<tr><td colspan="2">

Product Distribution Support Requirements
(Form number PDSR01)
Sheet _____ of _____ Date: _____
</td></tr>
<tr><td>

Entity: _____
Department: _____
Business process number: PD-0001
</td><td>

Facility number(s): 1000
Building number(s): 1000-001
</td></tr>
<tr><td>

Department location(s):
Name:
Address:

Main telephone:
Main fax number:
Main e-mail:
</td><td>

Disaster recovery contact(s):
Name:
Address:

Telephone:
Fax number:
E-mail:
</td></tr>
</table>

Support Requirements	Explanation:
Physical facilities	
Personnel	
Heavy equipment	
Light equipment	
Installed systems	
Information technology	
Office equipment	
Other	
Other	
Comments:	

3

Table 3-27   Service delivery support requirements sheet

<table>
<tr><td colspan="2" align="center">**Service Delivery Support Requirements**
(Form number SDSR01)
Sheet _____ of _____   Date: _____</td></tr>
<tr><td>Entity:_____
Department:_____
Business process number: SD-0001</td><td>Facility number(s): 1000
Building number(s): 1000-001</td></tr>
<tr><td>Department location(s):
Name:
Address:

Main telephone:
Main fax number:
Main e-mail:</td><td>Disaster recovery contact(s):
Name:
Address:

Telephone:
Fax number:
E-mail:</td></tr>
<tr><td>Support Requirements</td><td>Explanation:</td></tr>
<tr><td>Physical facilities</td><td></td></tr>
<tr><td>Personnel</td><td></td></tr>
<tr><td>Heavy equipment</td><td></td></tr>
<tr><td>Light equipment</td><td></td></tr>
<tr><td>Installed systems</td><td></td></tr>
<tr><td>Information technology</td><td></td></tr>
<tr><td>Office equipment</td><td></td></tr>
<tr><td>Other</td><td></td></tr>
<tr><td>Other</td><td></td></tr>
<tr><td colspan="2">Comments:</td></tr>
</table>

Table 3-28 Product manufacturing support requirements sheet

Product Manufacturing Support Requirements (Form number PMSR01) Sheet ____ of ____ Date: _____	
Entity:_____ Department:_____ Business process number: PM-0001	Facility number(s): 1000 Building number(s): 1000-001
Department location(s): Name: Address: Main telephone: Main fax number: Main e-mail:	Disaster recovery contact(s): Name: Address: Telephone: Fax number: E-mail:

Support Requirements	Explanation:
Physical facilities	
Personnel	
Heavy equipment	
Light equipment	
Installed systems	
Information technology	
Office equipment	
Other	
Other	
Comments:	

3

Table 3-29 Procurement support requirements sheet

Procurement Support Requirements (Form number PSR01) Sheet _____ of _____ Date: _____	
Entity: _____ Department: _____ Business process number: PP-0001	Facility number(s): 1000 Building number(s): 1000-001
Department location(s): Name: Address: Main telephone: Main fax number: Main e-mail:	Disaster recovery contact(s): Name: Address: Telephone: Fax number: E-mail:

Support Requirements	Explanation:
Physical facilities	
Personnel	
Heavy equipment	
Light equipment	
Installed systems	
Information technology	
Office equipment	
Other	
Other	
Comments:	

Table 3-30   Facility threat inventory sheet

Facility Threat Inventory Sheet (Form number FTIS01)	
Entity:_____	Facility number: 1000 Building number(s): 1000-001
Facility name and location: Name: Address: Main telephone: Main fax number: Main e-mail:	Disaster recovery contact: Name: Address: Telephone: Fax number: E-mail:

Describe the threats that may affect the physical facility and all operations there.

Describe additional threats that may affect the following assets:	
Personnel	
Heavy equipment	
Light equipment	
Installed systems	
Information technology	
Office equipment	
Products or parts	

3

Table 3-31 Facility threat mitigation sheet

Facility Threat Mitigation Sheet (Form number FTMS01)	
Entity: _____	Facility number: 1000 Building number: 1000-001
Facility name and location: Name: Address: Main telephone: Main fax number: Main e-mail:	Disaster recovery contact: Name: Address: Telephone: Fax number: E-mail:
Describe the mitigation steps that may reduce threats to the physical facility and all operations there.	
Describe additional mitigation steps that may reduce threats to the following assets:	
Personnel	
Heavy equipment	
Light equipment	
Installed systems	
Information technology	
Office equipment	
Products or parts	

Table 3-32 Business process threat inventory sheet

Business Process Threat Inventory Sheet (Form number BPTIS01)	

Entity:_____ Business process number:_____	Facility number(s): 1000 Building number(s): 1000-001
Facility name(s) and location(s): Name: Address: Main telephone: Main fax number: Main e-mail:	Disaster recovery contact(s): Name: Address: Telephone: Fax number: E-mail:

Describe the threats that may affect the overall business process.

Describe additional threats that may affect specific support requirements:

Personnel	
Heavy equipment	
Light equipment	
Installed systems	
Information technology	
Office equipment	
Products or parts	
Other	

3

Table 3-33 Business process threat mitigation sheet

Business Process Threat Mitigation Sheet (Form number BPTMS01)	
Entity:_____ Business process number:_____	Facility number(s): 1000 Building number(s): 1000-001
Facility name(s) and location(s): Name: Address: Main telephone: Main fax number: Main e-mail:	Disaster recovery contact(s): Name: Address: Telephone: Fax number: E-mail:
Describe the mitigation steps that may reduce threats to the overall business process.	
Describe additional mitigation steps that may reduce threats to the following:	
Personnel	
Heavy equipment	
Light equipment	
Installed systems	
Information technology	
Office equipment	
Products or parts	
Other	

Assessing Progress and Preparing to Move Ahead

Assessing risks in the enterprise is the second step in disaster recovery planning. This step enables the planning team to move forward in establishing roles across departments for developing disaster recovery procedures.

Depending on an organization's size and complexity, it may take several months to perform risk assessments for all facilities and business processes. The disaster recovery planning team and upper-level managers should agree on the priorities for performing these risk assessments. It is not difficult to rank the most important facilities or business processes, and then make the applicable risk assessments the highest priority for the planning team.

Once risk assessment reports have been compiled for the most critical facilities and business processes, the planning team can begin developing disaster recovery procedures. If resources allow, risk assessments can continue for less important facilities and business processes.

All facilities should have a disaster recovery plan in place. However, the reality of resource allocation dictates that disaster recovery planning must be prioritized to best serve the organization.

The disaster recovery planning team should meet to review risk assessment reports for thoroughness. The team must also question at this point whether risk assessment priorities are aligned with business goals. If the priorities are aligned, the team can start establishing roles across departments for developing and documenting necessary disaster recovery procedures.

Chapter Summary

- Risks are the potential consequences of events or conditions that can adversely affect an organization's operations and revenues, as well as its relationships with communities, business partners, suppliers, and customers. Before analyzing risks, the disaster recovery planning team must first determine the likelihood of an event's occurrence and their organization's related operating conditions.

- To understand the possible impact of adverse events and related conditions, the disaster recovery planning team must inventory the organization's exposure to such events. An exposure inventory is an annotated list of all facilities, processes, systems, and resources that an organization uses to maintain operations and sustain revenue.

- Individual exposure inventory sheets provide details for assets at the facility identified by the inventory overview sheet.

- The two primary types of organizations are product-focused and service-focused. A product-focused organization creates or distributes physical goods. A service-focused organization provides a specific service for a customer.

❏ A business process inventory is an annotated list of the key business processes necessary to maintain operations, including revenue collection, sales, distribution and delivery, manufacturing, and procurement. A business process inventory illustrates how a process works. It also lists the facilities and buildings in which the process occurs, the departments that perform the process, and the personnel who work in the departments. The inventory also lists the equipment, installed systems, information technology, and parts and supplies that the departments use.

❏ Organizations should maintain a series of business process inventory sheets for each facility or each group of related facilities in their business process. These inventory sheets provide details on the process, including which facilities, buildings, and departments support it, as well as the resources required to accomplish the process. Business process support requirements sheets provide detailed information about the resources needed to support the process, including physical facilities, personnel, heavy equipment, light equipment, installed systems, information technology, and office equipment.

❏ The key to successfully measuring the likelihood of threats being realized is to obtain data from as many sources as possible.

❏ A risk assessment report describes an asset that is exposed to risk, what the risks are, and the effectiveness of existing systems designed to mitigate these risks. The report ends by recommending which types of procedures an organization should include in its disaster recovery plan.

❏ A risk assessment report may include proprietary information on business processes, market conditions and positions, manufacturing procedures, and IT security. Therefore, the reports and the material used to compile them should be treated as confidential.

KEY TERMS

accidents — Events such as train derailments, motor vehicle collisions, construction mishaps, plane crashes, equipment fires, stored material explosions or fires, building collapses, and bridge outages. Such accidents can result in loss of utility services, loss of access to facilities, or loss of telecommunications and network services.

business process inventory — An annotated list of key business processes needed to maintain operations, including revenue collection, sales, distribution and delivery, manufacturing, and procurement.

business process inventory overview sheet — A form that keeps track of detailed business process inventories.

business process inventory sheet — A form that provides details on business processes, the facilities, buildings, and departments that support a process, and the resources required to accomplish a process.

business process support requirements sheet — A form that provides detailed information about the resources required to support business processes in an organization.

business process threat inventory sheet — A form that details potential threats to a business process, as well as specific threats to personnel, equipment, systems, and information technology.

business process threat mitigation sheet — A form that details the actions taken or the systems in place to reduce the impact of the threats described in the business process threat inventory sheet.

3

destructive or disruptive deliberate actions — Actions that halt or interrupt business operations, including arson, bombings, terrorist attacks, riots, looting, and sabotage of buildings or equipment.

distribution support requirements sheet — A form that provides detailed information about the resources required to support distribution in an organization.

exposure inventory — An annotated list of all facilities, processes, systems, and resources that an organization needs to maintain operations and sustain revenue.

exposure inventory sheet — A form that details assets at the facility identified by the facility exposure inventory overview sheet.

facility exposure inventory overview sheet — A form that keeps track of the detailed exposure inventories needed for each facility.

facility threat inventory sheet — A form that details the potential threats to an entire facility, as well as specific potential threats to personnel, equipment, systems, and information technology.

facility threat mitigation sheet — A form that details the actions taken or the systems in place to reduce the impact of the threats described in the facility threat inventory sheet.

heavy equipment exposure inventory sheet — A form that lists all of the heavy equipment in each building, along with an alternate facility where the equipment can be duplicated in case of disaster. Heavy equipment includes manufacturing, transportation, and industrial plant equipment.

information technology exposure inventory sheet — A form that lists all of the information technology in each building, along with an alternate facility where the equipment can be duplicated in case of disaster. Information technology includes large systems, servers, workstations, desktop computers, notebooks, PDAs, and related peripherals.

installed systems exposure inventory sheet — A form that lists all of the installed systems in each building, along with an alternate facility where the equipment can be duplicated in case of disaster. Installed systems include computer networks, telephone systems, fire prevention systems, and premises security systems.

light equipment exposure inventory sheet — A form that lists all of the light equipment in each building, along with an alternate facility where the equipment can be duplicated in case of disaster. Light equipment includes tools, cleaning and maintenance equipment, and emergency equipment.

material, parts, and supplies procurement — The raw materials, parts, and supplies required to support operations.

office equipment exposure inventory sheet — A form that lists all of the office equipment in each building, along with an alternate facility where the equipment can be duplicated in case of disaster. Office equipment includes furniture, built-in cabinetry, copiers, fax machines, and special lighting.

personnel exposure inventory sheet — A form that lists the personnel in each building. The form also lists the department(s) in the building, the number of employees in each department, and the business processes performed by each department in the building. Personnel includes all employees and contract workers.

physical facilities exposure inventory sheet — A form that includes relevant information about a building within an organization, including the business process it supports. The form also lists the dates of building construction, renovation, and the last safety inspections.

procurement inventory sheet — A form that provides detailed information about procurement for a specific division, product line, or location in an organization.

procurement support requirements sheet — A form that provides detailed information about the resources required to support procurement in an organization.

product distribution — The delivery of products to distributors or customers.

product distribution inventory sheet — A form that provides detailed information about product distribution for a specific division, product line, or location in an organization.

product manufacturing — The process and equipment required to create products.

product manufacturing inventory sheet — A form that provides detailed information about product manufacturing for a specific division, product line, or location in an organization.

product manufacturing support requirements sheet — A form that provides detailed information about the resources required to support product manufacturing in an organization.

product sales — The process of selling products to existing and new customers.

product-focused organization — An organization that creates or distributes physical goods.

products/parts exposure inventory sheet — A form that lists all of the products and parts in each building, along with an alternate facility where the equipment can be duplicated in case of disaster. Products or parts include all finished products created by an organization, as well as parts or raw material used to manufacture products.

recurring natural disasters — Events such as severe storms, lightning strikes, earthquakes, floods, landslides, and fires.

revenue collection — The process of collecting money from customers.

revenue collection inventory sheet — A form that provides detailed information about revenue collection for a specific division, product line, or location in an organization.

revenue collection support requirements sheet — A form that provides detailed information about the resources required to support revenue collection in an organization.

risk assessment report — A report that describes an asset or business process that is exposed to risk, what the risks are, and the effectiveness of existing systems designed to mitigate these risks. The report ends by recommending which types of procedures an organization should include in its disaster recovery plan.

risks — The potential consequences of events or conditions that can adversely affect an organization's operations and revenues, as well as its relationships with communities, business partners, suppliers, and customers.

sales inventory sheet — A form that provides detailed information about product or service sales for a specific division, product line, or location in an organization.

sales support requirements sheet — A form that provides detailed information about the resources required to support sales in an organization.

service delivery — The provision of services to customers.

service delivery inventory sheet — A form that provides detailed information about service delivery for a specific division, product line, or location in an organization.

service delivery support requirements sheet — A form that provides detailed information about the resources required to support service delivery in an organization.

service platform — The facility or equipment necessary to deliver services.

service sales — The process of selling services to existing and new customers.

service-focused organization — An organization that provides a specific service for a customer.

REVIEW QUESTIONS

1. The key to successfully measuring the likelihood of threats being realized is _____.

2. What types of systems are installed systems?

3. What information does the light equipment exposure inventory sheet provide?

4. Explain why risk assessment is the fundamental building block of disaster recovery planning, and why future steps in the planning process and successful disaster recovery depend on it.

5. Explain why financial requirements may affect the necessity to quickly recover a specific business process.

6. Explain what an exposure inventory is.

7. What is the purpose of the facility exposure inventory overview sheet?

8. What is the purpose of the heavy equipment exposure inventory sheet?

9. What are the five key goals of a typical product-focused organization?

10. What are the five key goals of a typical service-focused organization?

11. What information does a business process inventory illustrate?

12. The scope of exposure inventory has nothing to do with the size of the organization, the number of employees, or the number of locations. True or False?

13. The physical facilities exposure inventory sheet should be filled out only for very large buildings. True or False?

14. The personnel exposure inventory sheet should only cover employees who have worked for the organization for more than five years, because they are the most critical employees. True or False?

15. The information technology exposure inventory sheet only lists mainframes and servers. True or False?

16. Legal requirements or government regulations do not affect a disaster recovery plan. True or False?

17. When a business process spans more than one department, how can the disaster recovery planning team determine how the business process actually works?

18. Why should business process inventory sheets be maintained for each facility or each group of related facilities in the business process?

19. Why is it necessary to know which resources are required to support each business process?

20. What information does the business process threat mitigation sheet provide?

21. What is the purpose of a risk assessment report?

22. What factors influence the format and length of a risk assessment report?

23. When compiling a risk assessment report, what should the authors do to make it a more valuable tool?

24. Why should risk assessment reports be treated as confidential material?

25. Under what conditions should people outside an organization have access to a risk assessment report?

HANDS-ON PROJECTS

Complete the following inventory sheets and analyses for the organization for which you are developing a disaster recovery plan. When you finish, submit the materials to your instructor for review.

Project 3-1

1. Create a facility exposure inventory overview sheet. You should compile this inventory for facilities that the planning team considers most critical to the organization; these facilities should have the highest priority in disaster recovery planning.

2. Create and complete a physical facilities exposure inventory sheet.

3. Create and complete exposure inventory sheets for applicable personnel, heavy equipment, light equipment, installed systems, information technology, office equipment, and products or parts.

Project 3-2

Complete a business process inventory and support requirements analysis for revenue collection in the organization. The project includes the following steps:

1. Create and complete a business process inventory overview sheet.

2. Create and complete a revenue collection inventory sheet.

3. Create and complete a revenue collection support requirements analysis.

Project 3-3

Complete a business process inventory and support requirements analysis for sales in the organization. The project includes the following steps:

1. Create and complete a sales inventory sheet.

2. Create and complete a sales support requirements analysis.

Project 3-4

Depending on the organization your team is using for your projects, complete a business process inventory and support requirements analysis for the organization's product distribution or service delivery. The project includes the following steps:

1. Create and complete a product distribution inventory sheet or service delivery inventory sheet.

2. Create and complete a distribution support requirements analysis or service delivery support requirements analysis.

Project 3-5

If the organization for which you are developing a disaster recovery plan is a manufacturer, complete a business process inventory and support requirements analysis for its product manufacturing. The project includes the following steps:

1. Create and complete a product manufacturing inventory sheet.

2. Create and complete a product manufacturing support requirements analysis.

Project 3-6

Complete a business process inventory and support requirements analysis for procurement in the organization. The project includes the following steps:

1. Create and complete a procurement inventory sheet.

2. Create and complete a procurement support requirements analysis.

Project 3-7

1. Create and complete a facility threat inventory sheet for the organization. Compile this inventory for the facilities that the planning team considers most critical to the organization; these facilities should have the highest priority in disaster recovery planning.

2. Create and complete a facility threat mitigation sheet for your work in Step 1.

Project 3-8

1. Create and complete a business process threat inventory sheet for the organization. Compile this inventory for the processes that the planning team considers most critical to the organization; these processes should have the highest priority in disaster recovery planning.

2. Create and complete a business process threat mitigation sheet for your work in Step 1.

Case Projects

Case Project: Harris and Heartfield Manufacturing

Harris and Heartfield Manufacturing is a family-owned business that fabricates specialized metal parts for its North American clients. Most of its revenue comes from defense contracts, and from producing parts for heavy-equipment manufacturers. The company has an excellent reputation for quality and prompt deliveries.

The company has 200 employees at its only location in California. All 20 administrative employees have desktop PCs connected to the company's local area network (LAN). The 15 research and design engineers use Sun workstations that are also on the LAN. Three servers support administrative functions and six servers support design and manufacturing. About half the machining equipment on the shop floor is computerized.

Management is concerned about the company's future competitiveness, and about its ability to fulfill orders if a disaster hindered its operations. The board of directors is relatively business-savvy, but does not invest money unless it yields a positive return. As a result, the company hired you as a consultant to create a list of 10 key points that conveyed the importance of disaster recovery planning to the board. You also prepared 10 points for managers to discuss with employees about organizing and preparing to develop a plan.

Your assignment now is to work with company managers to develop a business process threat analysis for product manufacturing. Create a list of at least 20 questions that should be answered during this analysis.

OPTIONAL TEAM CASE PROJECTS

Team Case One

Your boss has asked you to identify data sources for assessing weather-related threats that could help complete a facility threat inventory sheet. Your assignment is to find five possible data sources for the disaster recovery planning team and write a one-paragraph description of each source. The description should include the name of the source and how it could help your planning team. If you use the Internet, identify the URL of the Web site where you found the information.

Team Case Two

Your boss has asked you to identify five data sources for assessing computer crime and hacking threats that could help complete a facility threat inventory sheet. Use the instructions in Team Case One to complete the assignment.

4

PRIORITIZING SYSTEMS AND FUNCTIONS FOR RECOVERY

After reading this chapter, you will be able to:

♦ Determine critical business activities

♦ Classify systems and functions for recovery priority

♦ Develop charts of responsibilities

♦ Assess insurance requirements and coverage needs

Once the disaster recovery planning team has compiled exposure inventories, risk inventories, and risk assessment reports, team representatives from all departments must determine which business activities are most critical to the organization. The planning team needs to develop recovery procedures to restore these activities as quickly as possible in case of disaster.

Next, the planning team classifies the organization's business support systems and resources, and establishes recovery priorities accordingly. If disaster recovery plans are already in place, the team must evaluate their adequacy.

The team then develops a chart of responsibilities to show which facilities, departments, and staff must participate in developing recovery procedures.

This is also an appropriate time to evaluate the organization's insurance coverage for business interruption and disaster recovery.

DETERMINING CRITICAL BUSINESS ACTIVITIES

To begin prioritizing systems and functions for recovery, the disaster recovery planning team must analyze the data collected during risk assessment and exposure inventories. (This data is described in Chapter 3.) During the business process inventory, the planning team determined if any extraordinary requirements dictated whether some business processes should have higher priorities for recovery planning. Those requirements were:

- Legal/regulatory requirements

- Contractual requirements

- Labor union contract requirements

- Competitive pressures

- Financial pressures

- Humanitarian or social expectations

- Management mandates

Any of these requirements can help determine priorities of business activities during disaster recovery. If business processes have enough of these requirements, then the disaster recovery planning team may have very few decisions to make about recovery priorities. In such cases, however, the planning team cannot be misled into thinking that its task is easy; planners must understand the possible consequences of not complying with the requirements. Table 4–1 shows some of these potential consequences.

Table 4-1 Consequences of noncompliance with recovery requirements

Requirement	Consequence of noncompliance
Legal/regulatory	Loss of license or permits, government investigations, fines, criminal charges, or other penalties as prescribed by law
Contractual	Loss of business, penalties for late delivery, or civil litigation
Labor union contract	Labor disputes, walkouts, strikes, or civil litigation
Competitive pressures	Loss of business, loss of major customers, or loss of market share
Financial pressures	Prolonged loss of revenue, shift in cash positions, or required borrowing of funds
Humanitarian or social expectations	Damaged reputation, class action lawsuits, or civil litigation
Management mandates	Board or stockholder actions against management, or termination of managers

Without such requirements, the planning team may face a more complicated effort when establishing priorities. In these cases, the team must ask: "What processes make the organization operate?" In Chapter 3, the team examined the following key processes during the business process inventory:

- Revenue collection

- Sales

- Product distribution

- Service delivery

- Product manufacturing

- Procurement

The planning team must consider input from all departments when prioritizing business processes for disaster recovery. If there is little immediate consensus about priorities among planners, the team must build consensus for their decisions before continuing.

Disputes among departmental representatives about disaster recovery priorities may not be difficult to resolve. If consensus building is necessary, the disaster recovery planning coordinator should start with the easiest process, which should enable the team to reach a straightforward consensus on its first try and gain confidence.

The planning coordinator should make a comprehensive list of all the business processes and facilities described in the inventory risk assessment reports. Departmental representatives should be given sufficient time to take the list back to their departments and rank all the processes and facilities from their own perspectives. These lists and rankings should be returned to the planning coordinator before the next team meeting, so the coordinator can compile the results and write a brief report for the team to review. Table 4-2 shows a sample business process ranking report.

Table 4-2 Sample business process ranking report

Business process	Average ranking	Department					
		A	B	C	D	E	F
Revenue collection	1.5	1	2	1	2	3	2
Sales	4.0	3	1	3	4	6	5
Product distribution	1.5	2	3	2	1	2	1
Service delivery	4.5	5	6	5	3	5	4
Product manufacturing	3.5	4	5	4	6	4	3
Procurement	6.0	6	4	6	5	6	6
Other business processes	7.0	7	7	7	7	7	7

At the subsequent meeting of the planning team, the coordinator should present a brief report that compares the rankings each department assigned to the business processes or facilities. If these rankings are relatively consistent from all departments, the planning team should be able to discuss the rankings and come to a consensus during the meeting.

In any consensus–building effort, all parties should have the opportunity to present their positions. Minority opinions and dissenters need to be heard just as much as the departmental representatives who are in agreement. During these discussions, the disaster recovery planning coordinator should remain as neutral as possible.

If the planning team cannot reach a consensus after independently ranking the possible recovery priorities, then the coordinator needs to decide how to move the team toward a consensus. If disagreements are not drastic, the coordinator can delay any decisions until the next meeting. Departmental representatives then have time to give the priorities further consideration.

If the planning team cannot reach a consensus at the next meeting, the coordinator should request that disagreeing parties prepare a presentation of their opposing perspectives for the following meeting. Each group should be allowed about 10 minutes to make its case. The presentations should all be structured in a similar manner to help the disaster recovery planning team make direct comparisons. Table 4-3 shows a sample outline for these presentations.

Table 4-3 Sample outline for discussing business process priorities

Presentation item	Recommended time allocation
Introduction and definition of business process	2 minutes
Existing requirements that affect recovery needs (if applicable)	2 minutes
Department position on recovery priority	2 minutes
Supporting data or material for department position	2 minutes
Summary on department position	1 minute
Final recommendation on all business process rankings	1 minute

Note the first item in the presentation, in which groups introduce and define the business process under discussion. This item's purpose is to ensure that all planning team members understand exactly what the department group is discussing. At times, disagreements may occur if team members do not define these business processes in the same way. Clarifying such information in the introduction is the best opportunity to avoid problems.

Next, a brief discussion of any existing requirements that affect recovery efforts helps to remind the team about external or internal requirements for setting recovery priorities. If any of these requirements were not properly documented or stated during the business process inventory, this review can help clarify outstanding issues.

The next sections of the presentation, in which speakers review their department's position on recovery priority and present supporting data, help the planning team make easier comparisons of opposing positions. The summary statement of the department's position helps to solidify its stance and provide a platform for further discussion. Finally, departmental representatives should explain their position on the overall rankings of all business processes for recovery priorities. Once the team sees these overall rankings, it might be easier to reach compromises on individual rankings.

After the opposing positions are presented, the planning team should be able to ask the presenters about data or material they used to support their positions. This discussion should further clarify issues and positions. In most cases, this process results in consensus, or at least in compromises.

If the presentations do not result in a shift in perspectives and a consensus, the disaster recovery planning coordinator should seek assistance from upper-level managers to resolve the dispute. Input from the CEO or CFO may help to build a consensus within the planning team. If not, then the most senior manager in the organization needs to meet with the opposing departments, hear opposing sides, and make a decision on the recovery priorities.

After the planning team or senior manager decides which business processes or facilities have the highest priority in disaster recovery, the team should compile a complete list of these business processes or facilities, and then rank their priorities numerically.

CLASSIFYING SYSTEMS AND FUNCTIONS FOR RECOVERY PRIORITY

After priorities are established for disaster recovery, the planning team must examine which systems or support functions need to be recovered or replicated in order for critical business processes to continue after a disaster. The analysis of the requirements for supporting the business process, which the planning team conducted during the risk assessment, should show all of the systems, facilities, and support material needed to recover the business process.

Under normal conditions, organizations try to maintain a full level of functionality and achieve their key goals. However, when a disaster occurs, business processes can be completely or partially disabled. Disaster recovery planners need to examine the processes that make their organization successful, and then classify these processes in the following categories:

- **Critical systems and functions** absolutely must be in place for any business process to continue at all.

- **Essential systems and functions** must be in place to support day-to-day operations.

- **Necessary systems and functions** contribute to smooth operations and comfortable working conditions for employees.

- **Desirable systems and functions** improve working conditions and help to enhance the organization's performance.

There are no absolute definitions for critical, essential, necessary, and desirable systems and functions. To begin classifying, disaster recovery planners should worry less about the definitions than the need to fully understand the nature, mission, and goals of their organization. In addition, upper management must agree with the team's classification of systems and functions.

When classifying systems, the planning team will discover that some systems support more than one business process. These discoveries provide an economy of scale for recovery efforts. Just as installed systems that were identified during the exposure inventories support numerous functions or processes, temporary or replacement systems can also support the recovery of multiple processes.

IT and network management staff play a crucial role at this point. They may be the best resource for explaining which processes are supported by each installed network, server, minicomputer, or mainframe, and the extent to which temporary or replicated systems can support multiple business processes. Other supporting departments can offer expertise and assistance as well, including Facilities Management, Human Resources, Shipping and Receiving, Security, and Telecommunications.

All planning team representatives from support departments need to take the prioritized list of business processes and facilities back to their departments for analysis. The support departments should perform detailed studies of the systems or support functions required to meet disaster recovery priorities. If disaster recovery procedures are already in place, the support departments need to compare the new priorities to the procedures and determine if they are still compatible.

Table 4-4 shows a sample numbering scheme for various system and support analysis sheets. Support departments should complete these sheets to help the team prepare to develop disaster recovery procedures. These forms can be printed and maintained on paper, but organizations can save considerable time and effort by maintaining the forms in a popular database or spreadsheet program, and by publishing the forms on an internal Web site for company-wide access.

Table 4-4 Sample numbering scheme for system and support analysis sheets

Form number	Sheet name
ITSS01	IT system and support analysis sheet
CNSS01	Computer network system and support analysis sheet
FMSS01	Facilities management system and support analysis sheet
TSS01	Telecommunications system and support analysis sheet
HRSS01	Human resources system and support analysis sheet
CSSS01	Corporate security system and support analysis sheet
SRSS01	Shipping and receiving system and support analysis sheet
Numbered accordingly	Other system and support analysis sheets

All support departments should prepare presentations for the planning team that clearly classify the importance of their systems and functions. Their presentations should also recommend a sequence for recovering or replicating these systems and functions to return to normal operations. Departments should use data from the exposure inventory sheets and process support requirements sheets as a starting point for their analysis.

During this step in disaster recovery planning, the support departments must provide considerable detail about high-priority systems or functions. This analysis can serve many purposes, including:

- Confirming the data that was collected during the business process inventory and support requirements analysis

- Establishing a foundation for cross-departmental disaster recovery procedures

- Showing which types of equipment and resources must be recovered or replicated during a disaster

- Providing a baseline to plan disaster recovery budgets

The following sections illustrate and describe each of the system and support analysis sheets listed in Table 4-4. As with all inventory and analysis sheets the planning team uses, each sheet has a number and a date. Each sheet has spaces for listing systems and functions required to support business processes that the planning team identifies as the most important for recovery.

Each analysis sheet also includes a space to indicate the classification of the system or function for recovery. Possible classifications are "critical," "essential," "necessary," or "desirable." The business processes that the system supports are also shown, along with the recovery priority for the business process.

IT System and Support Analysis Sheet

Table 4-5 shows a sample **IT system and support analysis sheet**, which describes specific IT systems and the business processes they support. The sample sheet shows that Mainframe #1 is most critical for supporting revenue collection and product distribution within the organization. The sheet should also list all the software needed to support the processes, as well as required personnel and any other required resources.

Table 4-5   Sample IT system and support analysis sheet

IT System and Support Analysis Sheet (Form number ITSS01) Sheet _____ of _____ Date: _____			
System or Function	Classification	Business Processes Supported	Recovery Priority of Business Process
Mainframe #1	Critical	Revenue Collection	1
	Critical	Product Distribution	2
(Add details as necessary)			

Computer Network System and Support Analysis Sheet

Table 4-6 shows a sample **computer network system and support analysis sheet**, which describes specific network systems and the business processes they support. The sample sheet shows that LAN #1 and WAN #1 are most critical to revenue collection in the organization. The sheet should also list the specific equipment required for connecting to WAN #1 or replicating LAN #1, as well as any software or communications connectivity needed for network access.

4

Table 4-6 Sample computer network system and support analysis sheet

Computer Network System and Support Analysis Sheet (Form number CNSS01) Sheet _____ of _____ Date: _____			
System or Function	Classification	Business Processes Supported	Recovery Priority of Business Process
WAN #1	Critical	Revenue Collection	1
LAN #1	Critical	Revenue Collection	1
(Add details as necessary)			

Facilities Management System and Support Analysis Sheet

Table 4-7 shows a sample **facilities management system and support analysis sheet**, which describes specific facilities and the business processes they support. The sample sheet shows that Data Center #1 is a critical system for supporting revenue collection, as is the 10,000 square feet of office space that the revenue collection staff occupies.

Table 4-7   Sample facilities management system and support analysis sheet

Facilities Management System and Support Analysis Sheet (Form number FMSS01) Sheet ____ of ____ Date: _____			
System or Function	Classification	Business Processes Supported	Recovery Priority of Business Process
Data Center #1	Critical	Revenue Collection	1
10,000 sq. ft. office space	Critical	Revenue Collection	1
(Add details as necessary)			

Telecommunications System and Support Analysis Sheet

Table 4-8 shows a sample **telecommunications system and support analysis sheet**, which describes specific telecommunications systems and the business processes they support. The sample sheet shows that Phone system #1 is critical for supporting revenue collection, as is the 4000 square feet of office space this phone system covers.

Table 4-8   Sample telecommunications system and support analysis sheet

Telecommunications System and Support Analysis Sheet (Form number TSS01) Sheet _____ of _____ Date: _____			
System or Function	Classification	Business Processes Supported	Recovery Priority of Business Process
Phone system #1	Critical	Revenue Collection	1
4000 sq. ft. office space	Critical	Revenue Collection	1
(Add details as necessary)			

4

Human Resources System and Support Analysis Sheet

A sample **human resources system and support analysis sheet** is shown in Table 4-9. This sheet describes specific human resources systems and the business processes they support. The sample sheet shows that the timekeeping and payroll system is most critical to supporting revenue collection. So is the 3000 square feet of office space that the staff occupies to run these systems.

Table 4-9   Sample human resources system and support analysis sheet

Human Resources System and Support Analysis Sheet (Form number HRSS01) Sheet ____ of ____ Date: _____			
System or Function	Classification	Business Processes Supported	Recovery Priority of Business Process
Timekeeping and payroll	Critical	Revenue Collection	1
3000 sq. ft. office space	Critical	Revenue Collection	1
(Add details as necessary)			

Corporate Security System and Support Analysis Sheet

A sample **corporate security system and support analysis sheet** is shown in Table 4–10. This sheet describes specific corporate security systems and the business processes they support. The sample sheet shows that the facility access control system is critical to supporting revenue collection. So is the 1000 square feet of office space occupied by the facility access control staff.

Table 4-10 Sample corporate security system and support analysis sheet

Corporate Security System and Support Analysis Sheet (Form number CSSS01) Sheet ____ of ____ Date: _____			
System or Function	Classification	Business Processes Supported	Recovery Priority of Business Process
Facility access control	Critical	Revenue Collection	1
1000 sq. ft. office space	Critical	Revenue Collection	1
(Add details as necessary)			

Shipping and Receiving System and Support Analysis Sheet

Table 4–11 shows a sample **shipping and receiving system and support analysis sheet**, which describes specific shipping and receiving systems and the business processes they support. The sample sheet shows that two shipping and receiving staff members and 500 square feet of related office space are critical to support revenue collection.

Table 4-11 Sample shipping and receiving system and support analysis sheet

Shipping and Receiving System and Support Analysis Sheet (Form number SRSS01) Sheet _____ of _____ Date: _____			
System or Function	Classification	Business Processes Supported	Recovery Priority of Business Process
2 staff	Critical	Revenue Collection	1
500 sq. ft. office space	Critical	Revenue Collection	1
(Add details as necessary)			

Developing Charts of Responsibilities

To determine which departments are responsible for developing recovery procedures for critical business processes or operations at specific facilities, the planning team should develop a series of **disaster recovery responsibilities charts**. Responsibilities are assigned based on the information in the support requirements sheets and the system and support analysis sheets. If a department does not have direct responsibility for recovery of a facility or business process, it may not be involved in developing recovery procedures.

The planning team should develop three disaster recovery charts of responsibilities:

- A facility chart of responsibilities

- A departmental chart of responsibilities

- A business process chart of responsibilities

Once these charts are developed, they should be completed for each facility, department, and business process in the organization. The following sections explain and illustrate each chart.

Facility Disaster Recovery Chart of Responsibilities

The **facility disaster recovery chart of responsibilities** is shown in Table 4-12. The chart lists the primary and alternate disaster recovery responders for a specific facility. The people listed on the form are responsible for designated tasks or functions at a facility. The form has spaces for the facility number, the number of buildings and employees at the facility, and contact information for responders.

Table 4-12   Sample facility disaster recovery chart of responsibilities

Facility Disaster Recovery Chart of Responsibilities (Form number FDRCR01) Sheet _____ of _____ Date: _____		
Facility number: 1000	Number of buildings: 3 Number of employees:	
Facility name and location: Name: Address: Main telephone: Main fax number: Main e-mail:	Primary disaster recovery contact: Name: Address: Telephone: Fax number: E-mail:	
Area of responsibility	Name and contact information for primary responder	Name and contact information for alternate responder
Disaster declaration		
Disaster response lead		
IT support		
Computer network support		
Facilities management support		
Telecommunications support		
Human Resources support		
Corporate security support		
Shipping and receiving support		
Other support functions (listed as necessary)		
Comments:		

Department Disaster Recovery Chart of Responsibilities

The **department disaster recovery chart of responsibilities** is shown in Table 4-13. The chart lists the primary and alternate disaster recovery responders for a specific department. The people listed on the form are responsible for designated tasks or functions within each department. The form has spaces for the business entity name, the department name, facility number, building number(s), and contact information for responders.

4

Table 4-13   Sample department disaster recovery chart of responsibilities

Department Disaster Recovery Chart of Responsibilities (Form number DDRCR01) Sheet _____ of _____ Date: _____		
Entity: _____ Department: _____	Facility number(s): 1000 Building number(s): 1000-001	
Facility name and location: Name: Address: Main telephone: Main fax number: Main e-mail:	Primary disaster recovery contact: Name: Address: Telephone: Fax number: E-mail:	
Area of responsibility	Name and contact information for primary responder	Name and contact information for alternate responder
Disaster declaration		
Disaster response lead		
IT support		
Computer network support		
Facilities management support		
Telecommunications support		
Human Resources support		
Corporate security support		
Shipping and receiving support		
Other support functions (listed as necessary)		
Comments:		

Business Process Disaster Recovery Chart of Responsibilities

The **business process disaster recovery chart of responsibilities** is shown in Table 4-14. The chart lists the primary and alternate disaster recovery responders for a specific business process. The people listed on the form are responsible for designated tasks or functions that support the business process. The form has spaces for the business entity name, the department name, facility number, building number(s), and contact information for responders. The business process number should match the number assigned during the business process inventory.

Table 4-14 Sample business process disaster recovery chart of responsibilities

Business Process Disaster Recovery Chart of Responsibilities (Form number BPDRCR01) Sheet _____ of_____ Date:_____		
Entity: _____ Department: _____ Business process number: RCP-0001	Facility number(s): 1000 Building number(s): 1000-001	
Facility name and location: Name: Address: Main telephone: Main fax number: Main e-mail:	Primary disaster recovery contact: Name: Address: Telephone: Fax number: E-mail:	
Area of responsibility	Name and contact information for primary responder	Name and contact information for alternate responder
Disaster declaration		
Disaster response lead		
IT support		
Computer network support		
Facilities management support		
Telecommunications support		
Human Resources support		
Corporate security support		
Shipping and receiving support		
Other support functions (listed as necessary)		
Comments:		

ASSESSING INSURANCE REQUIREMENTS AND COVERAGE NEEDS

At this point in the planning process, the team should have a qualified employee examine the organization's insurance for business continuity coverage in case of disaster. Of the more than 250 organizations surveyed for this book, respondents for two of every 10 said they had business continuity coverage (Figure 4-1). Another two of every 10 said they did not. Four of every 10 were not sure whether their organizations had business continuity insurance or not.

Surveyed organizations that reported having business continuity coverage	
Surveyed organizations that did not have business continuity coverage	
Respondents who were not sure whether their organization had business continuity insurance	
Respondents who said they could not reveal such information	

Figure 4-1 Survey of whether organizations have business continuity insurance

The survey respondents who said their organizations had business continuity insurance were also asked if they thought the insurance was adequate. Half of these respondents said they believed their company's insurance would cover potential losses. Slightly less than half of these respondents reported that their insurance company required minimum standards for disaster recovery planning.

The Need for Insurance

Organizations that have suffered through past disasters are well aware of the need for business continuity insurance. As a result of major hurricanes, tornadoes, floods, earthquakes, and terrorist attacks during the last decade, the nature of business continuity insurance has changed considerably. Most insurance companies now impose additional charges for covering natural disasters such as earthquakes, hail, or wind damage. The U.S. government is playing a stronger role in funding and regulating insurance coverage for terrorist attacks and floods.

From 1990 to 1999, the Federal Emergency Management Agency (FEMA) spent more than $25.4 billion for disasters and emergencies, compared with only $3.9 billion (current dollars) in the previous decade. Hurricanes and typhoons were the most costly weather-related disasters in the 1990s; to date, FEMA has obligated more than $7.78 billion for them. Nearly 90 declarations were issued for these storms, including 19 in 1999.[1]

Flooding was the most frequent type of U.S. disaster during the 1990s; FEMA committed more than $7 billion in response and recovery. The most costly floods were the 1993 Midwest floods ($1.17 billion), the Red River Valley floods in 1997 ($730.8 million), and flooding caused by Tropical Storm Alberto in 1994 ($544.2 million). Other major floods in Arizona, Houston, New Orleans, and California each required more than $100 million in FEMA funding.[2]

A total of 102 tornado-related disasters were declared during the 1990s, more than in any recent period. These tornados required more than $1.70 billion in FEMA aid.[3]

Among events not caused by weather, the 1994 Northridge earthquake in California was the decade's most expensive disaster recovery, requiring almost $7 billion in FEMA funding.[4]

Table 4-15 shows the top 10 natural disasters in U.S. history, based on the amount of funding that FEMA provided in response. Table 4-16 shows the total number of disasters declared from 1972 to 2000 in each of the 50 U.S. states, the District of Columbia, and nine U.S. territories.

Table 4-15 Top 10 natural disasters

Event (with states affected)	Year	FEMA funding
Northridge earthquake (CA)	1994	$6.999 billion
Hurricane Georges (AL, FL, LA, MS, PR, VI)	1998	$2.333 billion
Hurricane Andrew (FL, LA)	1992	$1.849 billion
Hurricane Hugo (NC, SC, PR, VI)	1989	$1.308 billion
Midwest floods (IL, IA, KS, MN, MO, NE, ND, SD, WI)	1993	$1.141 billion
Hurricane Floyd (CT, DE, FL, ME, MD, NH, NJ, NY, NC, PA, SC, VT, VA)	1999	$1.085 billion
Tropical Storm Allison (FL, LA, MS, PA, TX)	2001	$879.5 million
Loma Prieta earthquake (CA)	1989	$865.5 million
Red River Valley floods (MN, ND, SD)	1997	$734.0 million
Hurricane Fran (MD, NC, PA, VA, WV)	1996	$621.2 million

Source: FEMA

Notes: Amounts obligated from the President's Disaster Relief Fund for FEMA's assistance programs, hazard mitigation grants, federal mission assignments, contractual services, and administrative costs, as of February 28, 2002. Figures do not include funding provided by other participating federal agencies, such as the disaster loan programs of the Small Business Administration and the Agriculture Department's Farm Service Agency.

Table 4-16 U.S. disasters declared from 1972 to 2000

Rank	State/Territory	Number of disasters declared	Rank	State/Territory	Number of disasters declared
1.	Texas	51	27.	Indiana	17
2.	California	45	28.	Nebraska, South Dakota, Kansas	16
3.	Florida	35	31.	Vermont	15
4.	Alabama	34	32.	Alaska, New Hampshire, New Jersey, New Mexico	14
5.	Louisiana	33	36.	Massachusetts, Arizona, Maryland	13
6.	New York	31	39.	Hawaii, Oregon, Puerto Rico	12
7.	Oklahoma	30	42.	Montana	11
8.	Illinois, Washington	28	43.	Idaho	10
10.	Minnesota, Tennessee	26	44.	North Marianas, Connecticut, U.S. Virgin Islands	9
12.	Mississippi, Pennsylvania	25	47.	Micronesia, Colorado	8
14.	Arkansas, Kentucky, Ohio	24	49.	Marshall Islands, South Carolina	7
17.	Missouri, Virginia, Wisconsin	23	51.	American Samoa, Guam, Trust Territory of the Pacific Islands, Delaware	6
20.	Iowa, Georgia, Maine, North Carolina	21	55.	Nevada, Utah, District of Columbia, Wyoming	5
24.	West Virginia	20	59.	Rhode Island	4
25.	North Dakota	19	60.	Palau	1
26.	Michigan	18			

Source: FEMA

Notes: A total of 1037 major disasters were declared in these 29 years in 50 states, the District of Columbia, and nine U.S. territories.

Evaluating the Terms and Conditions of Insurance Policies

Far too many organizations do not clearly understand their insurance coverage, or the conditions under which insurance claims may not be paid. The disaster recovery planning team cannot afford the same misunderstandings. After working through Steps Two and Three of disaster recovery planning, the team should have a comprehensive knowledge of facilities, assets, business processes, equipment, installed systems, and personnel. Armed with this information, the planning team needs to form an insurance review subcommittee to evaluate the organization's existing coverage in relation to its needs. The subcommittee should work with staff from financial management, facilities management, legal counsel, and other departments as necessary. The subcommittee needs to evaluate the terms and conditions of the insurance coverage, and address the following questions:

- What perils or causes of loss are included and excluded?

- What are the deductibles?

- How is property valued?

- Does the policy cover the cost of required upgrades during renovation or reconstruction?

- What steps must be taken in the event of a loss?

- What types of records must the organization have to support claims?

- Can the disaster recovery plan help reduce insurance costs?

The subcommittee must also evaluate a policy's terms and conditions to know which resources are needed to recover from a disaster. Meanwhile, the planning team needs to examine more basic aspects of the policy. First it must determine the kinds of disasters for which the insurance policy will pay recovery expenses, either in part or in full. One approach to evaluating this event coverage is to examine the policies for exclusions.

The insurance review subcommittee should evaluate coverage for all the risks identified during the risk assessment. The subcommittee should report its findings back to the planning team using a form similar to the event coverage inventory sheet shown in Table 4–17.

Table 4-17 Sample event coverage inventory sheet

Type of event	Type of coverage and deductibles	Assessment of adequacy
Severe rainstorm		
Tornado		
Hurricane		
Earthquake		
Wilderness fire		
Flood		
Train derailment		
Auto/truck accident		
Toxic air pollution caused by accident		
Plane crash		
Building explosion or fire		
Militant group attacking facilities		
Riot or civil unrest		
Computer hack (external)		
Computer fraud (internal)		

A second key point the subcommittee must evaluate is whether the policy covers the cost of required upgrades during renovation or reconstruction. The subcommittee also needs to determine whether the existing coverage will pay for replacing buildings or equipment that meet current standards, or will only pay to replace buildings or equipment that are of the same age and condition as the destroyed capital.

For example, a disaster might destroy a 50,000–square-foot office building that is 45 years old. The subcommittee must determine whether the insurance will pay for the acquisition or construction of a new building with the same square footage, which meets current building design and construction standards, or whether the insurance will only pay to acquire a similar 45-year-old building.

As another example, a seven-year-old computer system might be destroyed. Will the insurance coverage pay the depreciated value of a seven-year-old computer as a replacement, or will it pay for a new model of the same type of computer? The cost differences can be significant. Understanding how the policy places values on physical property helps the planning team decide what kind of modifications to make in the coverage, and what kind of expenses to expect during disaster recovery.

The subcommittee must also evaluate exactly what the organization needs to do to collect insurance coverage if a disaster strikes. This is important, because recovering from disasters can consume large amounts of cash very quickly. An organization must be able to provide all necessary documentation to obtain funds as quickly as possible.

Finally, the insurance subcommittee needs to review the terms and conditions related to having a disaster recovery plan in place. Having a well-designed and tested plan may reduce the cost of insurance coverage, and may help to get funds from the insurance company more quickly.

Evaluating Insurance Coverage

In addition to examining terms and conditions of coverage, the insurance review subcommittee should evaluate insurance coverage and needs in the following areas:

- Physical assets, including buildings, light and heavy equipment, computers and networking technology, installed systems, and automobiles and trucks

- Stock, parts, supplies, raw material, and works in progress

- Assets that are in transit, at a subcontractor's location, in storage, or at exhibitions

- Financial assets, revenue, profits, and temporary operating expenses

- Intellectual properties, designs in process, patterns, and proprietary processes

- Records, stored files, electronic files, databases, and proprietary computer programs

- Impact of supplier or customer downtime

- Employee injury or death, key person loss, salary continuation, crisis counseling, and care packages

- Indemnity, director, and officer protection

The insurance review subcommittee should evaluate coverage for all the risks identified during the risk assessment. The subcommittee should report its findings back to the planning team using a form similar to the asset coverage inventory sheet shown in Table 4-18.

Table 4-18   Sample asset coverage inventory sheet

Type of asset	Type of coverage and deductibles	Assessment of adequacy
Physical facilities		
Heavy equipment		
Light equipment		
Installed systems		
Information technology		
Office equipment		
Products/parts		
Intellectual properties		
Records, files, data		
Supplier or customer downtime		
Indemnity		
Employee injury or death, salary continuation, crisis counseling, care packages		
Key person loss		

ASSESSING PROGRESS AND MOVING FORWARD

During this step of disaster recovery planning, the team ranked the importance of business processes and facilities for disaster recovery. Support departments also analyzed and classified the systems and support functions that must be in place to support each business process and facility. The planning team created charts of responsibilities for disaster recovery planning and response for facilities, departments, and business processes. The planning team's insurance review subcommittee evaluated the organization's insurance coverage and needs, as well as terms and conditions that affect insurance coverage.

All of this information helps to guide the work of the disaster recovery planning team during the next step of the planning process—developing specific disaster recovery procedures. Chapter 5 describes this step in detail.

By the end of Steps Two and Three in the planning process (assessing risk and establishing roles across departments, respectively), the disaster recovery planning coordinator will have accumulated large amounts of data. This is a good time to evaluate the condition of the records and the filing system in the coordinator's office. Files should be easily accessible, well organized, and clearly labeled. The filing system should allow a new coordinator to take over if the present coordinator is no longer available. These files should be secured against theft and backed up at multiple locations to prevent loss.

The following checklist (Table 4-19) is a helpful review tool to evaluate progress before the disaster recovery planning team moves on to develop recovery procedures. The checklist includes all major activities that the team must complete before continuing. The team should double-check the status of these activities before it develops procedures.

Table 4-19   Disaster recovery planning checklist

Activity	Status
Facility exposure inventories	(for example, complete, pending, or not applicable)
Business process inventories	
Business process support requirements analysis	
Evaluation of existing threat mitigation	
Risk assessment reports	
Recovery requirements analysis	
Business processes and facilities prioritized for disaster recovery	
Systems and functions prioritized for disaster recovery	
Charts of responsibilities completed	
Terms and conditions of insurance coverage evaluated	
Insurance coverage for assets evaluated	

CHAPTER SUMMARY

◻ The disaster recovery planning team needs to rank the importance of all business processes and facilities to establish priorities in the planning process, as well as determine the speed at which supporting systems and functions need to be recovered.

◻ The planning team must examine the systems and functions that support the most important business processes and facilities, then classify these systems as critical, essential, necessary, or desirable.

◻ Planners need to develop charts of disaster recovery responsibilities. These charts show which departments are responsible for developing recovery procedures for critical business processes or operations at specific facilities. Responsibilities are assigned based on the information in the support requirements sheets and the systems and support analysis sheets.

◻ Organizations that have suffered through past disasters are well aware of the need for business continuity insurance. As a result of major hurricanes, tornados, floods, earthquakes, and terrorist attacks during the last decade, the nature of business continuity insurance has changed considerably. Most insurance companies now impose additional charges for covering natural disasters such as earthquakes, hail, or wind damage. The U.S. government is playing a stronger role in funding and regulating insurance coverage for terrorist attacks and floods.

◻ After working through Steps Two and Three of disaster recovery planning, the team should have comprehensive knowledge of facilities, assets, business processes, equipment, installed systems, and personnel. Armed with this information, the planning team needs to form an insurance review subcommittee to evaluate the organization's existing coverage against its needs. The subcommittee should work with staff from financial management, facilities management, legal counsel, and other departments as necessary.

❏ By the end of Steps Two and Three in the planning process (assessing risk and establishing roles across departments, respectively), the disaster recovery planning coordinator will have accumulated large amounts of data. This is a good time to evaluate the condition of the records and the filing system in the coordinator's office. Files should be easily accessible, well organized, and clearly labeled. The filing system should allow a new coordinator to take over if the present coordinator is no longer available.

4

KEY TERMS

business process disaster recovery chart of responsibilities — A record of primary and alternate disaster recovery responders for a specific business process. The people listed on the form are responsible for designated tasks or functions that support the business process.

computer network system and support analysis sheet — A sheet that describes specific computer network systems and the business processes they support.

corporate security system and support analysis sheet — A sheet that describes specific corporate security systems and the business processes they support.

critical systems and functions — Systems and functions that absolutely must be in place for any business process to continue at all.

department disaster recovery chart of responsibilities — A record of primary and alternate disaster recovery responders for a specific department. The people listed on the form are responsible for designated tasks or functions within each department.

desirable systems and functions — Systems and functions that improve working conditions and help to enhance an organization's performance.

disaster recovery responsibilities charts — Charts that describe which departments are responsible for developing recovery procedures for business processes or operations at specific facilities. Responsibilities are assigned based on the information in the support requirements sheets and the systems and support analysis sheets.

facilities management system and support analysis sheet — A sheet that describes specific facilities and the business processes they support.

facility disaster recovery chart of responsibilities — A record of primary and alternate disaster recovery responders for a specific facility. The people listed on the form are responsible for designated tasks or functions at a facility.

human resources system and support analysis sheet — A sheet that describes specific human resources systems and the business processes they support.

IT system and support analysis sheet — A sheet that describes specific IT systems and the business processes they support.

necessary systems and functions — Systems and functions that contribute to smooth operations and comfortable working conditions for employees.

shipping and receiving system and support analysis sheet — A sheet that describes specific shipping and receiving systems and the business processes they support.

telecommunications system and support analysis sheet — A sheet that describes specific telecommunications systems and the business processes they support.

REVIEW QUESTIONS

1. What types of requirements or pressures can organizations face when deciding how to prioritize business processes and facilities for disaster recovery?

2. What potential consequences do organizations face if they fail to comply with disaster recovery requirements or expectations?

3. When the disaster recovery planning team is ranking business processes and requires consensus building to agree on the rankings, what should the planning coordinator do?

4. When departments present opposing views about prioritizing business recovery processes, what should their presentations cover?

5. What are critical systems and functions?

6. What are essential systems and functions?

7. What are necessary systems and functions?

8. What are desirable systems and functions?

9. What information does the IT system and support analysis sheet provide?

10. Which support departments need to participate in classifying systems and functions as critical, essential, necessary, or desirable?

11. What information does the business process disaster recovery chart of responsibilities provide?

12. What information does the facility disaster recovery chart of responsibilities provide?

13. What information does the department disaster recovery chart of responsibilities provide?

14. During the last decade, how has the nature of business continuity insurance changed?

15. Among events not caused by weather, what was the most costly natural disaster in the 1990s?

16. What was the most costly weather-related natural disaster in the 1990s?

17. In which areas should the insurance review subcommittee evaluate insurance coverage and needs?

18. What terms and conditions of an insurance policy should the insurance review subcommittee evaluate?

19. Why is it important to understand how an insurance policy values assets?

20. Why is it important to understand what an organization must do to collect insurance coverage if a disaster strikes?

21. Why should the insurance subcommittee review a policy's terms and conditions related to having a disaster recovery plan in place?

22. What research activities should be completed before the planning team starts to develop disaster recovery procedures?

23. Why is it important to ensure that the files of the disaster recovery planning coordinator are well organized?

24. Who should be on the insurance review subcommittee?

HANDS-ON PROJECTS

In the following projects you will create and complete various analysis sheets that you studied in this chapter. All of these sheets describe system and support requirements for revenue collection in the organization for which you are developing a disaster recovery plan. When you finish, submit the materials to your instructor for review.

Project 4-1

1. Create an IT system and support analysis sheet.

2. List all the computers, peripherals, operating systems, utility software, and applications software required to support revenue collection.

3. List all the office space needed to provide IT systems and support for revenue collection.

Project 4-2

1. Create a computer network system and support analysis sheet.

2. List all the networking hardware required to support revenue collection.

3. List all the network operating systems, utility software, applications software, and connectivity systems required to support revenue collection.

4. List all the office space needed to provide network connectivity systems and support for revenue collection.

Project 4-3

1. Create a facilities management system and support analysis sheet.

2. List all the office space required to support revenue collection.

3. List all amenities that must be in the office space to support revenue collection.

Project 4-4

1. Create a telecommunications system and support analysis sheet.

2. List all the telecommunications hardware required to support revenue collection.

3. List all the telecommunications operating systems, utility software, applications software, and connectivity systems required to support revenue collection.

4. List all the office space needed to provide telecommunications systems and support for revenue collection.

Project 4-5

1. Create a human resources system and support analysis sheet.

2. List all human resources system and support functions required for revenue collection.

3. List all the office space needed to provide human resources systems and support for revenue collection.

Project 4-6

1. Create a corporate security system and support analysis sheet.

2. List all the staff needed to provide corporate security systems and support for revenue collection.

3. List all the office space needed to provide corporate security systems and support for revenue collection.

Project 4-7

1. Create a business process chart of responsibilities for revenue collection.

2. Indicate which staff members have disaster recovery planning responsibilities for revenue collection.

CASE PROJECTS

CASE PROJECTS

Case Project: Harris and Heartfield Manufacturing

4

Harris and Heartfield Manufacturing is a family-owned business that fabricates specialized metal parts for its North American clients. Most of its revenue comes from defense contracts, and from producing parts for heavy-equipment manufacturers. The company has an excellent reputation for quality and prompt deliveries.

The company has 200 employees at its only location, in California. All 20 administrative employees have desktop PCs connected to the company's local area network (LAN). The 15 research and design engineers use Sun workstations that are also on the LAN. Three servers support administrative functions and six servers support design and manufacturing. About half the machining equipment on the shop floor is computerized.

Management is concerned about the company's future competitiveness, and about its ability to fulfill orders if a disaster hindered its operations. The board of directors is relatively business-savvy, but does not invest money unless it yields a positive return. As a result, the company hired you as a consultant to create a list of 10 key points that conveyed the importance of disaster recovery planning to the board. You also prepared 10 points for managers to discuss with employees about organizing and preparing to develop a plan. You worked with company managers to develop a business process threat analysis for their product manufacturing.

Your new assignment is to create a list of questions that the company should answer about its insurance coverage. The list should be as comprehensive as possible, and easy to understand. Make the questions as specific as possible.

OPTIONAL TEAM CASE PROJECTS

OPTIONAL CASE PROJECTS

Team Case One

Your boss has asked you to identify five insurance companies that provide disaster recovery insurance. Your assignment is to research the types of coverage offered by each company, and then write a one-page description of each coverage. The description should include the name of the insurance company and the types of coverage offered. If you use the Internet, identify the URL of the Web site where you found the information.

OPTIONAL CASE PROJECTS

Team Case Two

Your boss has asked you to create a chart that compares the coverage of the five insurance companies you identified in Team Case One. The chart should include the names of the insurance companies, the types of coverage offered, and other details that can assist in the selection of an insurance provider.

ENDNOTES

1. *www.fema.gov.*

2. *www.fema.gov.*

3. *www.fema.gov.*

4. *www.fema.gov.*

5

DEVELOPING PLANS AND PROCEDURES

After reading this chapter, you will be able to:

♦ Determine what disaster recovery procedures need to be developed

♦ Develop and write disaster recovery procedures

♦ Review and approve disaster recovery procedures

♦ Develop basic disaster recovery plans for a facility

♦ Publish the disaster recovery plan

The disaster recovery planning team must develop a set of recovery procedures for each facility that the organization operates. Although some basic procedures need to be in place for all facilities, some procedures must be tailored to address special conditions and staffing patterns at a facility. In addition, facilities might require procedures that address the specialized nature of their operations, the types of equipment they use, and their location.

Each disaster recovery procedure must be clearly written so that employees can quickly refer to it and understand their responsibilities during response and recovery. Procedures should follow a consistent format to make them easier to read and understand.

Each procedure should be reviewed by the disaster recovery planning team and the employees who must implement the procedure. In addition, managers of affected facilities, departments, and business processes should review any relevant procedures.

DETERMINING WHAT DISASTER RECOVERY PROCEDURES ARE NEEDED

The disaster recovery planning team needs to evaluate all facilities and business operations to determine what kinds of procedures it must help develop to facilitate recovery. These procedures fall into six major categories, as shown in Table 5-1. The procedures in each category must be coordinated to ensure that operations are disrupted as little as possible. The table shows examples of procedures in each category.

Table 5-1 Types of disaster recovery procedures

Category of procedures	Examples of procedures
Direction, control, and administration	Determining the level of disaster and type of response, controlling response activities, and performing administrative procedures for rescue and insurance claims
Internal and external communications	Initiating and managing communications in response to the disaster
Safety and health	Ensuring the safety and health of employees and disaster recovery workers
Containment and property protection	Ensuring that property is properly secured, and containing the disaster's impact to local areas or sections of facilities, when possible
Resuming and recovering operations	Relocating staff and resources to resume some level of business operation
Restoring facilities and normalizing operations	Rebuilding, restoring, or acquiring adequate facilities to support business operations in the same way they functioned before a disaster

Each of these categories requires its own team to develop procedures and execute them in a disaster. Members of each team should be listed on a separate page in the disaster recovery plan, along with their titles, departments, and contact information.

In addition, the planning team needs to develop disaster recovery procedures to account for various levels of damage and disruption of operations. Each level of disaster requires a different response. The three major classifications of disasters are shown in Table 5-2.

Table 5-2 Classifications of disaster

Disaster level	Description
Catastrophic disaster	Operations could be disrupted for more than a week unless disaster recovery procedures are implemented. Damage is severe; a facility might be destroyed, or might require replacement of equipment or major renovation.
Major disaster	Operations could be disrupted from two to seven days unless disaster recovery procedures are implemented. The damage can leave key business units without computer services, telecommunications, production resources, or personnel.
Minor disaster	Operations could be disrupted longer than one shift, but less than two days. Damage is relatively light; it can include minor damage to computer systems, office equipment, manufacturing equipment, or a facility.

DEVELOPING AND WRITING DISASTER RECOVERY PROCEDURES

As planning team members oversee the development of recovery procedures for the disaster recovery manual, they should continually monitor the drafts for thoroughness and consistency of formatting. Subcommittees of the disaster recovery team must work with the necessary departments to develop procedures. The procedures must be drafted and approved by all affected parties, as well as by employees who must implement the procedures.

These procedures can be printed and maintained on paper, but organizations can save considerable time and effort by maintaining procedures on an internal Web site that offers company-wide access.

Table 5-3 shows a generic **disaster recovery procedure sheet** that can be used whenever a specific form is not required. The sheet includes space for documenting the procedure and identifying the person who is responsible for implementing it. The sheet also includes space for other important details, including the facility name and number, building number, number of buildings and employees, and contact information for the facility and disaster recovery representative.

Table 5-3 Sample disaster recovery procedure sheet

Disaster Recovery Procedure Sheet _____ of _____ Date: _____	
Facility number: 1000 Building number: 1000-001	Number of buildings: 3 Number of employees:
Facility name and location: Name: Address: Main telephone: Main fax number: Main e-mail:	Disaster recovery contact: Name: Address: Telephone: Fax number: E-mail:
Procedure type (e.g., direction, control, and administration): Procedure number: Date approved:	Responsible parties: Name: Address: Telephone: Fax number: E-mail:
Procedure explanation (continue on additional sheet if necessary)	

REVIEWING AND APPROVING DISASTER RECOVERY PROCEDURES

The entire disaster recovery team should review drafts of all recovery procedures. Also, a team subcommittee that is not helping to develop procedures should perform an independent review. If this is not possible, then a group of middle-level managers who are not developing procedures can conduct the independent review.

Reviewers should ensure that the procedure is clearly documented, easy to read and understand, and consistent with other procedures being developed. Procedures must not contradict each other. If reviewers discover problems with a procedure, they must provide a written, detailed response to the subcommittee or department that developed the draft. A typewritten memorandum or e-mail is sufficient.

The drafters of the procedure should then revise it and submit it for another review. This process continues until the disaster recovery team and review subcommittees are satisfied with the procedure. The acceptance of the procedure should be a formal process; all members of the disaster recovery team should have the opportunity to comment.

DEVELOPING BASIC DISASTER RECOVERY PLANS FOR EVERY FACILITY

5

Every facility should have at least a basic disaster recovery plan in place. The plan should be straightforward, and should contain a sufficient amount of documentation and procedures to allow effective disaster response. Of course, plans become more complex for large facilities that have numerous departments and employees. Regardless of an organization's size, however, several basic rules apply to writing disaster recovery plans:

- Everything must be clearly documented.

- The plan and procedures must be written in straightforward language that all employees can understand.

- A disaster recovery plan can be computer-based, but paper copies of all related documents must be available for distribution if computer networks or servers are not working. Electronic and paper versions of plans and procedures must be kept at multiple locations to ensure their availability.

- All teams that work on disaster response and recovery need copies of the plan.

- Members of each team should be listed on a separate page in the disaster recovery plan, along with their titles, departments, and contact information.

The content of a disaster recovery plan varies among organizations. Numerous factors influence this content, including the industry in which the organization operates, laws and government regulations, the location and type of facility, and the type of operations supported at the facility.

The components of a basic disaster recovery plan are explained in detail in this section and outlined in Table 5-4.

Table 5-4 Outline for a basic disaster recovery plan

Section	Content
Title page	Name and location of facility
Table of contents	All contents of the document, with page numbers
Introduction	Overview and basic disaster recovery policies
Primary disaster recovery staff	Names, titles, addresses, phone numbers, and e-mail addresses of key contacts
Disaster classification	An explanation of how to classify the disaster
Direction, control, and administration procedures	Organizing the response team and recovery team, the emergency operations center, and first alerts; disaster confirmation and declaration; keeping activity logs
Safety and health procedures	Organizing the evacuation and rescue team, organizing the security team, facility evacuation, reentry, moving employees, crisis counseling
Procedures for internal and external communications	Organizing the communications team; notifying emergency medical services, such as fire, rescue, and police; notifying top management, insurance companies, employees and families, customers, suppliers, and service providers
Procedures for containment and property protection	Organizing the insurance and damage assessment team, securing buildings, utility shutoffs, asset security and retrieval, communications systems management, damage assessment
Procedures for resuming and recovering operations	Organizing the business continuation team; determining duration of shutdown; activating back-up systems and alternate systems; activating hot or cold sites to provide replicated computing environments; moving records, equipment, and supplies; recovering systems and functions that are critical, essential, necessary, and desirable
Procedures for restoring facilities and normalizing operations	Organizing the restoration team, restoration estimates, temporary repairs, restoration work, reoccupying facilities
Appendix A: Contact lists	Executives and department managers, disaster recovery team members, other key staff, emergency services, technology vendors, service providers, employees, customers, suppliers, and media
Appendix B: Building plans	Blueprints that show room layouts, hallways, exits, installed systems, emergency systems, locations of large equipment, locations of records and files, and locations of valuable assets, etc.
Appendix C: Risk assessment reports	Risk assessment reports and supporting documentation, including exposure inventories and business process support requirements
Appendix D: Organizational agreements	Memorandums of understanding and support agreements with other organizations
Appendix E: Requirements	Specific laws, regulations, or organizational policies that require actions during disaster response and recovery

Title Page

The title page of the disaster recovery plan should include the name and location of the facility or business process for which the plan was developed. If your organization uses facility numbers and building numbers on the various supporting forms, then the title page should include these numbers.

The title page can include the date that the plan was developed, along with revision dates. The title page should also state that the document is "company confidential for internal use only." If necessary, the disaster recovery team can work with the Legal Department to determine a similar phrase that is more acceptable to the organization.

The title page can also list the names and phone numbers of appropriate disaster recovery staff to contact for further information about the plan.

Table of Contents

The table of contents should be detailed enough to show all section headings, chapter titles, and subheadings within each chapter, as well as a separate list of tables and figures. The contents of the appendices should also be shown in detail, including risk assessment reports, exposure inventories, business process inventories, and business process support requirements.

Introduction

The introduction should provide an overview of the plan. It should also summarize any specific laws, regulations, or organizational policies that relate to disaster response and recovery. If necessary, include an appendix to the plan to provide more detailed exhibits or descriptions of these laws, regulations, and policies.

Primary Disaster Recovery Staff

Include the names, titles, addresses, phone numbers, and e-mail addresses of all key disaster recovery staff in this section. Keep this section current to reflect changes in the staff. As employees leave an organization, their disaster response and recovery responsibilities need to be reassigned and documented immediately.

Disaster Classification

This section should clearly explain how responders classify catastrophic, major, and minor disasters at a facility. This is often a difficult process. However, the classifications need to provide enough information to offer initial guidance to responders.

Catastrophic disasters are relatively easy to classify. If a building is destroyed or rendered inaccessible, the event can readily be classified as catastrophic. However, if an organization has several buildings that can be used for the same purpose, then the loss of a building may be classified as catastrophic until it is clear that no employees are dead or missing. The organization can then downgrade the event to a major disaster.

The disaster recovery planning team bears the burden of classifying damaging or disruptive events. The extensive study and analysis that goes into a plan should ensure that the planning team has as much information as possible to make these determinations during procedure development. The determinations also depend on the characteristics of the facility, its location, and the dangers and potential damages the facility faces.

Direction, Control, and Administration Procedures

Several important documents and procedures enable organization managers to direct, control, and administer the response to a disaster, and then move into the recovery phase:

- Organizing the response team

- Establishing an emergency operations center

- Establishing first alert notifications

- Confirming a disaster

- Declaring the disaster

- Keeping an activity log

The first document in this section of the disaster recovery plan should list the people designated as the **response team** . The response team should include employees from major departments and people with the necessary skills to deal with disasters at specific facilities. Table 5-5 shows typical response activities and indicates which team members might perform these activities.

Table 5-5 Composition of disaster response team

Response activities	Possible team members
Overall direction of activities	Middle- to upper-level managers, disaster recovery coordinator, facilities manager
Internal and external communications	Public relations manager, human resources manager, communications specialist
Safety and health	Corporate security staff, on-site nurse or medical specialist
Containment and property protection	Corporate security staff, facilities managers or staff, building maintenance staff, property management staff, manufacturing engineers
Resuming and recovering operations	Specialists in support functions, including IT and network management, operations directors, and department managers
Restoring facilities and normalizing operations	Facilities managers or staff, building maintenance staff, property management staff, operations directors, department managers

In many cases, and especially during catastrophic events, an organization may need to establish an **emergency operations center** . Leaders of the response team can direct activities from this facility, and team members can work and rest there. The disaster recovery plan must include primary and alternate locations for an emergency operations center. The plan should also document any necessary information for notifying facility managers of the move and relocating staff to the center.

If an organization has several facilities in the same community, any of them could be considered for use as an emergency operations center. If this is not possible, a local hotel with conference facilities may be adequate.

Table 5-6 is a sample **emergency operations center information sheet** . Use this document to describe the primary and alternate locations of emergency operations, and to list contact information for the facilities.

5

Table 5-6 Sample emergency operations center information sheet

Emergency Operations Center Information Sheet Sheet _____ of _____ Date: _____	
Facility number: 1000 Building number: 1000-001 Number of employess:	Facility name and location: Name: Address: Main telephone: Main fax number: Main e-mail:
Primary emergency operations center Facility name and location: Name: Address: Main telephone: Main fax number: Main e-mail:	**Alternate emergency operations center** Facility name and location: Name: Address: Main telephone: Main fax number: Main e-mail:
Contacts Name: Address: Main telephone: Main fax number: Main e-mail:	**Contacts** Name: Address: Main telephone: Main fax number: Main e-mail:
Comments	Comments

The next set of documents, the **first alert procedures** , provide a methodical and structured process for notifying managers, employees, and emergency service organizations that a disaster has occurred. The procedures should identify who is responsible for first alerts, which managers can authorize a first alert, and the names of people who must be contacted first after a disaster. An authorized manager must initiate a first alert; however, because so many people may need to be contacted during a first alert, staff from the manager's office or the disaster response team need to make the contacts. Table 5-7 shows a sample **first alert information sheet** , with spaces for the appropriate contact information.

Table 5-7   Sample first alert information sheet

First Alert Information Sheet Sheet _____ of _____ Date: _____	
Facility number: 1000 Building number: 1000-001 Number of employess:	Facility name and location: Name: Address: Main telephone: Main fax number: Main e-mail:
Contacts	**Contact information**
Name: Organization: Title:	Main telephone: Main fax number: Main e-mail:
Name: Organization: Title:	Main telephone: Main fax number: Main e-mail:
Name: Organization: Title:	Main telephone: Main fax number: Main e-mail:
Name: Organization: Title:	Main telephone: Main fax number: Main e-mail:
Name: Organization: Title:	Main telephone: Main fax number: Main e-mail:
Name: Organization: Title:	Main telephone: Main fax number: Main e-mail:

Use the **disaster confirmation procedure** to verify that a disaster occurred, to validate the impact of the event, and to determine the scope of its initial damage and disruption. Confirmation is important, because disaster response can consume considerable resources or even stop normal operations. Organizations cannot afford to shut down for a false alarm. The response team can confirm a disaster by conducting site visits and interviews.

Once an event is confirmed, the leader of the response team or another designate must issue a formal **disaster declaration** . This declaration initially classifies a disaster as catastrophic, major, or minor. The response team can adjust this classification as it obtains additional information.

Table 5-8 shows a sample **disaster confirmation and declaration report** . Use it to record who confirmed the disaster, how it was confirmed, and when it was declared. The report includes spaces for the affected facility and building numbers, their location, and contact information for the manager who confirmed the disaster. You can also describe the event and list the sources of confirmation.

Once a disaster is declared, the response team must maintain a **disaster response activity log** that tracks all response and recovery activities. Table 5-9 shows a sample activity log for disaster response. It provides space for describing each activity, the date and time of its occurrence, and contact information for the responsible party.

The disaster recovery plan should include samples of the activity log, along with several blank copies that the response team can use. The plan should include detailed instructions for how the organization wants the log to be maintained. Also, the risk assessment reports in the plan can provide information that helps the recovery team understand which operations an activity may affect. Individual teams can keep their own logs and integrate them into a master log that covers all activities.

5

Table 5-8 Sample disaster confirmation and declaration report

Disaster Confirmation and Declaration Report
Sheet _____ of _____ Date: _____

Facility number: 1000 Building number: 1000-001 Number of employees: Time of first report: Time of confirmation: Time of declaration:	Facility name and location: Name: Address: Main telephone: Main fax number: Main e-mail:
Classification of disaster (circle one): Catastrophic Major Minor	
Description of event:	
Manager who confirmed event Name: Organization: Title: Main telephone: Main fax number: Main e-mail:	**Sources confirming event** Name: Organization: Title: Main telephone: Main fax number: Main e-mail:
Sources confirming event Name: Organization: Title: Main telephone: Main fax number: Main e-mail:	**Sources confirming event** Name: Organization: Title: Main telephone: Main fax number: Main e-mail:
Comments	

Table 5-9 Sample disaster response activity log

Disaster Response Activity Log		
Sheet _____ of _____ Date: _____		
Facility number: _____ Building number: _____		
Team: _____ Team leader: _____		
Activity	**Date and time**	**Organization and contact information**

Safety and Health Procedures

Safety and health procedures are some of the most important procedures in any disaster recovery plan. Organizations should establish two teams to execute these procedures during disaster recovery: an evacuation and rescue team and a security team.

Both teams need access to building plans, which should be included as an appendix to the disaster recovery plan. Building plans can help the teams navigate facilities and locate personnel, utility systems, and valuable assets in an emergency.

The rescue and security teams should help to develop procedures for facility evacuation, reentry, movement of employees, and crisis counseling. Earlier in this chapter, Table 5-3 showed a generic form that can help the teams record all the procedures they develop for the disaster recovery plan.

During the first hectic hours after a disaster, the rescue and security teams must work quickly and urgently. However, one person from each team should still be assigned to maintain an activity log as accurately as possible. Team members can be debriefed later to complete the log if necessary.

The **evacuation and rescue team** should consist of trained employees who can supervise evacuation procedures and initiate rescue efforts at specific facilities. Table 5-10 shows evacuation and rescue activities that require recovery procedures and the team members who might perform these activities.

Table 5-10 Composition of evacuation and rescue team

Response activities for which procedures must be developed	Possible team members
Overall direction of activities	Middle- to upper-level managers, disaster recovery coordinator, facilities manager
Physically evacuating people from a facility	Corporate security staff, building engineers, maintenance staff, or medical specialist
Medical evacuation	Contract ambulance service or local emergency response service
Supervising assembly areas and conducting roll calls	Department managers
Search and rescue in damaged buildings	Local emergency services, building engineers

The **security team** ensures that facilities and valuable property are protected during evacuation, after evacuation, and while recovery is under way. Table 5-11 shows security activities that require recovery procedures and the team members who might perform these activities.

Table 5-11 Composition of security team

Response activities for which procedures must be developed	Possible team members
Overall direction of activities	Middle- to upper-level managers, corporate security director, facilities manager
Locking doors, gates, and other passages in and out of the building	Corporate security staff, building engineers, maintenance staff
Securing computers and essential computer data	IT and network staff
Securing valuable assets	Corporate security, department managers
Perimeter security	Corporate security, local police, contract security company
Security for emergency operations center or temporary quarters	Corporate security, local police, contract security company

Procedures for Internal and External Communications

During disaster recovery, it is very time consuming to contact all the people an organization depends on for day-to-day operations. However, these communications are necessary to keep the recovery running smoothly. For this reason, organizations need to establish a communications team for disaster recovery. The team contacts all necessary parties during recovery and provides them with consistent explanations of events. If the communications team wants to develop timelines for expected recovery activities, the director of the disaster response team should approve the timelines before distribution.

The communications team should keep an activity log that shows which organizations and people have been contacted, and when they were contacted. The team should also include its contact lists as an appendix to the disaster recovery plan. A sample contact list could include the following parties:

- Executives and department managers

- Disaster recovery team members

- Other key staff

- Emergency services

- Technology vendors

- Service providers

- Employees

- Customers

- Suppliers

- Media

Agreements between organizations, which are often documented in an appendix to the disaster recovery plan, can provide detailed information to the communications team about external relationships that have been established to assist in recovery.

The communications team should consist of trained employees who can manage internal and external communications and facilitate disaster response. The team is responsible for making necessary contacts with law enforcement agencies, government agencies that regulate the organization, the media, and the general public. Table 5-12 shows communications activities that require recovery procedures and the team members who might perform these activities.

Procedures for Containment and Property Protection

Procedures are needed to secure buildings, shut off utilities, retrieve valuable assets, and conduct damage assessments during a disaster. Organizations must form an **insurance and damage assessment team** to perform these activities. The team should consist of trained employees who can prepare initial, detailed damage assessments, file reports with insurance companies, and work with demolition crews or construction contractors to start cleanup or repairs.

Table 5-13 shows insurance and damage assessment activities that require procedures and the team members who might perform these activities.

Table 5-12 Composition of communications team

Response activities for which procedures must be developed	Possible team members
Overall direction of activities	Middle- to upper-level managers, public relations staff
Interactions with law enforcement agencies and emergency response organizations	Middle- to upper-level managers, corporate security director
Interactions with vendors and support organizations	Managers of support departments
Interactions with employees and families	Public relations staff, crisis counselors
Interactions with customers	Customer service staff, sales staff
Interactions with the media	Middle- to upper-level managers, public relations staff
Interactions with suppliers	Purchasing staff, shipping and receiving staff

Table 5-13 Composition of insurance and damage assessment team

Response activities for which procedures must be developed	Possible team members
Overall direction of activities	Middle- to upper-level managers, building engineers
Reporting to insurance companies	Financial Management Department, building maintenance staff, property management staff
Contract for cleanup	Building maintenance staff, purchasing director
Contract for emergency repairs to buildings	Building maintenance staff, purchasing director
Contract for renovation or reconstruction of buildings	Building maintenance staff, purchasing director
Assessment of damage to computer systems and networks	IT and network management staff
Assessment of damage to telecommunications systems	Telecommunications staff
Assessment of damage to manufacturing equipment	Manufacturing director, chief manufacturing engineer
Assessment of damage to vehicles	Motor pool staff

Procedures for Resuming and Recovering Operations

Several actions are necessary before an organization can resume operations after a disaster. The number of actions required increases with the severity of the disaster; for example, a new or temporary facility might be needed in the wake of a catastrophic disaster. The following disaster recovery procedures could be necessary to resume operations:

- Determining the duration of the shutdown

- Activating back–up systems

- Activating alternate systems

- Activating hot or cold sites

- Moving records

- Moving equipment

- Moving supplies

- Recovering critical systems and functions

- Recovering essential systems and functions

- Recovering necessary systems and functions

- Recovering desirable systems and functions

The organization should form a **business continuation team** to help develop these procedures and execute them in a disaster. The team should consist of trained employees with the skills to manage operations and restore critical business systems and functions. The team is responsible for moving employees into temporary quarters; providing telecommunications, computer networks, and computing support; and managing shipping and receiving.

Table 5-14 shows business continuation activities that require procedures, and the team members who might perform these activities.

Table 5-14 Composition of business continuation team

Response activities for which procedures must be developed	Possible team members
Overall direction of activities	Middle- to upper-level managers, department managers
Providing temporary office space and furniture	Property management staff, purchasing director
Providing computer and network support	IT and network management staff
Providing telephone and fax services	Telecommunications staff
Providing logistics support	Shipping and Receiving Department, Logistics Department
Providing support for incoming and outgoing mail	Mail room
Providing security for temporary facilities	Corporate security
Providing new or temporary vehicles	Motor pool staff, Purchasing Department

Procedures for Restoring Facilities and Normalizing Operations

The **restoration team** should consist of trained employees who can manage the restoration or rebuilding of facilities. The team is responsible for obtaining restoration estimates, managing temporary repairs, and preparing facilities for reoccupation. Table 5-15 shows restoration activities that require procedures and the team members who might perform these activities.

Table 5-15 Composition of restoration team

Response activities for which procedures must be developed	Possible team members
Overall direction of activities	Middle- to upper-level managers, property management staff, building maintenance staff
Obtaining restoration estimates	Property management staff, purchasing director
Temporary repairs and preparing to reoccupy facilities	Property management staff, building maintenance staff
Contract for renovating or reconstructing buildings	Building maintenance staff, purchasing director
Restoration work	Building maintenance staff, contract construction companies
Design and selection of replacement computer networks	Network management staff
Design and selection of replacement telecommunications systems	Telecommunications staff
Replacing light equipment	Department managers, purchasing director
Replacing heavy equipment	Department managers, manufacturing engineers, purchasing director

PUBLISHING THE DISASTER RECOVERY PLAN

Publishing the disaster recovery plan and procedures requires several steps. To organize and oversee this process, the planning team first needs to appoint a **plan publishing team leader** . The team leader should have a background in technical writing, publishing, or procedure documentation.

The team leader works with the planning team, departmental groups, and subcommittees to make sure that all published material has been approved and is accurate. The team leader also establishes a production process to manage the flow of documents from the disaster recovery planning team to the publishing team.

Next, the planning team must decide how the plan should be published. Many organizations now use their intranet to publish such documents. This form of distribution is acceptable, but paper copies of the plan must also be available for distribution if computer networks or servers are not working. Electronic and paper versions of disaster plans and procedures must be kept at multiple locations to ensure their availability.

Once published, the disaster recovery plan is distributed to all departments. Team members who are responsible for training employees on the plan and its procedures should have access to the electronic version of the plan. Trainers can use the electronic documents to create slides, handouts, and other instructional material.

The disaster recovery plan must be treated as a confidential document. The planning team should label the plan as "company confidential" and restrict access to it. At the same time, however, many team members and employees need copies. To keep track of this distribution, the planning team should maintain a log of employees who possess copies of the plan. Table 5-16 shows a sample distribution log for the disaster recovery plan.

5

Table 5-16 Sample distribution log for disaster recovery plan

Disaster Recovery Plan Distribution Log	
Name, title, and department of recipient	**Signature and date**
Name: _____ Title: _____ Dept.: _____	Signature: _____ Date: _____
Name: _____ Title: _____ Dept.: _____	Signature: _____ Date: _____
Name: _____ Title: _____ Dept.: _____	Signature: _____ Date: _____
Name: _____ Title: _____ Dept.: _____	Signature: _____ Date: _____

Because of the confidential nature of the disaster recovery plan and procedures, all employees or other parties who receive a copy should sign a confidentiality and nondisclosure agreement. Some organizations may have a blanket nondisclosure form that covers the contents of the disaster recovery plan.

Table 5-17 shows a sample confidentiality agreement for a disaster recovery plan. The agreement includes a confidentiality statement, as well as spaces to identify the person receiving the plan, the receiver's signature and date, and the name of the person who released the copy.

Table 5-17   Sample confidentiality agreement for a disaster recovery plan

Disaster Recovery Plan Confidentiality Agreement
The document you are receiving is the confidential disaster recovery plan for *<organization's name>*. As an employee, you are required to keep the contents of this plan confidential. You are not allowed to make copies of the plan in any form. If you misplace your copy or believe that it was lost or stolen, you must immediately report the incident to the *<department name>*.
I have read and will comply with the confidentiality requirements of the disaster recovery plan.
Name: _____ Title: _____ Department: _____ Address 1: _____ Address 2: _____ Address 3: _____ Address 4: _____ Phone number: _____ Employee ID Number: _____
Employee signature: _____ Date: _____ Plan released by: *Name of authorized person*

Assessing Progress and Moving Forward

This chapter provided an overview of the procedures needed to develop a basic disaster recovery plan. Organizations must develop detailed recovery procedures and document them to ensure that disaster recovery proceeds as smoothly as possible.

Chapter 6 explores the importance of organizational relationships in disaster recovery and provides more details on specific types of procedures. Chapter 7 explains how to develop procedures to respond to computer attacks. Chapter 8 covers how to document disaster recovery procedures for special circumstances.

Chapter Summary

- The disaster recovery planning team needs to evaluate all facilities and business operations to determine what kinds of procedures it must help develop to facilitate recovery. The procedures must be coordinated to ensure that operations are disrupted as little as possible.

- As planning team members oversee the development of recovery procedures for the disaster recovery manual, they should continually monitor the drafts for thoroughness and consistency of formatting. Subcommittees of the disaster recovery team must work with the necessary departments to develop procedures. The procedures must be drafted and approved by all affected parties, as well as by employees who must implement the procedures.

◻ The entire disaster recovery team should review drafts of all recovery procedures. Also, a team subcommittee that is not helping to develop procedures should perform an independent review. If this is not possible, then a group of middle-level managers who are not developing procedures can conduct the independent review.

◻ Every facility should have at least a basic disaster recovery plan in place. The plan should be straightforward, and should contain a sufficient amount of documentation and procedures to allow effective disaster response.

◻ A team leader should be appointed to oversee publication of the disaster recovery plan. The team leader should have a background in technical writing, publishing, or procedure documentation. The team leader works with the disaster recovery planning team, departmental groups, and subcommittees to make sure that published material has been approved and is accurate.

5

KEY TERMS

business continuation team — A team with the training and skills to manage operations after a disaster and restore critical business systems and functions. The team is responsible for moving employees into temporary quarters; providing telecommunications, computer networks, and computing support; and managing shipping and receiving.

catastrophic disaster — A disaster in which operations could be disrupted for more than a week unless disaster recovery procedures are implemented. Damage from a catastrophic disaster is severe; a facility might be destroyed, or might require replacement of equipment or major renovation.

containment and property protection procedures — Procedures to ensure that property is properly secured, and that a disaster's impact is contained to local areas or sections of facilities, when possible.

direction, control, and administration procedures — Procedures for controlling disaster response activities and administering the overall response.

disaster confirmation and declaration report — A report that details who confirmed a disaster and how the event was confirmed. The report includes a description of the event, contact information for the confirming manager, and confirmation sources.

disaster confirmation procedure — A procedure designed to validate the impact of a disaster and determine the scope of its initial damage and disruption.

disaster declaration — A formal announcement that a disaster has occurred. The declaration is made by the leader of the disaster response team or another designate within the organization. The declaration provides an initial classification of the disaster as catastrophic, major, or minor.

disaster recovery procedure sheet — A document that describes a disaster recovery procedure. The sheet should indicate who is responsible for implementing the procedure, identify the relevant facility, and provide appropriate contact information.

disaster response activity log — A document that the response team uses to track all activities related to disaster response and recovery. The log should detail each activity, the date and time of its occurrence, and the name of the person responsible for the activity.

emergency operations center — A facility from which leaders of the response team can direct activities, and where team members can work and rest.

emergency operations center information sheet — A document that describes the primary and alternate emergency operations centers.

evacuation and rescue team — A team with the training and skills to supervise evacuation procedures and initiate rescue efforts at specific facilities.

first alert information sheet — A list of managers, employees, and emergency service organizations that should be contacted first in case of disaster.

first alert procedures — A methodical and structured process to notify managers, employees, and emergency service organizations of a disaster.

insurance and damage assessment team — A team that prepares initial, detailed damage assessments after a disaster, files reports with insurance companies, and works with demolition crews or construction contractors to start cleanup or repairs.

internal and external communications procedures — Procedures for initiating and managing communications in response to a disaster.

major disaster — A disaster in which operations could be disrupted from two to seven days unless disaster recovery procedures are implemented. Damage from major disasters can leave key business units without computer services, telecommunications, production resources, or personnel.

minor disaster — A disaster in which operations could be disrupted longer than one shift, but less than two days. Minor disasters can include minor damage to computer systems, office or manufacturing equipment, or a facility.

plan publishing team leader — A person who oversees the publication of the disaster recovery plan. The team leader also works with the planning team, departmental groups, and subcommittees to make sure that published material has been approved and is accurate.

response team — A team of employees from major departments who are prepared to deal with disasters at specific facilities.

restoration team — A team of trained employees who manage the restoration or rebuilding of facilities after a disaster. The team is responsible for obtaining restoration estimates, managing temporary repairs, and preparing facilities for reoccupation.

restoring facilities and normalizing operations — Procedures for rebuilding, restoring, or acquiring adequate facilities to support business operations in the same way they functioned before a disaster.

resuming and recovering operations — Procedures for relocating staff and resources to resume some level of business operation after a disaster.

safety and health procedures — Procedures designed to ensure the safety and health of employees and disaster recovery workers during disaster response.

security team — A team of trained employees who can ensure that facilities and valuable property are secured during evacuation, after evacuation, and while recovery is under way.

REVIEW QUESTIONS

1. Explain the types of disaster recovery procedures that relate to direction, control, and administration.

2. Explain the types of disaster recovery procedures that relate to internal and external communications.

3. Explain the types of disaster recovery procedures that relate to safety and health.

4. Explain the types of disaster recovery procedures that relate to containment and property protection.

5. Explain the types of disaster recovery procedures that relate to resuming and recovering operations.

6. Explain the types of disaster recovery procedures that relate to restoring facilities and normalizing operations.

7. Define a catastrophic disaster.

8. Define a major disaster.

9. Define a minor disaster.

10. Explain the purpose of a disaster recovery procedure sheet.

11. List examples of the types of tasks the disaster response team performs.

12. What is the purpose of the emergency operations center?

13. What is the purpose of first alert procedures?

14. What is the purpose of the disaster confirmation procedure?

15. What is the purpose of the disaster response activity log?

16. What kind of staff should be on the evacuation and rescue team?

17. What is the role of the security team?

18. What is the role of the communications team?

19. What is the role of the insurance and damage assessment team?

20. What is the role of the business continuation team?

21. What is the purpose of the restoration team?

22. How can risk assessment reports help the disaster response team?

23. How do the rescue team and security team benefit from having access to building plans?

24. Why should the people who train employees on the disaster recovery plan have access to electronic documents used to publish the plan?

25. Why should paper copies of the plan be available for distribution to team members?

HANDS-ON PROJECTS

In the following projects, your team will develop materials on behalf of the organization for which you are creating a disaster recovery plan. When you finish, submit the materials to your instructor for review.

Project 5-1

Define which types of events would be catastrophic, major, and minor disasters for the organization. Your definitions should include the factors that influence the classification of disasters, the expected duration of disruption from each event, and the expected severity of damage from each event.

Project 5-2

Designate members of the organization's response team. Develop a list of team members for inclusion in the disaster recovery plan; include each member's title, department, and contact information. Explain the role of each team member, and explain why each person was chosen for the team.

Project 5-3

Complete an emergency operations center information sheet for the organization. Select a primary and alternate location for the emergency operations center. Explain your reasons for selecting these locations.

Project 5-4

Complete a first alert information sheet for the organization. Select which people should be contacted during the first alert process. Explain your selections.

Project 5-5

Designate members of the organization's evacuation and rescue team. Develop a list of team members for inclusion in the disaster recovery plan; include each member's title, department, and contact information. Explain the role of each team member, and explain why each person was chosen for the team.

Project 5-6

Designate members of the organization's security team. Develop a list of team members for inclusion in the disaster recovery plan; include the same types of information and explanations requested in Project 5-5.

5

Project 5-7

Designate members of the organization's insurance and damage assessment team. Develop a list of team members for inclusion in the disaster recovery plan; include the same types of information and explanations requested in Project 5-5.

Project 5-8

Designate members of the organization's business continuation team. Develop a list of team members for inclusion in the disaster recovery plan; include the same types of information and explanations requested in Project 5-5.

Project 5-9

Designate members of the organization's restoration team. Develop a list of team members for inclusion in the disaster recovery plan; include the same types of information and explanations requested in Project 5-5.

CASE PROJECTS

Case Project: Harris and Heartfield Manufacturing

Harris and Heartfield Manufacturing is a family-owned business that fabricates specialized metal parts for its North American clients. Most of its revenue comes from defense contracts, and from producing parts for heavy-equipment manufacturers. The company has an excellent reputation for quality and prompt deliveries.

The company has 200 employees at its only location, in California. All 20 administrative employees have desktop PCs connected to the company's local area network (LAN). The 15 research and design engineers use Sun workstations that are also on the LAN. Three servers support administrative functions and six servers support design and manufacturing. About half the machining equipment on the shop floor is computerized.

Management is concerned about the company's future competitiveness, and about its ability to fulfill orders if a disaster hindered its operations. The board of directors is relatively business-savvy, but does not invest money unless it yields a positive return. As a result, the company hired you as a consultant to create a list of 10 key points that conveyed the importance of disaster recovery planning to the board. You also prepared 10 points for managers to discuss with employees about organizing and preparing to develop a plan. You worked with company managers to develop a business process threat analysis for their product manufacturing, and developed questions that the company should answer about its insurance coverage.

Your new assignment is to help Harris and Heartfield decide which types of people should be on the disaster response team. Outline the basic responsibilities of the response team, and provide a list of recommendations for staffing the team.

OPTIONAL TEAM CASE PROJECTS

Team Case One

Your boss has asked you to identify local emergency and law enforcement agencies with which your company would work in a disaster. Your assignment is to research these organizations and write a one-page description of each, including its location, contact information, and a summary of the organization's services. Also, explain the best way to work with the organization to integrate its services into your disaster recovery plan.

Team Case Two

Your boss has asked you to identify local companies that can provide cleanup, demolition, and emergency repair services. Your assignment is to research the companies and write a one-page description of each, including its location, contact information, and a summary of the organization's services. Also, explain the best way to work with the company to integrate its services into your disaster recovery plan.

6

ORGANIZATIONAL RELATIONSHIPS IN DISASTER RECOVERY

After reading this chapter, you will be able to:

♦ Identify organizations to work with during a disaster

♦ Develop procedures for working with public service providers

♦ Create procedures for working with insurance companies

♦ Develop procedures for working with private service providers

♦ Create procedures for working with the business arena

♦ Communicate with the media

♦ Communicate with stakeholders

When responding to a disaster and starting recovery procedures, an organization needs to work with many other agencies that can assist with the recovery effort. These agencies include law enforcement, emergency services, contractors, utilities, equipment providers, business partners, and suppliers.

The organization must also communicate with other groups that may be affected by the disaster, including customers, employees and their families, and the surrounding community.

A disaster recovery plan must include procedures to guide all of these interactions. This chapter focuses on developing procedures that enable properly trained employees to work and communicate with other organizations in a disaster. The disaster response team must maintain a comprehensive list of these organizations.

IDENTIFYING ORGANIZATIONS TO WORK WITH DURING A DISASTER

Members of the disaster response and communications teams must contact numerous people and organizations in a disaster. The disaster recovery planning team needs to develop lists and procedures for establishing these communications. Required contacts vary by organization, and depend on the disaster's severity and specific disaster recovery needs. Typically, a disaster that is classified as catastrophic or major requires cooperation with the following organizations and groups:

- Local emergency services

- Local law enforcement

- Insurance companies

- Disaster recovery service providers

- Telecommunications service providers

- IT service providers

- Public utilities

- IT equipment providers and software companies

- Business partners

- Suppliers

- Customers

- Stakeholders

- Organizations in the local community

The disaster response team must quickly determine the extent of the disaster, and the expected duration of system downtime or facility closure. The team needs to develop contact instructions for the preceding organizations, alternate telephone and fax numbers, the names of disaster recovery liaisons, and other information to assist in recovery.

The disaster recovery planning team determines which organizations to contact, and then includes this information in the disaster recovery plan. Trained teams of disaster response workers are responsible for making contacts.

The response team should report all communications with other organizations in a disaster response activity log. The team should also complete a **disaster response contact sheet** for each contact it makes. The example sheet in Table 6-1 has spaces for recording information about the facility where the call originated, the staff who made the call, the organization contacted, and the results of the contact. If necessary, the team can use blank sheets to record additional information about the results.

Disaster response contact sheets can be useful for evaluating the response of service organizations, as well as the effectiveness of the disaster recovery plan and procedures. The contact sheets and other forms in this chapter can be printed and maintained on paper, but organizations can save considerable time and effort by maintaining the forms in a popular database or spreadsheet program, and by publishing the forms on an internal Web site for company-wide access.

Table 6-1 Sample disaster response contact sheet

Disaster Response Contact Sheet Sheet _____ of _____ Date:_____	
Entity name: Facility location: Main telephone: Main fax number: Main e-mail:	Organization to be contacted: Facility location: Contact name: Contact title: Contact address: Contact telephone: Contact fax number: Contact e-mail:
Staff making contact: Date contacted: Time contacted:	Nature of relationship:
Reason for contact:	Results of contact:
Comments:	

WORKING WITH PUBLIC SERVICE PROVIDERS

An organization works with several local agencies during disaster response and recovery, including emergency services, utilities, and public works organizations.

Developing Procedures for Working with Emergency Services

When a disaster occurs, particularly one that involves physical damage or destruction, one of the first series of necessary contacts is with local emergency services and law enforcement agencies. Because response time is critical in saving lives and minimizing damage to facilities, the disaster recovery planning team must develop thorough procedures for contacting the proper organizations and agencies quickly. These **emergency response organizations** include:

- Ambulance and emergency medical services

- Fire and police departments

- Hazardous material response teams

- Regional and local disaster agencies

- Vehicle removal and debris removal services

- Building maintenance and construction contractors

The need for emergency service varies based on the disaster. Obviously, the possibility of physical injury and death requires ambulances and emergency medical services. However, the scope and intensity of a disaster may require a wide range of emergency response, including firefighters, police, and contractors to remove debris or damaged vehicles.

To effectively use emergency services, the disaster response team needs to develop contact procedures that enable rapid response. Table 6–2 is a checklist that shows important items to include in emergency service contact procedures.

An organization needs to be prepared to work with emergency responders immediately upon their arrival, and needs to have the proper information ready. Having a knowledgeable liaison who can meet responders, answer questions, and provide assistance can save valuable time.

Table 6-2 Checklist for emergency service contact procedures

Items to include in emergency service contact procedures	Status (e.g., Completed, Pending, or N/A)
Names and titles of employees who are authorized to contact emergency services	
Contact information and locations of emergency service organizations	
Conditions that require emergency services to be contacted	
How events should be described to emergency service dispatchers	
How facilities and locations should be identified for emergency service responders	
Instructions that emergency service responders need before entering the facility	
Items that should be available upon arrival, such as copies of building plans	
Names and titles of people who should assist emergency service responders upon arrival, such as security staff or building maintenance staff	

Developing Procedures for Working with Public Utilities and Departments

Disaster recovery often requires working with public utilities to temporarily cut off services for safety reasons and then to restore them for normal operations. Public utilities are generally well-equipped and experienced when it comes to dealing with disasters. Electric utilities, for example, are continually faced with downed power lines or blown transformers. Water utilities battle broken water mains on a regular basis. Depending on the community where a facility is located, an organization may need recovery assistance from public utilities or Public Works departments in the following areas:

- Electric and gas power

- Water and sewer services

- Telephone lines

- Steam service

- Waste removal

- Road and highway maintenance and repair

- Forestry services

- Recycling services

- Environmental protection services

- Flood control services

- Animal control and protection

- Building inspection services

- Occupancy and use permits

The organizational structure and authority of public utilities and Public Works departments vary among communities. The disaster recovery planning team should study what each public department does, and determine whether and how to contact each during various types of disasters and emergencies. Table 6-3 is a checklist of items to consider when developing procedures to contact and work with utilities and Public Works departments.

Table 6-3 Checklist for working with public utilities and departments

Items to include in procedures for working with public utilities and departments	Status (e.g., Completed, Pending, or N/A)
Names and titles of employees who are authorized to work with public utilities	
Contact information and locations of public utilities and Public Works departments	
How facilities and locations should be identified for public utilities and Public Works departments	
A list of all services provided by public utilities, along with capacity and consumption patterns	
How to describe problems to public utility workers	
Blueprints and diagrams that show all public utility hookups and shutoffs for the facility	
A list of people who know the layout of a facility	

CREATING PROCEDURES FOR WORKING WITH INSURANCE COMPANIES

Once disaster response begins and dangerous circumstances have been addressed, the organization must contact its insurance companies. The insurance and damage assessment team assembles information to provide to insurance carriers.

The speed with which an organization initiates insurance claims makes a large difference in its ability to recover from a disaster. If an emergency operations center or temporary facilities are needed, some insurance policies may cover such expenses. If debris removal or emergency construction services are required, insurance may cover these costs as well.

Disaster recovery planning teams should consult with insurance companies while developing recovery plans and procedures to ensure that the organization can file successful insurance claims. Table 6-4 is a checklist that covers basic requirements for developing insurance company contact procedures.

Table 6-4 Checklist for insurance company contact procedures

Items to include in insurance company contact procedures	Status (e.g., Completed, Pending, or N/A)
Names and titles of employees who are authorized to contact insurance providers	
Contact information and locations of insurance providers	
How to describe the impact of a disaster to report damages to an insurance provider	
Current insurance policy numbers and information about coverage	
How facilities and locations should be identified for insurance claims	
How to develop initial and comprehensive insurance claims	
How to photograph, videotape, or otherwise report information that can support the extent of damage and the potential cost of recovery	

DEVELOPING PROCEDURES FOR WORKING WITH PRIVATE SERVICE PROVIDERS

An organization works with many types of private service companies and equipment vendors during disaster response and recovery. Some of these companies can provide specialized recovery services. Services are needed from a variety of contractors, telecommunications providers, IT service organizations, IT equipment suppliers, and software companies.

Developing Procedures for Working with Disaster Recovery Services

An organization may need to accomplish hundreds of tasks to thoroughly recover from a disaster. In many cases, in-house staff can accomplish these tasks. However, an organization probably does not have all the skills and equipment to respond to events that create extensive damage. The following **disaster recovery service providers** may be needed to provide assistance:

- Plumbing contractors

- Heating and air conditioning contractors

- Roofing contractors

- Electrical contractors

- General construction contractors

- Water removal specialists

- Hazardous material specialists

- Tree removal contractors

- Waste removal services

- Records restoration specialists

The disaster recovery planning team determines the necessity for restoring particular facilities to operable conditions and the priority in which they should be restored. After setting these priorities, the planning team develops disaster recovery procedures to restore the facilities accordingly.

The checklist in Table 6-5 covers many of the basic points to include in procedures for contacting disaster recovery service providers. The disaster response team probably needs to contact these contractors during the first few hours after a disaster. The restoration team may be responsible for making these contacts once the immediate danger has passed and the situation has stabilized.

Table 6-5 Checklist of procedures for contacting disaster recovery service providers

Items to include in procedures for contacting disaster recovery service providers	Status (e.g., Completed, Pending, or N/A)
Names and titles of employees who are authorized to contact disaster recovery service providers	
Contact information and locations of disaster recovery service providers	
How to describe needs to these service providers	
How facilities and locations should be identified for these service providers	
Information on negotiated contracts with these service providers	
Information on paying these service providers if there are no negotiated contracts	
How to access emergency funds to pay disaster recovery service providers	

Developing Procedures for Working with Telecommunications Service Providers

To maintain critical telecommunications services during a disaster, an organization should develop recovery procedures to ensure that services can be restored as quickly as possible, or rerouted to an alternate location if a facility is unusable. A disaster could affect the following types of telecommunications:

- Voice services

- Call center services

- Fax lines

- Data communications lines

- Electronic data interchange (EDI) systems

- Internet connections

- Web-based services and Web sites

- Toll-free customer service lines

- Voice mail

- E-mail services

- Access for remote workers, field staff, and regional offices

The priorities set by the disaster recovery planning team dictate which communications systems are most important to the organization's key business processes. Individual recovery procedures are required for each telecommunications service that an organization uses. Table 6-6 is a checklist for developing procedures to work with telecommunications service providers.

6

Table 6-6 Checklist for working with telecommunications service providers

Items to include in procedures for working with telecommunications service providers	Status (e.g., Completed, Pending, or N/A)
Names and titles of employees who are authorized to work with telecommunications service providers	
Contact information and locations of telecommunications service Help desks and customer service representatives	
How facilities and locations should be identified for telecommunications service providers	
A list of all telephone numbers, telephone lines and services, data communications lines, and contracted services for each provider	
Information on existing contracts with each service provider	
Information on paying these service providers if there are no current contracts for emergency services	
How to access emergency funds to pay for emergency telecommunications services	

Developing Procedures for Working with IT Service Providers

Most organizations cannot operate for very long without access to their computer systems. The disaster recovery planning team decides which systems are most critical to support business operations, and then determines what recovery procedures are required to restore these systems as quickly as possible in a disaster. The following types of computer systems could be affected:

- Enterprise systems that support business operations

- Servers that provide specialized business or manufacturing functions

- Servers that support supply–chain applications

- Workstations used in research and development

- Desktop systems that support office workers

- Web servers that support e-commerce applications

Some computer systems might be supported by IT service providers or set up for restoration through a hot site, which provides replicated computing environments. If so, procedures are necessary for activating backup computer facilities and emergency computer services. A variety of hot-site services are available, but the basic service is usually a replicated environment in a data center, which allows organizations to bring their computer systems back online quickly at a safe location. Table 6-7 is a checklist for developing procedures to work with IT service recovery providers.

Table 6-7 Checklist for IT service recovery procedures

Items to include in procedures for recovering IT services and computer systems	Status (e.g., Completed, Pending, or N/A)
Names and titles of employees who are authorized to work IT service recovery providers	
Contact information and locations of IT service recovery Help desks and customer service representatives	
How facilities and locations should be identified for IT service recovery providers	
A prioritized list of computer services and systems to be restored	
Information on existing contracts with each IT service recovery provider	
Information on paying these providers if there are no existing contracts for emergency services	
How to access emergency funds to pay for emergency IT services	

Developing Procedures for Working with IT Equipment Providers and Software Companies

In addition to working with IT service recovery providers, organizations must work with their IT equipment vendors and software companies to recover from a disaster. When developing procedures to restore computer systems and services, organizations must address the following concerns:

- The processes to move computer services to hot sites

- The staff needed to report to hot sites and maintain operations

- How a disaster may affect the need for equipment maintenance services

- How a disaster may affect the scope of software license use

- How using a hot site for computer support affects the cost of software licenses

- How IT equipment providers and software companies can assist in recovery

Computer and system recovery can run smoothly when procedures are well written and the IT staff is trained in disaster response. In past disasters, IT departments have demonstrated that they can sometimes restore high-priority services and systems within hours, and often within 24 hours, when recovery procedures are well designed and the organization subscribes to adequate hot-site services. Table 6-8 is a checklist for developing procedures to work with IT equipment providers and software companies during disaster recovery.

Table 6-8 Checklist for working with IT equipment providers and software companies

Items to include in procedures for working with IT equipment providers and software companies	Status (e.g., Completed, Pending, or N/A)
Names and titles of employees who are authorized to work with IT equipment providers and software companies	
Contact information and locations of IT equipment and software company Help desks and customer service representatives	
How facilities and locations should be identified for IT equipment providers and software companies	
A prioritized list of the computer services and systems to be restored	
Serial numbers for all IT equipment and license numbers for all software packages, along with the number of users covered by each license	
Information on existing contracts with each IT equipment provider and software company	
Information on paying these companies if there are no existing contracts for emergency services	
How to access emergency funds to pay for emergency IT equipment and software services	

CREATING PROCEDURES FOR WORKING WITH THE BUSINESS ARENA

An organization has many business relationships that it must address during disaster response and recovery. For example, organizations must maintain communications with a wide array of business partners that provide revenue or distribution channels for products and services. Organizations must also develop strategies for contacting and working with the many suppliers and service providers that make business operations possible. Above all, organizations must communicate with customers and assure them that transactions, deliveries, and relationships will continue to run smoothly.

These procedures have a public relations aspect as well. Contemporary business etiquette dictates that organizations maintain good relationships with business partners, suppliers, and customers by keeping in touch during a disaster.

Developing Procedures for Working with Business Partners

Organizations can have important economic relationships with a variety of **business partners**. A disaster can affect the operations of these partners, which include value-added resellers (VARs), original equipment manufacturers (OEMs), distributors, licensed resellers, and franchised operations. The planning team needs to develop recovery procedures for contacting and working with business partners to help mitigate the impact of a disaster. Table 6-9 is a checklist of these procedures.

Table 6-9   Checklist for contacting and working with business partners

Items to include in procedures for working with business partners	Status (e.g., Completed, Pending, or N/A)
Names and titles of employees who are authorized to work with business partners	
Contact information and locations of business partners	
How product lines or services should be identified when contacting business partners	
What to tell business partners about disasters	
What to tell them about recovery of operations	
What business partners should do if they need to contact the organization during the disaster	

Developing Procedures for Working with Suppliers and Business Service Providers

Organizations depend on their relationships with suppliers and service providers. Suppliers include organizations that provide raw materials, parts used in manufacturing, and consumable items that support business operations. Service providers include assembly contractors, testing contractors, logistics organizations, building cleaning services, and exterior maintenance services.

A disaster can damage supplier operations and result in a surfeit of materials arriving at an unusable facility. Disaster recovery procedures can help to reduce problems caused by suppliers who keep shipping material or service providers who show up to do work after a disaster. Table 6-10 is a checklist for developing procedures to work with suppliers and service providers during a disaster.

Table 6-10   Checklist for contacting and working with suppliers and service providers

Items to include in procedures for working with suppliers and service providers	Status (e.g., Completed, Pending, or N/A)
Names and titles of employees who are authorized to work with suppliers and service providers	
Contact information and locations of suppliers and service providers	
How product lines or services should be identified when contacting suppliers and service providers	
What to tell suppliers and service providers about disasters	
What to tell them about recovery of operations	
What suppliers and service providers should do if they need to contact the organization during the disaster	

Developing Procedures for Working with Customers

Organizations rely heavily on their relationships with customers, and vice versa—a disaster can adversely affect customer operations when shipments are delayed. Table 6-11 is a checklist for developing procedures to work with customers during a disaster.

Table 6-11 Checklist for contacting and working with customers

Items to include in procedures for working with customers	Status (e.g., Completed, Pending, or N/A)
Names and titles of employees who are authorized to work with customers	
Contact information and locations of key customers	
How product lines or services should be identified when contacting customers	
What customers should be told about disasters	
What they should be told about recovery of operations	
What customers should do if they need to contact the organization during the disaster	

COMMUNICATING WITH THE MEDIA

A disaster often results in extensive media coverage. An organization's dealings with the media during a disaster can reflect its management philosophy, and open communication is often interpreted as a mark of good citizenship. The disaster recovery plan should include procedures for the organization's external communications and designate an **official media spokesperson** to disseminate management-approved information. All media inquiries should be referred to the spokesperson.

All statements to the media *must be consistent*. Shareholders, investors, employees, and their families will see television and newspaper reports about the disaster, and everyone will have private concerns. Consistent statements help to ease these worries. On the other hand, inconsistent information supplied by executives, media spokespersons, and employees can only heighten concerns and intensify uncertainty.

The official spokesperson should have a background in working with the media; such employees often work in the Public Relations Department. Before top executives make statements to the media, they should seek assistance from the public relations staff. Table 6-12 is a checklist for developing procedures for media relations.

Table 6-12 Checklist for media relations procedures

Items to include in procedures for working with the media	Status (e.g., Completed, Pending, or N/A)
Names and titles of employees who are authorized to talk with the media	
Contact information and locations of local media and industry-focused media	
A list of executives who are assigned a public relations assistant to develop public statements	
A caution that trade secrets, proprietary information, and information restricted by law or regulation cannot be discussed publicly	
How to establish a media area at the emergency operations center	
How to establish a media area at affected facilities	
Preparation of media statements for distribution to all top executives and the on-site response team, along with information for contacting the official spokesperson	
A caution that names of missing, dead, or injured personnel cannot be released without clearance from upper management and victims' families	

6

COMMUNICATING WITH STAKEHOLDERS

An organization has a wide variety of stakeholders. A **stakeholder** is any person or organization that faces risks when disaster strikes a facility. Stakeholders include investors, employees and their families, and the surrounding community, all of whom depend on the facility in some way. The disaster recovery plan should include procedures for working with all stakeholders.

Stockholder and Investor Relations

Stockholders and investors naturally become concerned when one of their investments is affected by a disaster. An organization must respond quickly to inform stockholders and investors about any damages, and to assure them that steps are being taken to minimize the damage and restore normal operations.

The primary goal of stockholder and investor relations during a disaster is maintaining their confidence. Angry stockholders and investors can do considerable damage to an organization's reputation if they publicly question or criticize how the disaster response team is handling recovery.

If an organization has an Investor Relations Department or executives in charge of investor relations, they should be the primary contacts for stockholder and investor inquiries. In most cases, the investor relations staff or a lead executive know many of the large investors or stockholders. These employees have also worked with analysts who follow the industry in which the organization operates. They can use these existing relationships to communicate news and garner support for the organization's disaster recovery efforts. Table 6-13 is a checklist for developing procedures to maintain stockholder and investor relations during a disaster.

Table 6-13 Checklist of procedures for stockholder and investor relations

Items to include in procedures for working with stockholders and investors	Status (e.g., Completed, Pending, or N/A)
Names and titles of employees who are authorized to talk with stockholders and investors	
A list of executives assigned to stockholder and investor relations	
Contact information and locations of large stockholders and investors	
How to establish a stockholder and investor relations area at the emergency operations center	
A process to update stockholders and investors on the status of disaster recovery efforts	
A process to provide stockholders and investors with a final report when recovery is complete	

Communicating with Employees

Organizations have many obvious reasons for developing procedures to communicate with employees during disaster response and recovery. If a facility must be evacuated, employees need to know what to do next. For example, they might need to report to work at an alternate facility. If employees do not work on the disaster response team, they may not need to report at all for a period of time. Communicating such information to employees makes disaster recovery efforts run more smoothly.

Employees can also face great stress after the disaster, because they may be uncertain of their future or concerned about co-workers who were affected by the disaster. Organizations should develop a procedure that allows employees to check the status of operations, and that instructs them when and where to report to work again.

Employees deserve definitive and honest answers as quickly as possible. This not only helps to reduce stress, it builds confidence in management and disaster response efforts. Table 6-14 is a checklist for developing procedures for employee communications.

Table 6-14 Checklist for employee communications procedures

Items to include in procedures to communicate with employees	Status (e.g., Completed, Pending, or N/A)
Names and titles of authorized people who can provide official statements to employees	
A process that allows employees to check the status of operations, and that instructs them when and where to report to work again	
How to establish an employee communications area at the emergency operations center	
A process for department heads and supervisors to communicate with employees during recovery efforts	
A process to inform local media when and where employees should return to work	

Communicating with Families of Employees

An organization needs to communicate with families of employees and support them during a crisis. When disasters strike, families become frightened, and sometimes they even panic. Employees want to know that family members are kept informed of their health and safety; otherwise, the stress can hinder employees from focusing on recovery efforts. The organization must alleviate as much of this worry as possible.

If a crisis-counseling program is established for families of employees, it must be staffed with qualified and experienced counselors. Crisis counseling is not only stressful for families, it is emotional for the counselors. Experience is one of the best qualifications a crisis counselor can have.

Department managers and supervisors need to be sensitive and sympathetic to the needs of families during a disaster. However, they should not attempt to provide counseling themselves; instead, they should refer family members to the crisis-counseling program. Table 6-15 is a checklist for developing procedures to communicate with families of employees during a disaster.

Table 6-15 Checklist of procedures for communicating with families of employees

Items to include in procedures for communicating with families of employees	Status (e.g., Completed, Pending, or N/A)
Names and titles of authorized employees who can provide official statements to families	
A process that allows families to check the status of operations, and that tells employees in the family when and where to report to work again	
A process for obtaining names and contact information for families, to ensure that information is not given to prank callers and impostors	
How to establish an area at the emergency operations center to support communications with families	
A process for department heads and supervisors to communicate with families during disaster recovery	
A process to inform local media of messages the organization wants to relay to families	
How to establish crisis-counseling systems when necessary	

Working with the Local Community

All organizations have a complex set of relationships with their surrounding communities. People in the community have friends, neighbors, or relatives who work at a facility. Employees at the facility have children who attend community schools. A disaster naturally increases children's fears and anxieties.

Local businesses have economic dependencies on a facility, and disasters can create concerns about the future of their community. Some businesses may supply goods to an organization, while others may provide some type of service to it. Other businesses might not have direct relationships with the organization, but they may depend on the contribution a facility makes to the local economy.

An organization must be sympathetic in its relationships with businesses, institutions, schools, civic organizations, and the community at large. To maintain these relationships, organizations must appropriately handle inquiries from the community during a disaster. Table 6-16 is a checklist for developing procedures to work with the local community.

Table 6-16 Checklist of procedures for working with the local community

Items to include in procedures for working with the local community	Status (e.g., Completed, Pending, or N/A)
Names and titles of authorized employees who can provide official statements to the local community	
A process for local organizations to check the status of operations	
A process for department heads and supervisors to deal with inquiries from the community during disaster recovery	
A process to inform local media of messages for the community	

6

CHAPTER SUMMARY

❏ Members of the disaster response and communications teams must contact numerous people and organizations in a disaster. These agencies include law enforcement, emergency services, contractors, utilities, business partners, and suppliers. The disaster recovery planning team needs to develop lists and procedures for making these contacts. Trained teams of disaster response workers are then responsible for making the actual contacts, for reporting them in the disaster response activity log, and for documenting the details of each contact.

❏ When a disaster occurs, one of the first series of necessary contacts is with local emergency services and law enforcement agencies. Because response time is critical in saving lives and minimizing damage to facilities, the disaster recovery planning team must develop thorough procedures for contacting the proper organizations and agencies quickly. Also, disaster recovery often requires working with public utilities to temporarily cut off services for safety reasons and then to restore them for normal operations. Depending on the community where a facility is located, an organization may need to contact many public utilities or Public Works departments.

❏ Once disaster response begins and dangerous circumstances have been addressed, the organization must contact its insurance companies. The insurance and damage assessment team assembles information to provide to insurance carriers. The speed with which an organization initiates insurance claims makes a large difference in its ability to recover from a disaster.

❏ To maintain critical telecommunications services during a disaster, an organization should develop recovery procedures to ensure that services can be restored as quickly as possible, or rerouted to an alternate location if a facility is unusable. Also, most organizations cannot operate for very long without access to their computer systems. The disaster recovery planning team decides which systems are most critical to support business operations, and then determines what recovery procedures are required to restore these systems as quickly as possible in a disaster.

❏ An organization has many important economic relationships that it must address during disaster response and recovery. For example, organizations must contact and work with a variety of business partners, including VARs, OEMs, distributors, licensed resellers, and franchised operations. Organizations also need to maintain relationships with important suppliers and service providers. Most importantly, organizations rely heavily on their relationships with their customers, and vice versa—a disaster can adversely affect customer operations when shipments are delayed.

❑ The disaster recovery plan should include procedures for the organization's external communications and designate an official media spokesperson. All media inquiries should be referred to the spokesperson. The official spokesperson should have a background in working with the media; such employees often work in the Public Relations Department. Before top executives make statements to the media, they should seek assistance from the public relations staff.

❑ A stakeholder is any person or organization that faces risks when disaster strikes a facility. Stakeholders include investors, employees and their families, and the surrounding community, all of whom depend on the facility in some way. An organization's disaster recovery plan should include procedures for working with all stakeholders.

Key Terms

business partners — Organizations with which companies have important economic relationships. These partners include value-added resellers (VARs), original equipment manufacturers (OEMs), distributors, licensed resellers, and franchised operations.

disaster recovery service providers — Contractors and specialists that can provide services for disaster recovery, including heating and air conditioning, roofing, electrical services, general construction, water removal, hazardous material treatment, tree removal, and waste removal.

disaster response contact sheet — A sheet that describes the contacts an organization makes after a disaster.

emergency response organizations — Organizations that can respond to emergencies and disasters, including ambulance and emergency medical services, fire departments, police departments, and hazardous material response teams.

official media spokesperson — A person who provides management-approved information to the media. All media inquiries should be referred to the official spokesperson.

stakeholder — Any person or organization that faces risks when disaster strikes a facility. Stakeholders include investors, employees and their families, and the surrounding community, all of whom depend on the facility in some way.

Review Questions

1. What is the purpose of the disaster response contact sheet?

2. List five examples of emergency response organizations that may need to be contacted after a disaster.

3. What information should be included in the emergency service contact procedures?

4. List five examples of public utilities, departments, or agencies that may need to be contacted after a disaster.

5. What information should be included in the insurance company contact procedures?

6. List five types of disaster recovery service providers that an organization may need to work with during recovery.

7. What types of telecommunications could be affected during a disaster?

8. What information should an organization include in its procedures for working with telecommunications service providers?

9. What types of computer systems could be affected during a disaster?

   a. enterprise systems that support business operations

   b. servers that provide specialized business or manufacturing functions

   c. servers that support supply-chain applications

   d. all of the above

10. When developing procedures to restore computer services, which of the following considerations is important?

    a. the processes to move computer services to hot sites

    b. the staff needed to report to hot sites and maintain operations

    c. how a disaster may affect the need for equipment maintenance services

    d. all of the above

11. What types of organizations can be considered business partners?

12. What information should be included in procedures for working with business partners?

13. Why should organizations communicate with their customers during a disaster?

14. What is the role of the official media spokesperson during a disaster?

15. Why is it important to make consistent statements to the media about disaster recovery efforts?

16. What is the primary goal when working with stockholders and investors during a disaster?

17. Why is it important to have procedures for communicating with employees during disaster response and recovery efforts?

18. What information should be included in procedures for working with the local community during a disaster?

19. Who should be available to work with emergency responders upon their arrival at a facility?

20. Why is it important to communicate with suppliers and service providers during a disaster?

HANDS-ON PROJECTS

In this chapter you studied the importance of working with other organizations when responding to a disaster and initiating recovery procedures. In the following projects, you will demonstrate what you learned by creating materials and procedures on behalf of the organization for which you are developing a disaster recovery plan.

In Project 6-1, you will create a list of all the organizations and agencies that your organization may need to contact during a disaster. In Projects 6-2 to 6-16, you will develop procedures for contacting and working with these organizations. When developing procedures, use the generic disaster recovery procedure sheet from Chapter 5, or create your own procedure sheet.

Because this section contains a large number of projects, your instructor might want to assign only a subset of these projects, rather than all of them. When you finish your work, submit the materials and procedures to your instructor for review.

HANDS-ON PROJECTS

Project 6-1

Create a list of the organizations and agencies that your organization may need to contact during a disaster. Provide reasons for listing each organization; include contact names, titles, and contact information for each. Your list should include local emergency services, local law enforcement, insurance companies, contractors for disaster recovery services, telecommunications service providers, IT service and equipment providers, public utilities, software companies, business partners, suppliers, and customers.

HANDS-ON PROJECTS

Project 6-2

Develop procedures for contacting emergency service providers after a disaster. The procedures should include the items listed in Table 6-2 earlier in this chapter.

HANDS-ON PROJECTS

Project 6-3

Develop procedures for working with public utilities or Public Works departments to recover electric power, water service, sewer service, telephone lines, steam service, waste removal, road and highway maintenance and repair, forestry services, recycling services, environmental protection services, flood control services, animal control and protection, building inspection services, and occupancy and use permits. The procedures should include the items listed in Table 6-3 earlier in this chapter.

Project 6-4

Develop procedures for contacting insurance companies after a disaster. The procedures should include the items listed in Table 6-4 earlier in this chapter.

Project 6-5

Develop procedures for contacting disaster recovery service providers after a disaster. The procedures should include the items listed in Table 6-5 earlier in this chapter.

Project 6-6

Develop procedures for working with service providers to recover the organization's tele-communications, including voice services, call center services, fax lines, data communications lines, EDI systems, Internet connections, Web-based services, Web sites, toll-free customer service lines, voice mail, and e-mail services. The procedures should cover communications access for remote workers, field staff, and regional offices. The procedures should include the items listed in Table 6-6 earlier in this chapter.

Project 6-7

Develop procedures for working with IT service providers to recover the organization's IT services. These services include enterprise systems that support business operations, servers that provide specialized business or manufacturing functions, servers that support supply-chain applications, workstations used in research and development, desktop systems that support office workers, and Web servers that support e-commerce. The procedures should include the items listed in Table 6-7 earlier in this chapter.

Project 6-8

Develop procedures for working with IT equipment providers and software companies during disaster recovery. Your procedures should address the following needs and issues:

- Moving computer services to hot sites

- The staff needed to report to hot sites and maintain operations

- How a disaster may affect the need for equipment maintenance services and the scope of software license use

- How using a hot site for computer support affects the cost of software licenses
- How IT equipment providers and IT software companies can assist in recovery

Project 6-9

Develop procedures for working with business partners after a disaster. The procedures should include the items listed in Table 6-9 earlier in this chapter.

Project 6-10

Develop procedures for working with suppliers and service providers after a disaster. The procedures should include the items listed in Table 6-10 earlier in this chapter.

Project 6-11

Develop procedures for working with customers after a disaster. The procedures should include the items listed in Table 6-11 earlier in this chapter.

Project 6-12

Develop media relations procedures for your organization's disaster recovery plan. The procedures should include the items listed in Table 6-12 earlier in this chapter.

Project 6-13

Develop procedures for stockholder and investor communications after a disaster. The procedures should include the items listed in Table 6-13 earlier in this chapter.

Project 6-14

Develop procedures for communicating with employees after a disaster. The procedures should include the items listed in Table 6-14 earlier in this chapter.

Project 6-15

Develop procedures for communicating with the families of employees after a disaster. The procedures should include the items listed in Table 6-15 earlier in this chapter.

Project 6-16

Develop procedures for working with local communities after a disaster. The procedures should include the items listed in Table 6-16 earlier in this chapter.

CASE PROJECTS

Case Project: Harris and Heartfield Manufacturing

Harris and Heartfield Manufacturing is a family-owned business that fabricates specialized metal parts for its North American clients. Most of its revenue comes from defense contracts, and from producing parts for heavy-equipment manufacturers. The company has an excellent reputation for quality and prompt deliveries.

The company has 200 employees at its only location, in California. All 20 administrative employees have desktop PCs connected to the company's local area network (LAN). The 15 research and design engineers use Sun workstations that are also on the LAN. Three servers support administrative functions and six servers support design and manufacturing. About half the machining equipment on the shop floor is computerized.

Management is concerned about the company's future competitiveness, and about its ability to fulfill orders if a disaster hindered its operations. The board of directors is relatively business-savvy, but does not invest money unless it yields a positive return. As a result, the company hired you as a consultant to create a list of 10 key points that conveyed the importance of disaster recovery planning to the board. You also prepared 10 points for managers to discuss with employees about organizing and preparing to develop a plan. You worked with company managers to develop a business process threat analysis for their product manufacturing, developed questions for the company to answer about its insurance coverage, and advised Harris and Heartfield how to build a disaster response team.

Your next assignment is to develop a list of organizations that Harris and Heartfield needs to contact and work with during disaster recovery. The list should help prompt discussions about developing contact procedures, and the scope of operations of Harris and Heartfield.

OPTIONAL TEAM CASE PROJECTS

Team Case One

Your boss has asked you to identify companies that can provide hot sites to restore your organization's computer systems and operations in a disaster. Your assignment is to research these providers and write a one-page description of each, including its location, contact information, what the organization provides, and how to integrate its services into your disaster recovery plan. If possible, you should also obtain information about the cost of the services.

Team Case Two

Your boss has asked you to identify companies that can provide emergency telecommunic-ations services for your organization in a disaster. Your assignment is to research these companies and write a one-page description of each. These descriptions should include the same type of information you provided in Team Case One.

7

PROCEDURES FOR RESPONDING TO ATTACKS ON COMPUTERS

After reading this chapter, you will be able to:

♦ Understand computer crimes and cyberattacks

♦ Understand the evolution of privacy laws

♦ Explain how computer systems are attacked

♦ Develop recovery procedures after a breach in computer security

♦ Develop procedures for working with law enforcement

♦ Develop procedures to determine economic losses

♦ Develop procedures to ease IT recovery

♦ Establish a computer incident response team

Not all disasters have natural causes. More often, they result from human error, accidents, or deliberate attacks. Although computer networks have contributed to dramatic increases in business revenue and worker productivity, their increased use has also made them more vulnerable to security threats. Any business that uses computers and network technology must incorporate computer security into its disaster recovery planning.

Past attacks have demonstrated how vulnerable systems are, and how devastating a successful attack can be. The Love Bug attack in 2000 cost more than $8.75 billion worldwide, and the Code Red worm in 2001 cost $2.6 billion.[1]

Understanding how systems can be penetrated, and then developing response procedures as part of a sound recovery plan, can help mitigate losses and minimize downtime. Developing these procedures requires extensive analysis, along with cooperative efforts from local, state, and federal law enforcement, community members, and service providers. Recovery planning is only a part of the process; planners also need to develop procedures to assess damages, report incidents to the appropriate agencies, and assist law enforcement in capturing and prosecuting offenders.

COMPUTER CRIME AND CYBERATTACKS

Threats to an organization's computer systems come from a variety of sources. The motivations for computer attacks are as different as the attackers themselves. For example, a group of organized criminals may carefully execute an attack on your computer system, hoping to gain confidential information they can sell to competitors or use to extort money from your organization. Industrial spies may try to steal a company's secret plans for a new product. Cyberterrorists with political or religious motivations may attack an organization or government with which they disagree. Amateur hackers may access systems to plant their virtual flag and earn merit badges in the hacker community. Occasionally, bored teenagers may hack into a system just to prove they can.

The trends in computer crime are alarmingly clear. From 1997 to 1999, the Computer Crime and Security Survey, conducted by the Computer Security Institute (CSI) and the San Francisco FBI, detailed an average annual loss of $120 million from survey respondents. In 2000, the reported losses rose to $265 million, and in 2001, losses increased again to $377 million. Survey participants included government agencies, medical facilities, financial institutions, and universities.[2] Not all respondents were able or willing to quantify losses, so the true losses were undoubtedly much higher.

The 2002 CSI/FBI Computer Crime and Security Survey involved a wider range of respondents from government, high tech, telecommunications, health care, and industry. More than 500 respondents participated in the survey, but only 44% were willing or able to quantify losses. These reported losses totaled almost $456 million. Theft of proprietary information was the source of the most serious financial losses (nearly $171 million), and financial fraud was responsible for losses of almost $116 million.[3]

According to the 2002 survey, Internet connections were the most frequent point of attack. Other commonly reported breaches of computer security included internal attacks, viruses, denial-of-service attacks, and abuse of Internet connections, such as inappropriate e-mail use and downloading of pornography and pirated software. Ninety percent of the respondents detected security breaches in the 12 months preceding the survey.

Cyberattack Scenarios

Threats against technology infrastructure are real, and very frightening. Food, water, electricity, transportation, industry, finance, emergency services, gas, telephones, and national security all depend on technology to function properly. In January 2002, Senator John Edwards of North Carolina introduced S-1900, The Cyberterrorism Preparedness Act of 2002, and S-1901, The Cybersecurity Research and Education Act, to the U.S. Senate. Edwards stated:

"Computer networks have brought extraordinary improvements in the way we live and work. We communicate more often, more quickly, more cheaply. With the push of a button in a classroom or a bedroom, our children can get more information than most libraries have ever held. Yet there is a dark side to the Internet, a new set of dangers. Today, if you ask an expert quietly, he or she will

tell you that cyberspace is a very vulnerable place. Terrorists could cause terrible harm. They might be able to stop all traffic on the Internet. Shut down power for entire cities for extended periods. Disrupt our phones. Poison our water. Paralyze our emergency services—police, firefighters, and ambulances. The list goes on. We now live in a world where a terrorist can do as much damage with a keyboard and a modem as with a gun or a bomb." [4]

The Senate isn't alone in writing cybersecurity legislation. Many bills have been introduced in the House of Representatives as well, as legislators struggle to catch up with technology. The explosive growth of the Internet in recent years has presented new concerns for businesses, government, and citizens.

As an example, consider the repercussions of a successful attack on a power grid that could leave the entire U.S. Northeast without power for a week in the middle of winter. The damage to business would be horrendous, putting many people out of work entirely. The lack of heating could cause hundreds or even thousands of deaths. Emergency services and transportation would be severely affected—ambulances, police, and firefighters are all dispatched using computerized systems that rely on electricity to operate. Air-traffic control systems would shut down, and planes in the air would be hard-pressed to avoid collisions and land safely. Granted, most of these systems include redundancies for power, but how long would they last, and what would happen when backup power supplies were exhausted? The lack of answers demonstrates our vulnerability to attack.

Economic Impact of Malicious Code Attacks

A **malicious code attack** occurs when people write computer code intended to damage or disrupt computer systems and networks, and then release that code across the systems. Malicious code attacks include viruses and worms of all types. Attacks of this nature are increasing, and the cleanup costs to restore systems to working order are growing as well. The impact from virus attacks has been mitigated somewhat since the "Love Bug" attack, mainly because the process of cleaning up virus damage has become highly automated. Table 7-1 summarizes the economic impact of some high-profile code attacks. Table 7-2 lists economic losses by year.

Table 7-1 Code attack analysis, by incident

Year	Code name	Worldwide economic impact ($U.S.)
2001	Nimda	$635 million
2001	Code Red	$2.62 billion
2001	SirCam	$1.15 billion
2000	Love Bug	$8.75 billion
1999	Melissa	$1.10 billion
1999	ExploreZip	$1.02 billion

Source: Computer Economics [5]

Table 7-2   Code attack analysis, by year

Year	Worldwide economic impact ($U.S.)
2001	$13.2 billion
2000	$17.1 billion
1999	$12.1 billion
1998	$6.1 billion
1997	$3.3 billion
1996	$1.8 billion
1995	$0.5 billion

Source: Computer Economics[6]

Table 7-2 is particularly alarming. From 1995 through 2001, losses increased by nearly 2800%. While steps have been taken to mitigate losses from malicious code attacks, the sheer number of attacks and attackers makes it nearly impossible to remove the threat.

Including Cyberattacks in Definitions of Terrorism

The FBI defines a **terrorist incident** as a violent act that endangers human life, violates U.S. or state criminal law, and intimidates a government and its citizens, all in service of advancing a group's political or social objectives. Barry Collin, a senior research fellow at the Institute for Security and Intelligence in California, was credited for creating the term "cyberterrorism" —the convergence of cybernetics and terrorism. In the same year, FBI Special Agent Mark Pollitt offered a working definition: " **Cyberterrorism** is the premeditated, politically motivated attack against information, computer systems, computer programs, and data, which result in violence against noncombatant targets by sub-national groups or clandestine agents." [7]

News media have used the term "cyberterrorism" to describe everything from a 14-year-old hacker to organized groups that plan and execute attacks against major targets, such as a nuclear power plant or municipal water supply. Such incidents receive extensive media coverage and public attention, but the FBI investigates many other incidents that often escape public scrutiny. For example, suspected terrorist incidents are violent acts that cannot yet be attributed to a terrorist or group. Even more gratifying to law enforcement is terrorism prevention, a documented instance of known or suspected terrorists being thwarted by investigative activity.[8]

The FBI classifies terrorists as domestic or international. Domestic terrorists operate entirely within the United States and Puerto Rico, without foreign direction. Their acts are directed at the U.S. government or people. International terrorism is the unlawful use of force or violence by a group or person with connections to a foreign power, or by a group whose activities transcend national boundaries.

In the past, terrorism was limited to the physical world, but its definition has expanded over time to include computers and cyberspace. Since the September 11 attacks on the World Trade Center and the Pentagon, local, state, and federal governments have closely examined their roles in national security. The Department of Homeland Security (DHS) was formed as a central authority to coordinate these efforts and develop a seamless flow of information. Securing cyberspace is a prominent part of this work, because it is the medium through which information flows and communications take place. It is also a major source of vulnerability to attack.

In February 2003, DHS published *The National Strategy for the Physical Protection of Critical Infrastructures and Key Assets*. The document calls for cooperation among government, industry, and private citizens to protect the following key assets:

- Agriculture, food, and water

- Public health and emergency services

- Defense industrial base and commercial key assets

- Telecommunications, energy, transportation, banking, and finance

- Chemical industry and hazardous materials

- Nuclear power plants, dams, government facilities, and national monuments[9]

Disaster recovery planners should become familiar with the DHS strategy; they can find more information at *www.dhs.gov*. The strategy includes several points for protecting computer systems and telecommunications systems. Before organizations can fully participate in this effort and determine whether their assets are critical to national infrastructure, they must complete the exposure inventories and mitigation analyses described in earlier chapters.

DHS also released *The National Strategy to Secure Cyberspace* in February 2003, to provide a framework for protecting technology assets from electronic or hacking attacks. The document sets several priorities for a national cyberspace program, such as creating a national security response system, reducing security threats and vulnerability, creating a security awareness and training program, and securing government cyberspace.[10]

Organizations can take several steps to cooperate with the DHS cyberspace strategy:

- Participate in a public/private architecture for responding to national cyber incidents, and for developing continuity and contingency planning efforts.

- Contribute to the development of tactical and strategic analyses of cyberattacks and vulnerability assessments.

- Assist in enhancing law enforcement's ability to prevent and prosecute cyberspace attacks. Organizations must report more incidents and file necessary complaints to support criminal prosecution.

- Provide information that contributes to national vulnerability assessments, so that all organizations can better understand the potential consequences of cyberspace threats.

- Deploy new and more secure protocols, routing technology, digital control systems, supervisory control and data acquisition systems, and software that can reduce vulnerability.

- Participate in a comprehensive national awareness program to help businesses and the general population secure their own parts of cyberspace.

- Improve internal training and education programs to support security in cyberspace.

- Provide information to the government that helps to continuously assess threats to federal computer systems, and that helps to keep computer networks secure.

Expectations of Cyberattacks

When people or groups use computer technology, software, and networks to attack systems, they launch a **cyberattack**. According to a 2002 survey conducted by Computer Economics, respondents believed that terrorists were most likely to launch large-scale cyberattacks in less than two years. Table 7-3 shows more detailed survey responses about the possibility of large-scale cyberattacks.[11]

Table 7-3   When survey respondents expect large-scale cyberattacks

Response	When large-scale cyberattacks will be launched by military	When large-scale cyberattacks will be launched by terrorists
Less than two years	48.4%	69.6%
Two to five years	28.2%	20.9%
Five to 10 years	11.7%	4.2%
More than 10 years	5.9%	1.6%
Never	5.9%	3.7%

Source: Computer Economics

Even though many respondents believed that cyberattacks were imminent, far fewer thought their country or organization was prepared to defend against them (Table 7-4).

Table 7-4   Survey opinions about preparedness for cyberattacks

Response	Country is prepared to defend against large-scale cyberattacks	Organization is prepared to defend against large-scale cyberattacks
Yes	9.4%	36.1%
No	80.1%	57.1%
Don't know	10.5%	6.8%

Source: Computer Economics

Dale Watson of the FBI says the agency has identified a wide array of cyberthreats in the past several years. In 2002, Watson, an Executive Assistant Director of Counterterrorism and Counterintelligence, told the U.S. Senate Intelligence Committee that the "threats range from defacement of Web sites by juveniles to sophisticated intrusions sponsored by foreign powers." [12] Watson said that some of these incidents obviously pose more significant threats than others. For example, the theft of national security information from a government agency or the interruption of electrical power to a major metropolitan area would be more serious than the defacement of a Web site.

Regardless of the threat to national security, all cyberattacks can have real consequences, and can violate privacy or property rights. An attack that closes down an e-commerce Web site can be disastrous to a Web-based business, and can undermine public confidence in e-commerce. An intrusion that results in the theft of millions of credit card numbers from an online vendor can create significant financial loss, reduce consumers' willingness to engage in e-commerce, and possibly bring legal action against the vendor. Significant national security concerns, including greater threats from terrorists, arise from cyberspace. Terrorist organizations are increasingly using new technology and the Internet to plan and execute attacks, raise funds to support their efforts, and use the Internet to spread propaganda. [13]

Information Warfare

Information warfare has a number of possible definitions and models. For example, it could be described as an organized effort to use cyberattacks to damage or disrupt important computer systems. Categorizing threats is another matter for debate. One popular model separates information warfare into three categories:

- Personal information warfare

- Corporate information warfare

- Global information warfare

In this model, victims are classified as individuals, corporations, or governments. While the model works in some instances, a better viewpoint for disaster recovery planners is to consider each threat as either internal or external to their organization. This approach allows planners to readily identify the risks to their company's computing and information assets.

An internal threat would originate from any employee who has physical access to equipment and legitimate rights to information within the organization. Dangers from inside the organization are usually created by accident. For example, employees might unknowingly download a virus with their e-mail. Other threats, such as industrial espionage or a malicious act toward a senior staff member, are deliberate.

External threats originate from people outside the organization who have no legitimate interests or rights to corporate systems or information. Organizations may face targeted attacks on their systems, or may become innocent victims of an attack aimed at someone else. Their systems may become a pawn in an attack on another system. This is the case with denial of service (DoS) attacks, when an intruder takes control of many systems to launch an attack. While the controlled systems are not directly under attack, they have been compromised, and recovery procedures are still necessary.

Managing internal threats is much easier than managing the risks from outside the organization. Access controls, physical security of sensitive systems, and system audits are all important parts of comprehensive IT security policies and procedures. Once the threats move outside, the task of identifying and controlling them becomes much more difficult.

Securing systems against direct or indirect attack requires dividing internal and external threats into cohesive and manageable elements early in the security analysis. These "clusters" can then be addressed in a logical fashion. By methodically identifying each threat, planners can design policies and procedures to address each cluster, mitigate the potential damages, and reduce their probability.

When developing procedures to deal with information warfare threats and damages, organizations should consider:

- Developing security policies for information systems to address legitimate uses and system operations

- Implementing security measures and policies to protect information systems

- Training employees in the evidence handling and forensics used to investigate computer crimes

- Developing contact information for law enforcement agencies that deal with computer crime

- Staying abreast of current and future legislation regarding computer crime, as well as related international standards and laws

Because every organization has different needs and operating environments, planners must consider the specific factors that affect a given facility. Although organizations cannot possibly identify all of the threats against their computer systems, they can take steps to reduce the likelihood of damage from most common threats.

Protecting Against Cyberattacks

The threat of cyberattacks is real, and the damages can be disastrous. An unfortunate fact of information systems security is that defenders must protect against all possible means of intrusion or damage, while attackers only need to find a single point of entry into a system. If an attack is successful, organizations could face a huge cleanup task, irrecoverable damage to information, destruction of equipment, and even the loss of jobs.

Securing a system against intrusion is an immense and difficult task. This battle is waged daily across the globe, as attackers seek open doors and defenders try to close them all. The battlefield of cyberspace includes all government, military, corporate, and private systems. Any machine or network that is linked to another network is a potential target—the only secure system is one with no outside connections.

New methods of compromising computer systems are developed by the "black hats" every day, so the "white hats" must constantly be aware of emerging threats. To protect against cyberattacks and create an appropriate defense plan, organizations need a combination of training, manual procedures, technology, and awareness efforts. Information security personnel and disaster recovery planners should use the following resources to find current information about computer threats (Table 7-5).

Table 7-5 Computer security information and resources

Name	Description	Contact information
Cisco Systems, Inc.	Cisco offers white papers on information security, threats, and business issues related to technology	*www.cisco.com*
Microsoft Corporation	Microsoft offers searchable databases on security, planning, and recovery	*www.microsoft.com*
Alternative Power Systems	Their information can serve as an introduction to disaster recovery planning	*www.aapspower.com*
Creative Data Concepts Limited	They provide data on the hidden cost of downtime from a variety of articles, research reports, and consulting firms	*www.creativedata.net*
Computer Security Products, Inc.	They offer physical security products and information	*www.computersecurity.com*
The SANS Institute	The institute provides training and useful resources	*www.sans.org*
Network Security Center	The center, at the University of Chicago, covers information technology security from a variety of perspectives	*www.security.uchicago.edu*
Downtime Central	The Web site provides data on the cost of downtime	*www.downtimecentral.com*
Department of Homeland Security (DHS)	The U.S. government's new security agency covers a wide range of topics	*www.dhs.gov/dhspublic*
NIPC (National Infrastructure Protection Center)	NIPC operates under DHS; it unites representatives from government agencies and the private sector in a partnership to protect U.S. infrastructure	*www.nipc.gov*

7

Name	Description	Contact information
NIST (National Institute of Science and Technology)	NIST's mission is to develop and promote measurement, standards, and technology to enhance productivity, facilitate trade, and improve the quality of life	www.nist.gov
Federal Emergency Management Agency (FEMA)	FEMA provides guidelines and information for disaster recovery planning and procedure development	www.fema.gov
National Security Institute	NSI provides professional information and security awareness services to defense contractors, governments, and industrial security executives	www.nsi.org
FedCIRC	The Federal Computer Incident Response Center offers guidelines for creating incident response teams	www.fedcirc.gov
National Security Agency (NSA)	NSA's goal is to ensure secure communications for all U.S. government agencies; NSA also provides information on cryptology and offers security recommendations	www.nsa.gov
Federal Bureau of Investigation (FBI)	The FBI provides reporting, investigation, and prevention topics	www.fbi.gov
CERT Coordination Center	CERT provides information for protecting computer systems and handling computer security incidents	www.cert.org
The Forum of Incident Response and Security Teams	Its goals include cooperative efforts to effectively prevent, detect, and recover from computer security incidents	www.first.org
Safe harbor principles	The Web site provides full details on safe harbor principles (European Union privacy legislation)	www.ita.doc.gov/td/ ecom/shprin.html
Gramm-Leach-Bliley Act	This legislation protects nonpublic financial data	www.ftc.gov/privacy/
Health Insurance Portability and Accountability Act (HIPAA)	The law encourages electronic transactions in the health care field, but requires safeguards to keep information secure and confidential	www.hhs.gov/ocr/hipaa/

EVOLVING PRIVACY LAWS

Cybercrimes have a direct impact on privacy. An organization's failure to adequately protect information can lead to disaster, so the necessity for good data security is absolute, and a fiduciary responsibility of corporate management. However, even though data security and privacy have a relationship, the concept and practice of data security is generally geared toward restricting data access. This restriction does not automatically safeguard the privacy of users. If organizational policies on the use or sale of sensitive information are not appropriate, privacy problems can still surface, even though the information and technology are secure.

In theory, law enforcement agencies in most major countries become involved when unauthorized parties access information systems or misappropriate trade secrets. Unfortunately, the reality is different; most law enforcement agencies are not equipped to deal with cybercrimes. Officials may write a report and be helpful when physical property is stolen, but they probably cannot assist in information theft or the intentional violation of information privacy.

Most organizations do not have insurance that covers damage produced by major privacy violations, although they should check to make sure. Unless an organization has demonstrated due care in protecting its data, and has clear policies for privacy management, coverage may be unavailable. Organizations must conduct an insurance audit to determine whether there is coverage, and the extent of the coverage. This audit includes a legal review of the policies, as well as conferences with their insurance companies.

Social pressures on organizations to protect personal information are increasing. As concerns mount, governments are working to develop legislation and cooperative efforts to protect privacy. Guidelines vary considerably from nation to nation, and the global nature of communications makes it difficult for organizations to determine their responsibilities.

Until recently, the Organization for Cooperation and Development has been at the forefront of addressing privacy issues. Now the European Union has taken the lead with the development of their safe harbor principles (Table 7-6). These principles state that transfers of personal data must take place only between countries that provide acceptable levels of privacy protection. Currently, compliance with the directive is voluntary, and may be achieved in different ways.

Table 7-6 Principles of safe harbor

An organization must inform people why information is collected about them, how to contact the organization with inquiries or complaints, what types of third parties can see the information, and how people can limit the use and disclosure of their information. Notice must be immediately provided in clear language when people are asked to provide personal information, or as soon as possible afterward. Organizations must always inform people before using their information for purposes that were not discussed originally, or before disclosing information to a third party.
An organization must allow people to opt out of the arrangement if personal information is used or disclosed to third parties without their consent. People must be given clear, readily available, and affordable means to exercise this option. Before using sensitive information such as medical and health records, racial or ethnic origin, political opinions, religious or philosophical beliefs, trade union membership, or sexual preferences, the organization must receive specific consent from a person.
An organization can disclose personal information to third parties if it observes the original principles of notice and choice. Before an organization passes on information that a person has approved, it must first determine that the receiving party subscribes to safe harbor principles. As an alternative, the receiving party can enter into a written agreement that it will provide the same level of privacy protection as that required by relevant safe harbor principles.
Organizations that create, use, or disseminate personal information must take reasonable measures to ensure that the systems are reliable for the intended use. In addition, organizations must take reasonable precautions to protect information from loss, misuse, unauthorized access, disclosure, alteration, and destruction.
An organization may only process personal information for the purposes for which it was originally collected. In doing so, an organization must ensure that the data is accurate, complete, and current.
People who provide personal information must have reasonable access to it from the organization, and must be able to correct or amend inaccurate information.

Source: Cisco Systems[14]

In the United States, privacy legislation is a thorny area—the needs for national security and the public's right to privacy can conflict at times, especially in a climate of increased concerns about terrorism. Since passage of the Privacy Act of 1974, many new challenges have arisen, requiring new laws. The most recent laws address telecommunications, health care, video, motor vehicle information, and surveillance techniques. Some of the more important legislation is summarized in the following list. [15]

- **Privacy Act of 1974** —The act was implemented to protect the privacy of people identified in information systems maintained by federal executive branch agencies, and to control the collection, use, and sharing of information.

- **Computer Matching and Privacy Protection Act of 1988** —This act provides an exemption to allow information disclosure to an intelligence agency for preventing terrorist acts. The exemption for foreign counterintelligence in the act, which amended the Privacy Act, legitimizes information sharing through data matching among agencies for national security purposes.

- **The Cable Communications Policy Act of 1984** —This legislation limits the disclosure of cable television subscriber names, addresses, and other information.

- **The Video Privacy Protection Act of 1988** —The act regulates the treatment of personal information collected during video sales and rentals. The act prohibits videotape providers from disclosing customers' names, addresses, and specific videotapes rented or purchased, unless the customer consents, or pursuant to a federal or state search warrant, grand jury subpoena, or court order.

- **Telecommunications Act of 1996** —This legislation limits the use and disclosure of customer proprietary network information (CPNI) by telecommunications service providers. The statute does not include specific provisions for the disclosure of CPNI to law enforcement or government officials. Except as required by law or with customer consent, a telecommunications carrier must only use, disclose, or permit access to individually identifiable CPNI in providing the telecommunications service.

- **The Health Insurance Portability and Accountability Act of 1996 (HIPAA)** —The rule establishes privacy protections for individually identifiable health information held by health care providers, health care plans, and health care clearinghouses. It establishes a series of regulatory permissions for uses and disclosures of health information. To lower health care costs, the law encourages electronic transactions in the health care field, but also requires safeguards to protect the security and confidentiality of information.

- **Driver's Privacy Protection Act of 1994** —The act regulates the use and disclosure of personal information from state motor vehicle records.

- **The Electronic Communications Privacy Act of 1986** —ECPA regulates government access to wire and electronic communications such as voice mail and e-mail, transactional records access, and other devices.

- **The USA PATRIOT Act of 2001** —The act substantively amended previous federal legislation and authorized the disclosure of wiretap and grand jury information to "any federal, law enforcement, intelligence, protective, immigration, national defense, or national security official" for the performance of his duties. It permits surveillance when foreign intelligence gathering is a "significant" reason for surveillance rather than the only reason.

- **The Homeland Security Act of 2002** —The act authorizes sharing of the federal government's information-gathering efforts with relevant foreign, state, and local officials.

- **The Gramm-Leach-Bliley Act of 1999** —This legislation requires financial institutions to disclose their privacy policies to customers.

- **Children's Online Privacy Protection Act of 1998** —This legislation requires Web site operators and online service providers to obtain parental consent to collect a child's personal information, and requires sites that collect information from children to disclose how they plan to use the data.

Considering the variations in privacy laws among countries, states, and even different municipalities, it is wise to seek legal counsel regarding your company's stance on privacy management. The legal representative on the disaster recovery planning team, if there is one, should be the primary source for research and information regarding legal and contractual requirements of privacy. This representative can draft guidelines and recovery procedures to protect against a breach of privacy obligations. If the organization has no permanent legal department, recovery planners should seriously consider retaining legal counsel for such matters.

How Computer Systems Are Attacked

In many ways, IT security specialists are at a disadvantage in their struggle against hackers. Attackers can mount assaults at their leisure, and can choose their targets at will. IT workers don't enjoy the same luxury—they can never let their guard down, and must keep their systems secure at all times. This disadvantage is only the beginning:

- The original architects of the Internet never anticipated how widespread its use would become, so they didn't design security into the specification when developing the Internet Protocol (IP). Most IP implementations are therefore inherently insecure, and prone to many types of attacks.

- The explosive growth of networks and Internet connections gives attackers almost limitless opportunities to probe until they find a network with a security flaw they can exploit.

- Attackers have access to the same hardware, software, and applications that information security specialists have. This access makes it relatively easy for skilled attackers to discover weaknesses in the technology.

- Hackers can monitor Internet communications such as chat rooms and bulletin boards to obtain product information and learn about the latest security measures designed to repel their attacks. Attackers can use false identities and remain anonymous as they collect data.

- Because of the Internet and global networks, computer attacks can come from anywhere. Attackers can work together from different continents to exchange information, form their own support networks, and coordinate their attacks.

Types of Attacks

Attackers can target routers, switches, hosts, networks, and applications. Some attacks are elaborate and complex; in other cases, well-intentioned operators may unwittingly perform the attacks themselves. This section explains several common computer attacks.

Application-layer attacks exploit well-known weaknesses in commonly used server software such as sendmail, HTTP, and FTP. Hackers use these weaknesses to access computers with permissions of the account that runs the application, usually a privileged system-level account. Application-layer attacks often use ports that are allowed through a firewall. For example, a hacker often exploits Web server weaknesses by using TCP port 80 in an attack. Because the Web server makes pages available to users, a firewall needs to allow access on the port. From a firewall's perspective, the attack is standard port 80 traffic.

Autorooters are programs that automate the entire hacking process. Computers are sequentially scanned, probed, and captured. The capture installs a "rootkit" on the computer and then uses the newly captured system to automate the intrusion. As a result, intruders can scan hundreds of thousands of systems quite quickly.

Denial-of-service (DoS) attacks and distributed denial-of-service (DDoS) attacks focus on making a service unavailable for normal use, typically by exhausting some resource within a network, operating system, or application. These attacks are different from most others, because they are not usually targeted at gaining access to your network or its information. DoS and DDoS attacks are among the most difficult to eliminate. Many hackers regard them as trivial, and even consider them bad form because they require so little effort. Still, their ease of implementation and potential for significant damage make DoS and DDoS attacks worthy of special attention from security administrators.

TCP SYN flood attacks can occur during the client-server "handshake," a sequence of messages required when a client attempts to establish a TCP connection to a server. The client system sends a SYN message to the server, which acknowledges receipt by sending back a SYN-ACK message to the client. The client establishes the connection by responding with an ACK message, and then data can be exchanged. However, in the interim between sending the SYN-ACK acknowledgment and receiving the ACK message, the server leaves a half-open connection. Hackers can attack this connection, then create so many partially open connections that the server's data structure overflows.

Ping of death attacks occur when hackers modify the PING command to send Internet Control Message Protocol (ICMP) packets that exceed their maximum size. The extra bytes in the packet can cause unprotected TCP/IP software to overflow the buffer space, resulting in computer crashes, freezing, and rebooting.

IP-spoofing attacks occur when a hacker inside or outside a network pretends to be a trusted computer. The hacker can either use an IP address within the range of a network's trusted IP addresses, or use an authorized external IP address that allows access to specific network resources. IP-spoofing attacks are often used to launch other attacks. The classic example is to launch a DoS attack using spoofed source addresses that hide the hacker's identity.

Tribe Flood Network (TFN) and Tribe Flood Network 2000 (TFN2K) are distributed tools used to launch coordinated DoS attacks from many sources against one or more targets. TFN can generate packets with spoofed source IP addresses. An intruder can instruct a master to send attack instructions to a list of TFN servers.

Stacheldraht (German for "barbed wire") combines features of several DoS attacks, including TFN. The attack begins with a mass intrusion, in which automated tools remotely compromise large numbers of systems to be used in the attack. Next, a DoS attack uses the compromised systems to attack one or more sites. Stacheldraht uses encrypted communication between attackers and Stacheldraht masters, and automated updates.

Packet sniffers are software applications that use a network adapter card in "promiscuous" mode. In this mode, the card sends all packets received on the physical network wire to an application for processing. The application then captures all network packets sent across a particular collision domain. Sniffers are used legitimately in networks to assist in troubleshooting and traffic analysis. However, because some network applications send data in clear text (including Telnet, FTP, SMTP, and POP3), a packet sniffer can provide meaningful and often sensitive information, such as user names and passwords.

Man-in-the-middle attacks can occur when a hacker has access to packets that come across a network. For example, an ISP employee might have access to all packets transferred between the ISP's network and any other network. Hackers can implement these attacks using network packet sniffers and routing and transport protocols. Attackers can then steal information, hijack a communications session to gain access to private network resources, find information about a network and its users, deny service, corrupt transmitted data, and introduce new information into network sessions.

Network reconnaissance is the gathering of information about a target network using publicly available data and applications. Before hackers attempt to penetrate a network, they often learn as much about it as they can, using DNS queries, ping sweeps, and port scans. DNS queries can reveal who owns a domain and the addresses assigned to it. Ping sweeps of these addresses can present a picture of the live hosts in a particular environment. After a list is generated, port-scanning tools can cycle through all well-known ports to provide a complete list of services running on the hosts discovered by the ping sweep. Hackers can also examine the characteristics of applications running on the hosts, which can provide information that helps them compromise the service.

Trojan horse attacks and **viruses** refer to malicious software that is attached to another program to execute an unwanted function on a user's workstation. An example of a virus is a program that a hacker attaches to command.com, the primary interpreter for Windows systems. The unwanted program then deletes certain files and infects any other versions of command.com it can find. A Trojan horse is so named because it is written to look like a harmless application, when in fact it is an attack tool. For example, a Trojan horse application might resemble a simple game that runs on the user's workstation. While the user plays the game, the Trojan horse mails a copy of itself to everyone in the user's address book.

Backdoors are paths into systems that an attacker can create during a successful intrusion or with specifically designed Trojan horse code. Unless the backdoor is detected and patched, an intruder can use it again and again to enter a computer or network. Often intruders use the computer to gain access to other systems, or to launch DoS attacks when they have no further use for the computer.

Password attacks are repeated attempts to identify a user account and password. When hackers find a valid account name and password, they gain access to system resources and have the same rights as authorized users. Hackers can use several methods to get passwords, including brute-force attacks, Trojan horse programs, IP spoofing, and packet sniffers. Often, a brute-force attack uses a program that runs across the network and attempts to log in to a shared resource, such as a server. If the compromised accounts have sufficient privileges, the hackers can create backdoors for future access, without concern for future password changes to the accounts.

In **trust exploitation attacks** , hackers take advantage of a trust relationship within a network to attack several interconnected servers. The classic example is a corporation's perimeter network connection, which often houses DNS, SMTP, and HTTP servers. Because the systems all reside on the same segment and might trust other systems attached to the same network, a compromise of one system can lead to others being compromised.

Port redirection attacks are a type of trust exploitation attack that uses a compromised host to pass traffic through a firewall that would otherwise be dropped. Consider a firewall with three interfaces and a host on each interface. The host on the outside can reach the host on the public services segment (commonly referred to as a DMZ), but not the host on the inside. The host on the public services segment can reach the host on both the outside and the inside. If hackers can compromise the public services segment host, they can install software to redirect traffic from the outside host directly to the inside host.

DEVELOPING PROCEDURES IN THE WAKE OF A SECURITY BREACH

If an organization detects and confirms a breach in system security, its next step should be to collect as much information as it can about the intrusion. To prevent prolonged business disruptions, the disaster recovery planning team, IT specialists, and network staff need to develop procedures to recover quickly from computer system attacks. These procedures should incorporate guidelines from the FBI and the National Infrastructure Protection Center (NIPC), as listed in Table 7-7.

Table 7-7 Responding to a computer attack

Do not contact the suspect; let law enforcement officials deal with suspects.
Immediately contact local law enforcement, the FBI, and the organization's computer incident response team. Experts might be able to trace the attack or find valuable evidence if they can examine the systems soon enough after the intrusion. The response team can help prevent further damage and protect evidence.
Develop a list of these contacts and include them in the recovery procedures; preparing this list in advance increases the speed of response.
Develop a list of people who are authorized to handle evidence of the attack, and develop a chain of custody for the evidence; improper evidence handling can impede the investigation.
Do not shut down the system or alter any files; you might inadvertently delete evidence of the attack.
Because attackers may be monitoring e-mail, use the telephone to communicate.
If possible, copy any files the attacker may have used; these files could assist the investigation.

Source: www.nipc.gov[16]

The disaster recovery planning team and IT staff need to develop several procedures for dealing with an intrusion. The procedures should include steps for determining how an incident occurred, and how to prevent similar attacks in the future. The information systems security staff then executes these procedures, many of which are listed in Table 7-8. The procedures were developed with assistance from the Information Systems Security Association (ISSA), the High-Tech Crime Investigation Association (HTCIA), and the National Cyber Security Alliance (NCSA).

Table 7-8 Procedures to follow after an attack

Determine the scope of damage, collect evidence about the attack, and then examine the evidence in a structured manner.
Review system logs for clues about the attacker's point of entry.
Prepare for law enforcement to enter the facilities.
Determine whether other corporate systems could fall prey to the same type of attack, and then provide steps to IT managers for protecting these systems.
Recommend security upgrades or changes, and help develop new security procedures as needed.

The IT employees who maintain systems should follow several procedures after systems security personnel or law enforcement officers finish their investigations of the intrusion. After inspecting systems, applications, and files to determine damage, IT staff should remove any malicious code, reload operating system software and other software as needed, install patches, and restore configurations and other system operations. IT staff should also restore files from backup as needed and replicate damaged files when backups are not available. If the investigations take several days, IT personnel must install and configure a replacement machine. Finally, IT staff should test the repaired system and have users confirm that the restored data is usable.

DEVELOPING PROCEDURES FOR WORKING WITH LAW ENFORCEMENT

The NIPC, with help from private industry, the academic community, and government agencies, developed the InfraGard initiative to share information about cyberintrusions, exploited vulnerabilities, and infrastructure threats. All 56 FBI field offices have established an InfraGard chapter, and over 800 organizations across the United States are members. The national InfraGard program provides four basic services to members:

- An alert network using encrypted e-mail

- A secure Web site for communication about suspicious activity or intrusions

- Local chapter activities and a Help desk for questions

- A way to send information about intrusions to the local FBI field office using secure communications

General membership in InfraGard is open to anyone who wants to support its purposes and objectives. On the local level, InfraGard is organized into 56 chapters; each is associated with an FBI field office. InfraGard members are responsible for promoting the protection and advancement of critical infrastructure, exchanging knowledge and ideas, supporting the education of members and the general public, and maintaining the confidentiality of information obtained through their involvement.[17]

Before reporting a computer crime to law enforcement agencies, be sure to have the contact's name, title, telephone and fax numbers, and e-mail address, as well as the full address of your own organization.

The disaster recovery planning team needs to develop procedures for collecting and providing information about intrusions to law enforcement investigators. This information is shown in Table 7-9; it was developed with assistance from ISSA, the HTCIA, and the NCSA.

7

Table 7-9   Questions to answer for law enforcement agencies after a computer attack

What was the nature of the attack? When did it occur, and for how long?
Where are the affected computer systems and networks? Are they critical to the organization?
Are these systems managed internally, by contractors, or by service providers?
Has the problem occurred before?
What method was used to attack the system? For example, was a virus used? A Trojan horse?
Are there any suspects, such as a disgruntled employee, a former employee, or a competitor? If the suspect is (or was) an employee, what type of system access does the person have?
What was the source (IP address) of the attack? Was there any evidence of spoofing?
What systems, hardware, software, and data were affected or damaged? Was any sensitive, classified, or proprietary information affected?
Were any security measures in place at the time of the attack, such as encryption, firewalls, and packet filtering?
What was done after the attack? Did IT staff or other employees disconnect the system from the network, check system data, back up systems, or review logs? Did the organization call the police, the Computer Emergency Response Team (CERT), or other agencies?
When was the system last modified or updated, and who made these changes?

DEVELOPING PROCEDURES TO DETERMINE ECONOMIC LOSSES

An organization could endure several types of negative economic effects as a result of computer attacks or intrusions:

- **Immediate** —These impacts include damage to systems, the direct costs of repairing or replacing systems, and disrupted business and revenues.

- **Short-term** —These impacts might include lost contracts, sales, or customers, a tarnished reputation, and problems in developing new business.

- **Long-term** —These effects include reduced market valuation, stock prices, investor confidence, and goodwill toward the organization.

The adverse impact of a hacking attack or intrusion can also be described in terms of the following losses:

- **Loss of integrity** —System and data integrity refers to the need to protect information from improper modification. Integrity is lost if unauthorized changes are made to the data or IT system, either intentionally or accidentally. If this loss of integrity is not corrected, continued use of the corrupted system or data could result in inaccuracy, fraud, or erroneous decisions. Also, loss of integrity may be the first step in another attack against a system's availability or confidentiality.

- **Loss of availability** —Lost system functionality and effectiveness can result in lost productivity, which impedes users' performance and their support of the organization's mission.

- **Loss of confidentiality** —Confidentiality refers to the protection of systems and data from unauthorized disclosure. The impact of such disclosures can range from jeopardized national security to the disclosure of Privacy Act data. Unauthorized disclosure could result in loss of public confidence, embarrassment, or legal action against the organization.

An organization may have to develop monetary estimates for damages, business losses, and system restoration after a computer attack. This information might be needed by insurance companies, law enforcement, and attorneys. The information shown in Table 7-10 was developed with the help of the HTCIA.

Table 7-10   Possible costs of computer system damage after an attack

Invoices from contractors who assisted in recovery and repairs
Labor costs of internal staff to repair and restore systems, including hourly wages, benefits, and associated overhead
The value of transactions or sales that were disrupted by the attack (organizations can use an average value if precise figures are not available)
The cost of disrupting the production of goods, delivery of services, and management of operations
The purchase price and installation costs of any systems that were physically damaged or stolen
The labor costs of ensuring that data from stolen systems cannot be used to access other systems
The value of any stolen intellectual property or trade secrets, and the monetary impact on the organization if a competitor uses this information
The monetary impact of compromised data privacy or confidentiality

DEVELOPING PROCEDURES TO EASE IT RECOVERY

An organization needs to develop disaster recovery procedures for several types of computer and network hardware, operating system software, and user applications. Information technology is unique in disaster recovery, in the sense that organizations can build in redundancy and automate processes to address many problems that can occur when a disaster strikes.

NIST sponsored the development of the *Contingency Planning Guide for Information Technology Systems: Recommendations of the National Institute of Standards and Technology* (NIST Special Publication 800-34). This section summarizes several concepts and recommended actions from the guide, including the value of frequent backups, offsite data storage, redundant system components, well-documented system configurations and requirements, power management systems, and environmental controls.[18]

Types of Systems and Networks

An organization has several types of systems and networks, and it needs recovery procedures for each:

- PCs and portable computers are often used to perform automated routines within IT departments, and are therefore important to an organization's contingency plan. They can be connected to a local area network (LAN), or used to dial into the network from a remote location, or they can act as stand-alone systems.

- Web sites communicate corporate information to the public or internal users. External Web sites can be used for e-commerce, and internal Web sites can provide corporate information to employees.

- Servers support file sharing, storage, data processing, application hosting, printing, and other network services. Users log in to a server via networked PCs.

- Mainframes are centralized groups of interconnected processors. Clients that access a mainframe are often "dumb" terminals with no processing capabilities—they only accept output. PCs can access a mainframe via terminal emulation software.

- Distributed systems use LAN and wide area network (WAN) resources to link clients and users at different locations. These systems require synchronization to prevent disruptions and processing errors. For example, a large database management system (DBMS) coordinates business functions in different geographic locations; data is replicated among servers at each location, and users access the system from local servers.

- LANs are networks within an organization; they might connect two or three PCs through a hub, or they could link hundreds of employees and multiple servers. To connect a LAN to a WAN, organizations use the communication links shown in Table 7-11.

Table 7-11 Types of WAN communication links

Type of link	Description	Transfer rate
Dial-up modem	Transfers data using a temporary connection	Up to 56 kilobits per second (Kbps)
Integrated Services Digital Network (ISDN)	Standard for transmitting voice, video, and data over digital telephone lines	64 or 128 Kbps
T-1	Dedicated phone line with 24 separate 64-Kbps channels for transmitting voice or data; fractional T-1 access is possible if multiple lines are needed	1.544 megabits per second (Mbps)
T-3 (also called DS3)	Dedicated phone line with 672 channels, each of which supports 64 Kbps	Approx. 43 Mbps
Frame relay	Packet-switching protocol for connecting devices on a WAN; data is routed over virtual circuits	Comparable to T-1 and T-3 speeds
Asynchronous transfer mode (ATM)	Network technology that transfers data at high speeds with guaranteed throughput, using packets of fixed size	25 to 622 Mbps
Synchronous Optical Network (SONET)	Standard for synchronous data transmission on optical media	Gigabit
Wireless LAN bridge	Can connect multiple LANs to form a WAN	Distances of 20 to 30 miles with a direct line of sight
Virtual Private Network (VPN)	Encrypted channel between Internet nodes	

7

Recovery of Small Computer Systems

Desktop PCs, laptops, and hand-held computers are often networked to other devices, applications, and the Internet. To help recover these small systems after a computer attack, organizations should:

- Train users to regularly back up data if PC backups are not automated from the network.

- Store backup media offsite in a secure, environmentally controlled facility. If users back up data on a stand-alone system instead of to the network, they should have access to an offsite location for storing their backups, along with copies of software licenses, vendor contracts, and other important documents.

- Standardize hardware, software, and peripherals throughout the organization. If this is not possible, then the equipment should at least be standardized by department, or by machine type or model.

- Make important hardware components compatible with off-the-shelf computer components, to avoid delays caused by ordering custom equipment.

- Document system configurations in the disaster recovery plan, along with vendor and emergency contact information, in case replacement equipment is needed quickly.

Recovery of Large Computer Systems

For the purpose of this analysis, large systems consist of file servers, applications servers, workstation servers, Web servers, and mainframes. Because so many users in an organization rely on large systems, they require more effort than small systems to ensure maximum availability. These efforts include the following steps:

- The use of uninterruptible power supplies

- The replication of databases

- The use of fault-tolerant computer and networking systems

- The use of redundant, critical system components. A popular technology in this area is **Redundant Array of Independent Disks (RAID)**.

RAID ensures that data is always available by providing disk redundancy and spreading data storage across multiple disk drives, rather than one. Organizations can install RAID through hardware or software; the redundant drives appear to the operating system as a single drive. Several levels of RAID are available; RAID-1 and RAID-5 are the most popular.

RAID uses several techniques to ensure data availability and redundancy. For example, the mirroring technique saves data simultaneously to separate hard drives or drive arrays. This approach reduces system downtime, makes data easy to recover, and increases performance in reading from the disk. If one hard drive fails, the system can switch to another hard drive. The system can also use different hard drives to process different requests.

RAID also uses a technique called parity to determine whether data has been lost or over-written. Although parity has lower fault tolerance than mirroring, it can protect data without requiring storage of it, as mirroring requires. Another technique, called striping, improves performance by separating data into sections and distributing them to different drives. Data transfer works better with striping because the drives can access each section of data simultaneously. RAID-0, the simplest RAID level, relies exclusively on striping to provide better performance in read/write speeds than the other levels, but does not provide data redundancy. RAID-2 uses bit-level striping, RAID-3 uses byte-level striping with dedicated parity, and RAID-4 and RAID-5 use block-level striping.

Network Recovery

The procedures described for small systems and large systems in the preceding sections can also apply to most networking devices. Again, documentation is important to quick recovery or replication. Other practices can also help to reduce network downtime:

- Redundant communications links

- Multiple network service providers

- Duplicate network connecting devices

- Deployment of segmented networks

- Use of off-the-shelf network technology

- Network security systems

- Intrusion detection and prevention systems

7

ESTABLISHING A COMPUTER INCIDENT RESPONSE TEAM

The disaster recovery planning team needs to give special attention to disasters that may affect computer systems and networks, but that do not have a physical impact on facilities. The team should consider establishing a subcommittee of team members to focus on computer and network issues. Table 7-12 shows the types of procedures the subcommittee needs to address.

The planning team needs to establish a well-rounded computer incident response team. Appropriate IT and network management staff certainly need to be on the team, but assistance may also be required from corporate security, legal counsel, and the Public Relations Department.

Table 7-12 Checklist for computer incident response procedures

Items to include in computer incident response procedures	Status (e.g., Completed, Pending, or N/A)
Names and titles of people on the computer incident response team	
People in the organization who should be contacted when a computer incident occurs	
How to determine if law enforcement agencies should be contacted	
If necessary, people in the organization who should contact law enforcement agencies	
How computer incidents should be described to vendors or law enforcement agencies	
How computer systems and networks should be identified for vendors or law enforcement agencies	
How to restore computer systems and networks	
What to tell end users about computer incidents	

CHAPTER SUMMARY

❑ Threats to an organization's computer systems come from a variety of sources, including organized criminals, cyberterrorists, industrial spies, disgruntled employees, and amateur hackers. The motivations for computer attacks are as different as the attackers themselves.

❑ Cybercrimes have a direct impact on privacy. An organization's failure to adequately protect information can lead to disaster, so the necessity for good data security is absolute, and a fiduciary responsibility of corporate management. However, even though data security and privacy have a relationship, the concept and practice of data security is generally geared toward restricting data access. This restriction does not automatically safeguard the privacy of users.

❑ In many ways, IT security specialists are at a disadvantage in their struggle against hackers. Attackers can mount assaults at their leisure, and can choose their targets at will. IT workers don't enjoy the same luxury—they can never let their guard down, and must keep their systems secure at all times.

❑ If an organization detects and confirms a breach in system security, its next step should be to collect as much information as it can about the intrusion. To prevent prolonged business disruptions, the disaster recovery planning team, IT specialists, and network staff need to develop procedures to recover quickly from computer system attacks.

❑ The disaster recovery planning team needs to develop procedures for collecting and providing information to authorities after a computer attack. Before reporting a computer crime to law enforcement agencies, be sure to have the contact's name, title, telephone and fax numbers, and e-mail address, as well as the full address of your own organization.

❑ An organization could endure several types of negative economic effects as a result of computer attacks or intrusions. Immediate impacts include damage to systems, the direct costs of repairing or replacing systems, and disrupted business and revenues. Short-term impacts might include lost contracts, sales, or customers. Long-term effects include reduced market valuation, stock prices, and investor confidence.

❑ An organization needs to develop disaster recovery procedures for several types of computer and network hardware, operating system software, and user applications. Information technology is unique in disaster recovery, in the sense that organizations can build in redundancy and automate processes to address many problems that can occur when a disaster strikes.

❑ The disaster recovery planning team needs to give special attention to disasters that may affect computer systems and networks, but that do not have a physical impact on facilities. The team should consider establishing a subcommittee of team members to focus on computer and network issues.

KEY TERMS

application-layer attacks — Attacks that exploit well-known weaknesses in commonly used server software such as sendmail, HTTP, and FTP. Hackers use these weaknesses to access computers with permissions of the account that runs the application, usually a privileged system-level account.

autorooters — Programs that automate the entire hacking process. Computers are sequentially scanned, probed, and captured. The capture installs a "rootkit" on the computer and then uses the newly captured system to automate the intrusion.

backdoors — Paths into systems that an attacker can create during a successful intrusion or with specifically designed Trojan horse code.

cyberattack — The use of computer technology, software, and networks to attack computer systems.

cyberterrorism — A premeditated, politically motivated attack against information, computer systems, or computer programs.

denial-of-service (DoS) attacks — Attacks that focus on making a service unavailable for normal use, typically by exhausting some resource within a network, operating system, or application.

information warfare — An organized effort to use cyberattacks to damage or disrupt important computer systems.

IP-spoofing attacks — Attacks that occur when a hacker inside or outside a network pretends to be a trusted computer.

loss of availability — Lost system functionality and effectiveness that can result in lost productivity, which impedes users' performance and their support of the organization's mission.

loss of confidentiality — Confidentiality refers to the protection of information from unauthorized disclosure. The impact of such disclosures can range from jeopardized national security to the disclosure of Privacy Act data.

loss of integrity — System and data integrity is lost if unauthorized changes are made to the data or IT system, either intentionally or accidentally.

malicious code attack — Computer code that is meant to damage or disrupt computer systems and networks.

man-in-the-middle attack — Attacks that can occur when a hacker has access to packets that come across a network. For example, an ISP employee might have access to all packets transferred between the ISP's network and any other network. Hackers often implement such attacks using network packet sniffers and routing and transport protocols.

network reconnaissance — The gathering of information about a target network using publicly available data and applications. Before hackers attempt to penetrate a network, they often learn as much about it as they can.

packet sniffers — Software applications that use a network adapter card in "promiscuous" mode, a mode in which the card sends all packets received on the physical network wire to an application for processing. The application then captures all network packets that are sent across a particular collision domain.

password attacks — Repeated attempts to identify a user account and password. When hackers find a valid account name and password, they gain access to system resources and have the same rights as authorized users.

ping of death — Attacks that send oversized IP packets to a computer system and create unpredictable behavior such as crashing, freezing, and rebooting.

port redirection attack — A type of trust exploitation attack that uses a compromised host to pass traffic through a firewall that would otherwise be dropped.

Redundant Array of Independent Disks (RAID) — A popular technology that ensures data availability by providing disk redundancy and fault tolerance for data storage.

Stacheldraht — An attack that combines features of several DoS attacks, including TFN. The attack uses encrypted communication between the attacker and Stacheldraht masters, and automated updates. Stacheldraht is German for "barbed wire."

TCP SYN flood — Attacks that can occur through the half-open connection created during the client-server "handshake," a sequence of messages required when a client attempts to establish a TCP connection to a server.

terrorist incident — A violent act that endangers human life, violates U.S. or state criminal law, and intimidates a government or its citizens, all in service of advancing a group's political or social objectives.

Tribe Flood Network (TFN) and Tribe Flood Network 2000 (TFN2K) — Distributed tools used to launch coordinated DoS attacks from many sources against one or more targets. TFN can generate packets with spoofed source IP addresses. An intruder can instruct a master to send attack instructions to a list of TFN servers.

Trojan horse attacks — Malicious software that is attached to another program to execute an unwanted function on a user's workstation.

trust exploitation attack — An attack in which a hacker takes advantage of a trust relationship within a network to attack several interconnected servers (e.g., DNS, SMTP, and HTTP servers on a perimeter network connection).

virus — Malicious software that is attached to another program to execute an unwanted function on a user's workstation.

REVIEW QUESTIONS

1. Which of the following should be considered threats to computer security? (Choose all that apply.)

    a. organized criminals, who are economically motivated and seek information they can use to extort money from victims

    b. terrorists, who are politically motivated and often religiously motivated

    c. the FTC, when investigating crimes

    d. industrial spies, who seek competitive information

2. IT professionals must always successfully protect their systems, while hackers can attack at their leisure or move on to easier targets. True or False?

3. Which groups of people respond to computer hacking incidents? (Choose all that apply.)

    a. in-house information systems security staff

    b. IT staff responsible for system operation and maintenance

    c. law enforcement officers

    d. FTC staff dispatched from Washington, D.C.

4. Define a terrorist incident.

5. What is a cyberattack?

6. What is cyberterrorism?

7. What is HIPAA?

8. What is the ping of death?

9. Explain the principles of safe harbor.

10. Explain how application-layer attacks are implemented.

11. What is an autorooter?

12. How does network reconnaissance help hackers?

13. When responding to a hacking incident, why should you use the telephone to communicate?

14. What steps should IT staff take after a computer attack has been investigated?

15. When first reporting a computer crime to law enforcement agencies, what information must you have?

16. What type of immediate impact can hacking attacks have on an organization?

7

17. What is loss of system or data integrity?

18. What general procedures does NIST recommend to ease the recovery of damaged computer systems?

19. Because so many users in an organization rely on large systems, what should an organization do to ensure their maximum availability?

20. What types of practices can help to reduce network downtime?

HANDS-ON PROJECTS

Project 7-1

Designate members of a computer incident response team within the organization for which you are developing a disaster recovery plan. List all team members in the disaster recovery plan, along with their titles, departments, and contact information. Explain the role of each team member, and explain why each person was chosen to the team.

When you finish, submit the list to your instructor for review.

Project 7-2

Develop procedures for reporting computer incidents to law enforcement agencies. Use the generic disaster recovery procedure sheet from Chapter 5, or develop your own procedure sheet. Your procedures should include the following information:

- How to determine whether law enforcement agencies should be contacted

- Which members of the organization must contact law enforcement agencies, if necessary

- How to describe computer incidents to vendors or law enforcement agencies

- How to identify computer systems and networks for vendors or law enforcement agencies

When you finish, submit the procedures to your instructor for review.

Project 7-3

Develop procedures for reporting computer hacking incidents to end-user departments if an intrusion results in downtime. Use the generic disaster recovery procedure sheet from Chapter 5, or develop your own procedure sheet. Your procedures should include the following information:

- What end-user departments should be told about computer incidents

- How to describe computer incidents to users

- How to identify computer systems and networks for users

When you finish, submit the procedures to your instructor for review.

CASE PROJECTS

Case Project: Harris and Heartfield Manufacturing

Harris and Heartfield Manufacturing is a family-owned business that fabricates specialized metal parts for its North American clients. Most of its revenue comes from defense contracts, and from producing parts for heavy-equipment manufacturers. The company has an excellent reputation for quality and prompt deliveries.

The company has 200 employees at its only location in California. All 20 administrative employees have desktop PCs connected to the company's LAN. The 15 research and design engineers use Sun workstations that are also on the LAN. Three servers support administrative functions and six servers support design and manufacturing. About half the machining equipment on the shop floor is computerized.

Management is concerned about the company's future competitiveness, and about its ability to fulfill orders if a disaster hindered its operations. The board of directors is relatively business-savvy, but does not invest money unless it yields a positive return. As a result, the company hired you as a consultant to create a list of 10 key points that conveyed the importance of disaster recovery planning to the board. You also prepared 10 points for managers to discuss with employees about organizing and preparing to develop a plan.

You worked with company managers to develop a business process threat analysis for their product manufacturing, developed a list of questions for the company to answer about insurance coverage, advised the company how to develop and staff a disaster response team, and developed a list of organizations that Harris and Heartfield should contact and work with in a disaster.

Your next assignment is to develop general guidelines for determining when and if the company should report computer hacking incidents to law enforcement agencies. The guidelines should be designed to prompt discussions about developing procedures for reporting such incidents.

OPTIONAL TEAM CASE PROJECTS

Team Case One

Your boss has asked you to identify law enforcement agencies in your area that could assist your organization during a computer hacking incident. Your assignment is to research these agencies and write a one-page description of each, including its location and contact information, what services the agency provides, and how to best work with each agency to integrate its services into your disaster recovery plan.

Team Case Two

Your boss has asked you to identify consultants and service providers in your area that could assist your organization during a computer hacking incident. Your assignment is to research these companies and then create the same types of materials you provided in Team Case One.

ENDNOTES

1. Computer Economics press release, January 21, 2002.

2. FBI/CSI Computer Crime and Security Survey, Vol. II–VI, Computer Security Institute, San Francisco, 1997-2001, *www.gocsi.com*.

3. Richard Power, FBI/CSI Computer Crime and Security Survey Vol. VII, No 1, Computer Security Issues and Trends, Computer Security Institute, San Francisco, Spring 2002.

4. Congressional Record: January 28, 2002 (Senate), pages S176–S183, *The Cybersecurity Research and Education Act of 2002, The Cyberterrorism Preparedness Act of 2002*, Senator John Edwards, *www.fas.org/irp/congress/2002_cr/s1900.html*.

5. *www.computereconomics.com/article.cfm?id=133*.

6. *Ibid.*

7. Serge Krasavin, *www.crime-research.org/eng/library/Cyber-terrorism.htm*.

8. FBI Web site, FBI Laboratory Annual Report, 2001, *www.fbi.gov/hq/lab/labannual01.pdf*.

9. *The National Strategy for the Physical Protection of Critical Infrastructures and Key Assets*, U.S. Department of Homeland Security, February 2003.

10. *The National Strategy to Secure Cyberspace*, U.S. Department of Homeland Security, February 2003.

11. Michael Erbschloe, *IT Security: Perceptions, Awareness, and Practices* (Carlsbad, California: Computer Economics, 2002).

12. FBI Web site, *www.fbi.gov*.

13. Cisco Systems, Inc., *Economic Impact of Network Security Threats*, White paper, 2001, *www.cisco.com/en/US/netsol/ns110/ns170/ns172/networking_solutions_audience_business_benefit09186a008010e48d.html*.

14. Cisco Systems, Inc., *Privacy Protection Depends on Network Security*, White paper, 2002.

15. Gina Marie Stevens, Legislative Attorney, American Law Division, *Privacy: Total Information Awareness Programs and Related Information Access, Collection, and Protection Laws*, Congressional Research Service (CRS), Library of Congress, Order Code RL31730, 2003.

16. NIPC Web site, *www.nipc.gov*.

17. *Ibid.*

18. *Contingency Planning Guide for Information Technology Systems: Recommendations of the National Institute of Standards and Technology.* NIST Special Publication 800-34 (Washington, D.C. June 2002).

7

8

DEVELOPING PROCEDURES FOR SPECIAL CIRCUMSTANCES

After reading this chapter, you will be able to:

♦ Evaluate the need for special procedures

♦ Develop procedures for hazardous materials

♦ Develop procedures for art, antiques, collectibles, and historic documents

♦ Develop procedures for perishable foods and materials

♦ Develop procedures for controlled substances

♦ Develop procedures for trade secrets

♦ Develop procedures for animals and other life forms

♦ Develop procedures for precision equipment and rare materials

Many organizations have specialized missions and work that dictate the need for additional disaster recovery procedures. These special circumstances should be covered in the exposure inventory and risk assessments conducted for key business processes, facilities, and assets.

Organizations need to protect special assets and develop procedures for their maintenance and storage in a disaster. Insurance companies may require specific documentation for special assets before paying to cover their loss.

Organizations must also give special attention to facilities that contain hazardous materials and supplies. Not only must these assets be protected, numerous laws and government regulations govern the use of hazardous materials and regulated substances.

This chapter covers special circumstances and materials that might require attention from the disaster recovery planning team. Not all organizations have such unusual materials and assets; if so, they needn't concern themselves with all the topics in this chapter.

EVALUATING THE NEED FOR SPECIAL PROCEDURES

A key to successful disaster recovery is understanding an organization's exposures and associated risks. The extensive inventories, risk assessments, and recovery procedures discussed in previous chapters are designed to identify these exposures and mitigate risks.

It is easy to get lost in the volumes of information that must be analyzed during disaster recovery planning. Since the terrorist attacks of September 11, 2001, many organizations have expanded efforts to improve or develop their recovery plans. The attacks motivated organizations to refocus their efforts and save lives during a disaster. Evaluating the need for special procedures is consistent with this motivation.

The disaster recovery planning team should determine whether the materials and assets listed in Table 8-1 must be addressed in the recovery plan. The planning team should use the exposure inventory and risk assessment reports to make these determinations. The team should also poll all departments and facilities to discover other special needs. Representatives from each department or facility should conduct their own assessments and inform the planning team whether they require special procedures.

Once departmental representatives have evaluated the need for special procedures, the disaster recovery planning team should meet to prioritize these needs. Next, the planning team should form subcommittees of specialists and affected departments to develop the procedures.

As with other procedures described in preceding chapters, the planning team and other independent teams should review each proposed procedure and suggest modifications before final approval. The planning team may also need to consult with appropriate regulatory agencies to ensure that the procedures meet current requirements and standards.

Table 8-1 Checklist for evaluating the need for special procedures

Materials and assets that might need special procedures	Status (e.g., Completed, Pending, or N/A)
Hazardous materials are defined by FEMA as chemical substances that can pose a threat to the environment or public health if released or misused; hazardous materials are explosives, flammable and combustible substances, poisons, and radioactive materials[1]	
Art, antiques, and collectibles are rare and expensive items that may not be replaceable	
Historic documents include rare or unique items such as photographs, letters, books, and music that may not be replaceable	
Perishable foods and materials are items that need to be stored at certain temperatures to prevent spoilage; they are subject to handling and storage regulations by national, state, and local governments	
Controlled substances, such as drugs or the materials used to manufacture them, are subject to national, state, and local regulation	
Trade secrets and proprietary processes are ideas, patents, plans, and manufacturing processes on which an organization depends	
Life forms include animals, plants, lab specimens, and experimental organisms	
Precision equipment includes electronics, test devices, and optical devices	
Rare materials and expensive supplies include precious metals, gemstones, chemicals, and solvents	

8

DEVELOPING PROCEDURES FOR HAZARDOUS MATERIALS

Hazardous materials can create disasters at a facility, and they can compound problems caused by an unrelated disaster. Hazardous materials include explosives, flammable and combustible substances, poisons, and radioactive materials. These materials can explode, intensify fires, and release toxic fumes when burning. They can contaminate and injure employees and emergency responders.

To effectively work with emergency service responders who specialize in hazardous materials, an organization must develop procedures to make contacts during a disaster and enable rapid response. Table 8-2 lists some of the most important items to include in the procedures.

An organization must be prepared to work with emergency responders immediately upon their arrival, and must have the proper information ready. Having a knowledgeable liaison waiting to meet responders, answer questions, and provide assistance can save valuable time.

Table 8-2 Checklist of procedures for dealing with hazardous materials

Items to include in procedures for dealing with hazardous materials	Status (e.g., Completed, Pending, or N/A)
Names and titles of knowledgeable employees who are responsible for hazardous materials	
Applicable laws and regulations for handling hazardous materials during a disaster	
Contact information and locations of emergency service organizations that specialize in hazardous materials	
Conditions that require these organizations to be contacted	
How events should be described to the dispatchers for these organizations	
How facilities and locations should be identified for these organizations	
Instructions that should be given to responders about entering the facility	
Items that should be available to responders upon arrival, such as copies of building plans, and locations and types of hazardous materials	
The names and titles of employees who should assist responders upon arrival, such as security or building maintenance staff	
How to secure areas where hazardous materials are stored or used	

Organizations that routinely deal with hazardous materials probably have staff members who understand these materials, and who know the laws and regulations for using and storing them. However, some organizations may not be aware of the presence of hazardous materials. The disaster recovery planning team must examine equipment, materials, and supplies used at each facility to determine if they are hazardous or potentially hazardous.

The planning team should not try to interpret scientific data or government regulations on hazardous materials, because they require extensive knowledge and training. Information is available from several organizations, including local fire departments, the U.S. Environmental Protection Agency (EPA), and the Occupational Health and Safety Administration (OSHA).

The Emergency Planning and Community Right to Know Act (EPCRA) gives communities access to information concerning the release of toxic chemicals into the environment. EPCRA requires facilities that use significant amounts of toxic chemicals to file annual reports about their releases. The reports describe the types and amounts of toxic chemicals that are released into the air, water, and soil, along with information on the quantities of toxic chemicals sent to other facilities for further waste management.[2] A complete list of the materials covered under EPCRA is available at *www.epa.gov/tri*.

The EPA places the reports into a database called the Toxics Release Inventory (TRI), which is available on the Internet. In 2000, nearly 24,000 facilities submitted more than 90,000 forms for entry into TRI. Releases totaled 7.10 billion pounds for 2000; manufacturing industries accounted for 32 percent of this total.[3] Figures 8-1 through 8-4 illustrate data from the 2000 reports and trend data from 1998 to 2000.[4]

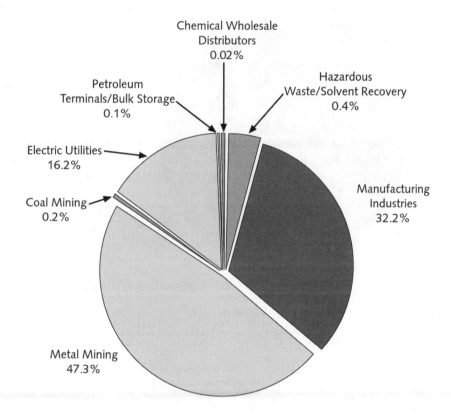

TRI Total Releases, 2000: 7.10 billion pounds (*Source: EPA*)

Figure 8-1   Total reported releases in 2000, by industry

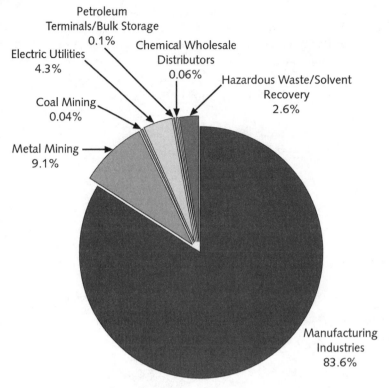

TRI Total Production-related Waste Managed, 2000: 37.89 billion pounds (*Source: EPA*)

Figure 8-2 Total production-related waste in 2000

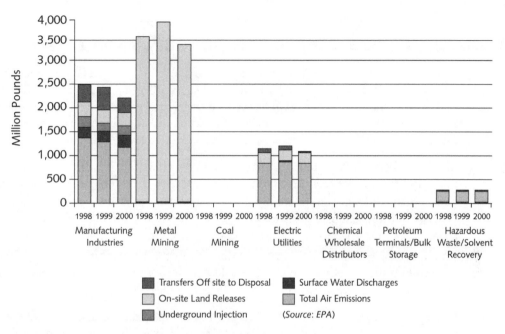

Figure 8-3   Total releases by industry from 1998 to 2000

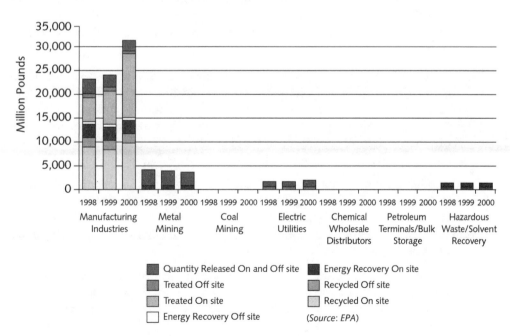

Figure 8-4   Total production-related waste from 1998 to 2000

8

DEVELOPING PROCEDURES FOR ART, ANTIQUES, AND COLLECTIBLES

Many public and private organizations own valuable art, antiques, and collectible items. For example, Progressive Casualty Insurance began collecting prints in the 1970s, with the goal of bringing the creative experience into the work environment. Progressive now has more than 5000 works of art in offices nationwide, making it one of the top collections in the United States.[5]

In November 2002, Sotheby's auctioned more than 90 artworks from John Fairfax Publications for more than $2.5 million.[6] In 2000, Sara Lee donated 52 masterpieces from its corporate art collection to 40 museums around the world, including the Art Institute of Chicago.[7] Microsoft has a collection of 2700 works in its buildings in Washington and California.[8] Over the last 30 years, SAFECO has collected more than 2200 works by contemporary regional artists, many of them from the Pacific Northwest. The collection was built on the belief that SAFECO could enrich its working environment while recognizing and supporting artists.[9]

Despite these examples, however, relatively few organizations really know the value of their art holdings. A manufacturing company, for example, may display models of past products dating from the founding of the company, without realizing that the items could be worth hundreds of thousands of dollars. Christie's, the auction house, can assist these companies with a variety of services, including appraisals and valuations for proper insurance coverage.[10]

Dealing with art, antiques, and collectibles during a disaster requires specific procedures. For example, these items may need to be removed from a facility and restored, which requires the services of specialized contractors. If art, antiques, and collectibles are destroyed or damaged beyond repair, insurance companies may require complete documentation about their purchase, condition, and appraised value. This documentation should be kept off site, and should include receipts, appraisal reports, and photographs.

When items have not been appraised, the documentation can help to place values on items that were destroyed. Several guidebooks are available to provide basic pricing information for a wide range of art, antiques, and collectibles; these books may also be helpful for making identifications and supporting insurance claims. In many cases, organizations may need to consult an appraiser when filing these claims.

The planning team must also develop procedures to secure art, antiques, and collectibles that are not damaged or destroyed, in case a facility must be closed for repairs or renovation. The team may need to contract for an off-site storage facility to provide temporary safe-keeping.

Table 8-3 lists some of the most important items to include in procedures for dealing with art, antiques, and collectibles.

Table 8-3 Checklist of procedures for dealing with art, antiques, and collectibles

Items to include in procedures for dealing with art, antiques, and collectibles	Status (e.g., Completed, Pending, or N/A)
Names and titles of knowledgeable employees who are responsible for art, antiques, and collectibles	
Contact information and locations of contractors who specialize in removing and restoring art, antiques, and collectibles	
Conditions that require these contractors to be contacted	
How events should be described to the dispatchers for these contractors	
How facilities and locations should be identified for these contractors	
Instructions that should be given to responders about entering the facility	
Items to provide to responders upon their arrival, such as copies of building plans, and locations and types of art, antiques, and collectibles	
The names and titles of employees who should assist responders upon arrival, such as security or building maintenance staff	
Documentation on the acquisition and value of art, antiques, and collectibles	
How art, antiques, and collectibles should be secured during disaster response	

DEVELOPING PROCEDURES FOR HISTORIC DOCUMENTS

Historic preservation is an eclectic activity that spans public, private, and nonprofit industries.[11] Many organizations possess valuable documents that describe their own history or that of the surrounding community. In long-established organizations, most employees may have no idea that such documents even exist.

Corporations have played a major role in American society; their history is intertwined with the history of American politics, society, and culture. Corporate archives can be valuable tools for an organization's management training, public relations, and advertising. These documents can also help preserve institutional memories that serve corporate planning purposes, and they can provide an accurate legal record for a corporation.[12]

Historic documents can be exceptionally fragile, and might require the services of a specialized contractor to restore after a disaster. These documents are also difficult to value. An organization should keep extensive records of the following types of documents, and have them periodically appraised by a certified specialist:

- Autographed photos, photos of company founders, and photos of facilities during construction

- Letters signed by founders or employees

- Technical drawings of significant inventions

- Maps and navigational aids

- Advertising and marketing materials

- Documents related to wars, political conflicts, and national or cultural heritage

- Sheet music

For legal reasons, organizations may need to protect older documents that include customers' names, client identities, patrons of medical facilities, or correspondence that relates to past litigation. If exposed to the wrong parties, these materials could be used in extortion attempts against organizations or the people named in the documents. When developing security and disaster recovery procedures to deal with historic documents, an organization should err on the side of caution to avert lawsuits and legal fees.

To make effective use of contractors who specialize in removing and restoring historic documents, an organization must develop procedures to make contacts during a disaster and enable rapid response. Table 8-4 lists some of the most important items to include in these procedures.

Table 8-4 Checklist of procedures for dealing with historic documents

Items to include in procedures for dealing with historic documents	Status (e.g., Completed, Pending, or N/A)
Names and titles of knowledgeable employees who are responsible for historic documents	
Contact information and locations of contractors who specialize in removing and restoring historic documents	
Conditions that require these contractors to be contacted	
How events should be described to the dispatchers for these contractors	
How facilities and locations should be identified for these contractors	
Instructions that should be given to responders about entering the facility	
Items that should be available to responders upon arrival, such as copies of building plans, and locations and types of historic as documents	
The names and titles of employees who should assist responders, such as security or building maintenance staff	
Documentation on the acquisition and value of historic documents	
How historic documents should be secured during disaster response	

DEVELOPING PROCEDURES FOR PERISHABLE FOODS AND MATERIALS

During a disaster, an organization must deal with perishable foods and materials in accordance with a variety of complex food and health laws. The disaster recovery planning team should seek expert help from the U.S. Food and Drug Administration (FDA), as well as state and local health agencies, when developing procedures for handling perishable foods and materials.

After the September 2001 attacks, concerns about food safety surfaced as the U.S. government worked to improve its antiterrorism efforts. The FDA, Cabinet-level departments, and other federal agencies began developing guidelines and support materials to assist organizations in making these improvements. The issue is important for some organizations—failure to properly handle perishable foods and materials during a disaster can cost thousands of dollars in wasted goods. Worse yet, these materials can create health hazards if they are used after spoiling. Again, organizations should err on the side of caution to ensure that perishable foods and materials are handled properly during a disaster. Table 8-5 lists some of the most important items to include in these procedures.

Table 8-5 Checklist of procedures for dealing with perishable foods and materials

Items to include in procedures for dealing with perishable foods and materials	Status (e.g., Completed, Pending, or N/A)
Names and titles of knowledgeable employees who are responsible for perishable foods and materials	
Applicable laws and regulations for handling perishable foods and materials during a disaster	
Contact information and locations of contractors who specialize in perishable foods and materials	
Conditions that require these contractors to be contacted	
How events should be described to the dispatchers for these contractors	
How facilities and locations should be identified for these contractors	
Instructions that should be given to responders about entering the facility	
Items that should be available to responders upon arrival, such as the locations and types of perishable foods and materials	
The names and titles of employees who should assist responders upon arrival, such as security or building maintenance staff	

8

DEVELOPING PROCEDURES FOR CONTROLLED SUBSTANCES

During a disaster, an organization must deal with controlled substances in accordance with many drug control laws and regulations. The disaster recovery planning team should seek expert help from the FDA, state agencies, and local health agencies when developing procedures for dealing with controlled substances. Table 8-6 lists some of the most important items to include in these procedures.

Controlled substances that are improperly moved or handled during a disaster could be misplaced or stolen, and end up on the illegal drug market. If these stolen substances are involved in a criminal incident or law enforcement agencies can trace the substances back to an organization, there is high potential for litigation and fines.

Table 8-6 Checklist of procedures for dealing with controlled substances

Items to include in procedures for dealing with controlled substances	Status (e.g., Completed, Pending, or N/A)
Names and titles of knowledgeable employees who are responsible for controlled substances	
Applicable laws and regulations for handling controlled substances during a disaster	
Contact information and locations of contractors who specialize in handling, removing, or storing controlled substances	
Conditions that require these contractors to be contacted	
How events should be described to the dispatchers for these contractors	
How facilities and locations should be identified for these contractors	
Instructions that should be given to responders about entering the facility	
Items that should be available to responders upon arrival, such as copies of building plans, and locations and types of controlled substances	
The names and titles of employees who should assist responders upon arrival	
How controlled substances should be secured during disaster response	

DEVELOPING PROCEDURES FOR TRADE SECRETS

The focus of most disaster recovery planning since the 2001 terrorist attacks has focused on saving lives, and rightfully so. However, organizations must also protect their intellectual property. Trade secrets and proprietary processes are some of the most valuable assets a company can have.

The Economic Espionage Act, which became effective in 1996, authorizes stiff fines and imprisonment for people and organizations that knowingly steal or misappropriate another company's trade secrets. The act also covers the downloading and uploading of trade secrets using computers and the Internet. Penalties for individual defendants include up to a $500,000 fine, 10 years imprisonment, or both. Penalties for corporations include up to a $5 million fine. If trade secrets are stolen on behalf of a foreign government, the fines and prison terms are increased.[13]

The precise definition of what constitutes a trade secret has been argued in many lawsuits, but for the purposes of this discussion, a trade secret has the following criteria:

- It is any form of corporately owned information that has economic value.

- An organization must be able to prove that it owns the information, either through development or purchase.

- The organization has taken reasonable measures to keep the information secret from the public and its competitors.[13]

The last point is often the most crucial in lawsuits involving trade secrets. For example, the question of whether information was secret before it was obtained by another party is important. Companies must make sure that the information has not been publicly disclosed through technical journals or other publications. Also, the "secrets" cannot be obvious to industry competitors—information that a company regards as its "crown jewels" could be well known within a particular field, and therefore not protected. On the other hand, if a scientist can review technical publications and then deduce a proprietary formula, but only after extensive laboratory testing and analysis, the scientist's work could violate the Economic Espionage Act. The work would probably not qualify as "reasonably ascertainable by the public." [13]

In 1996, FBI Director Louis Freeh testified before the House Judiciary Subcommittee on Crime in a hearing on economic espionage. Freeh said that theft and misappropriation of U.S. corporate trade secrets, particularly by foreign governments and their agents, "directly imperils the health and competitiveness of our economy. The ever increasing value of proprietary economic information in the global and domestic marketplaces, and the corresponding spread of technology, have combined to significantly increase both the opportunities and motives for conducting economic espionage." [14]

Freeh said the FBI was concerned about the theft by foreign corporations of trade secrets from U.S. telecommunications companies, automotive manufacturers, biotechnology firms, and microprocessor companies. Although Freeh emphasized that the FBI had not systematically evaluated the costs of economic espionage, he cited studies and surveys showing that U.S. companies had lost billions of dollars and hundreds of thousands of jobs as a result of stolen trade secrets by foreign interests. For example, FOCUS magazine estimated in 1995 that illegal copying and counterfeiting of medicines in Argentina, Brazil, India, and Turkey cost U.S. pharmaceutical companies more than $1.5 billion each year.[14]

When disaster strikes, procedures must be in place to ensure that trade secrets and proprietary processes are preserved and kept confidential. The disaster recovery planning team needs to develop these procedures. In many cases, confidential material must be quickly secured and even removed from a facility to maintain security during disaster response and recovery. In some organizations, procedures could require thousands of documents to be moved and secured. The checklist in Table 8-7 shows several issues to consider when dealing with trade secrets and proprietary processes.

Table 8-7 Checklist of procedures for dealing with trade secrets

Items to include in procedures for dealing with trade secrets	Status (e.g., Completed, Pending, or N/A)
Names and titles of knowledgeable employees who are responsible for the confidentiality of trade secrets and proprietary processes	
Conditions that require a lockdown of confidential materials	
A confidential building plan that indicates where confidential materials are kept	
Procedures for locking down confidential materials	
Procedures for relocating confidential materials during disaster response and recovery	
An off-site, secure location for storing confidential materials	
Procedures for returning confidential materials after disaster response and recovery have ended	

DEVELOPING PROCEDURES FOR ANIMALS AND OTHER LIFE FORMS

Many organizations use test animals or organisms in their research and development. Millions of laboratory animals are used across the United States to test the safety of chemicals, drugs, vaccines, cosmetics, household cleaners, pesticides, foodstuffs, and packing materials.[15]

If an organization uses animals for any purpose, the disaster recovery planning team must develop procedures to preserve them in an emergency. In many cases, animals and life forms must be moved to another part of a facility or completely removed to ensure their safety during disaster response and recovery.

A valuable resource for recovery planners is The American Veterinary Medical Association's *Disaster Preparedness and Response Guide*. The guide is designed to help veterinarians, technicians, and emergency managers work with animals in disasters. It includes instructions for animal care, handling, and feeding; appropriate operations of veterinary medical assistance teams (VMATs); VMAT enrollment procedures; sample forms; foreign animal diseases; and vaccination guidelines after a disaster.[16]

Many advocacy groups around the world are concerned about the use of animal testing in product research and development. Failure to properly protect animals and other life forms during a disaster could fuel the animosity of these groups, leading to embarrassing news stories and even litigation. The desire to avoid such embarrassment should motivate recovery planners to ensure the protection of all life forms in a crisis.

Organizations should retain a local veterinarian near each applicable facility to provide emergency services and to help develop animal care procedures. The checklist in Table 8-8 shows several issues an organization must cover when developing procedures to deal with animals and other life forms.

Table 8-8 Checklist of procedures for dealing with animals and other life forms

Items to include in procedures for dealing with life forms	Status (e.g., Completed, Pending, or N/A)
Names and titles of knowledgeable employees who are responsible for the life forms at risk	
Contact information and locations of contractors who can move animals or organisms	
Conditions that require these contractors to be contacted	
How events should be described to the dispatchers for these contractors	
How facilities and locations should be identified for these contractors	
Instructions that should be given to responders about entering the facility	
The names and work locations of employees who have companion animals that accompany them to work	
Items that should be available to responders upon arrival, such as copies of building plans, and locations and types of life forms	
The names and titles of employees who should assist responders upon arrival, such as security or research and development staff	

8

DEVELOPING PROCEDURES FOR PRECISION EQUIPMENT

Precision equipment, electronics, and optics are often expensive items, so the disaster recovery planning team must develop procedures to preserve them during an emergency. Precision tools and lab equipment can cost thousands of dollars apiece, and some precision instruments can be worth more than $100,000. These items are easy to resell on Internet auction sites, and can be very difficult to trace back to their rightful owners.

Because expensive equipment could be stolen during the chaos of a disaster, these items must be quickly secured or removed to a safe location. Afterward, the equipment can be reinstalled or restarted to help resume normal operations. The checklist in Table 8-9 shows several issues an organization must consider when developing procedures to secure and preserve precision equipment.

Table 8-9   Checklist of procedures for dealing with precision equipment

Items to include in procedures for dealing with precision equipment	Status (e.g., Completed, Pending, or N/A)
Names and titles of knowledgeable employees who are responsible for precision equipment	
Contact information and locations of contractors who specialize in moving precision equipment	
Procedures for locking down precision equipment	
Conditions that require contractors to be contacted	
How events should be described to the dispatchers for these contractors	
How facilities and locations should be identified for these contractors	
Instructions that should be given to responders about entering the facility	
Items that should be available to responders upon arrival, such as copies of building plans, and locations and types of precision equipment	
The names and titles of employees who should assist responders, such as security or lab personnel	

DEVELOPING PROCEDURES FOR RARE MATERIALS

Rare materials are often used in manufacturing or test environments. They can include precious metals and gemstones, and expensive chemicals, solvents, or paints. Such items could be stolen in the confusion after a disaster, lost during cleanup procedures, or misplaced during remodeling or renovation.

Even small amounts of rare materials can cost thousands of dollars, and larger quantities can be difficult to replace. Although prices fluctuate with the markets, gold typically costs more than $300 per ounce, and platinum costs more than $600 an ounce. Lesser-known materials such as palladium are worth more than $200 an ounce, and rhodium costs more than $400 per ounce.

Many organizations that use rare materials often stockpile them when prices drop during market fluctuations. Such purchases can save organizations hundreds of thousands of dollars over the long term. The planning team must develop procedures for quickly securing these materials or removing them to a safe location during a disaster. Afterward, the materials can be returned to help resume normal operations.

The checklist in Table 8-10 shows several issues an organization must consider when developing procedures to deal with rare materials.

Table 8-10 Checklist of procedures for dealing with rare materials

Items to include in procedures for dealing with rare materials	Status (e.g., Completed, Pending, or N/A)
Names and titles of knowledgeable employees who are responsible for rare materials	
Contact information and locations of contractors who move and store rare materials	
Procedures for locking down rare materials	
Conditions that require contractors to be contacted	
How events should be described to the dispatchers for these contractors	
How facilities and locations should be identified for these contractors	
Instructions that should be given to responders about entering the facility	
Items that should be available to responders upon arrival, such as copies of building plans, and locations and types of rare materials	
The names and titles of employees who should assist responders, such as security or lab personnel	

OTHER AREAS THAT MAY NEED SPECIAL ATTENTION

As you have seen, disaster recovery planning can be a seemingly endless process. The planning team and department representatives must evaluate what special procedures are needed, considering the nature of their organization and the location of its facilities. Some scenarios can present significant challenges:

- Health care facilities must deal with patient needs if a facility must be evacuated and renovated after a disaster.

- Government offices must be prepared to continue serving their constituencies and meet statutory requirements for activity.

- Child care facilities face strict safety requirements, and must be prepared to use alternate facilities or refer clients to other service providers.

- Banks must provide services at other branches or open emergency facilities to serve customers.

- Food service providers may need to have their facilities inspected before the local Health Department allows them to resume operations.

- An automobile repair shop may need to provide quick insurance payments to customers whose vehicles were in its custody during a destructive tornado.

- People with handicaps or disabilities must be considered in every disaster recovery plan.

The disaster recovery planning team should not stop developing procedures once a basic recovery plan is in place. The more an organization plans for contingencies, and the better that managers and employees understand the organization's needs, the better the chances that disaster recovery can proceed smoothly.

CHAPTER SUMMARY

❏ The disaster recovery planning team should determine whether it needs to develop procedures for dealing with special materials or assets in the recovery plan. The team should use the exposure inventory and risk assessment reports to make these determinations. The team should also poll all departments and facilities to discover other special needs. Representatives from each department or facility should conduct their own assessments and inform the planning team whether they require special procedures.

❏ Hazardous materials can create disasters at a facility, and they can compound problems caused by an unrelated disaster. Hazardous materials include explosives, flammable and combustible substances, poisons, and radioactive materials. These materials can explode, intensify fires, and release toxic fumes when burning. They can contaminate and injure employees and emergency responders. To effectively work with emergency service responders who specialize in hazardous materials, an organization must develop procedures to make contacts during a disaster and enable rapid response.

❏ Dealing with art, antiques, and collectibles during a disaster requires specific procedures. These items may need to be removed from a facility and restored, which requires the services of specialized contractors. If art, antiques, and collectibles are destroyed or damaged beyond repair, insurance companies require complete documentation about their purchase, condition, and appraised value. This documentation should be kept off site, and should include receipts, appraisal reports, and photographs.

❏ Historic documents such as photographs, letters, books, and music can be exceptionally fragile, and might require the services of a specialized contractor to restore after a disaster. Historic documents are also very difficult to value. An organization should keep extensive records of its historic documents, and have them periodically appraised by a certified specialist.

❏ During a disaster, an organization must deal with perishable materials and controlled substances in accordance with a variety of laws and regulations. The disaster recovery planning team should seek expert help from the FDA, state agencies, and local health agencies when developing procedures for dealing with perishable materials and controlled substances.

❏ Trade secrets and proprietary processes are some of the most valuable assets of an organization. When disaster strikes, procedures must be in place to ensure that trade secrets and proprietary processes are preserved and kept confidential. The planning team needs to develop these procedures.

❑ Many organizations use test animals or organisms in their research and development. If so, the planning team must develop procedures to safely preserve these life forms in an emergency. In many cases, they must be moved to another part of a facility or completely removed to ensure their safety and preservation during disaster response and recovery.

❑ Precision equipment, electronics, and optics are often expensive items. Because this equipment could be stolen during the chaos of a disaster, the planning team must develop procedures to quickly secure it or remove it to a safe location. Afterward, the equipment can be reinstalled or restarted to help resume normal operations.

❑ Rare materials are often used in manufacturing or test environments. They can include precious metals and gemstones, and expensive chemicals, solvents, or paints. Such items could be stolen in the confusion after a disaster, lost during cleanup procedures, or misplaced during remodeling or renovation. Therefore, the planning team must develop procedures for quickly securing these materials or removing them to a safe location. Afterward, the materials can be returned to help resume normal operations.

8

KEY TERMS

art, antiques, and collectibles — Rare and expensive items that may not be replaceable.

controlled substances — Drugs or the materials used to manufacture them. These substances are subject to regulation by national, state, and local governments.

hazardous materials — Substances that can pose a threat to the environment or public health if released or misused. Hazardous materials include explosives, flammable and combustible substances, poisons, and radioactive materials.

historic documents — Rare or unique items such as photographs, letters, books, and music that may not be replaceable.

life forms — Animals, plants, lab specimens, and experimental organisms.

perishable foods and materials — Items that must be stored at certain temperatures to prevent spoilage. They are subject to handling and storage regulations by national, state, and local governments.

precision equipment — Electronics, test devices, and optical devices.

rare materials — Special supplies and goods, such as precious metals, gemstones, chemicals, and solvents.

trade secrets and proprietary processes — Ideas, patents, plans, and manufacturing processes on which organizations depend.

REVIEW QUESTIONS

1. List several types of hazardous materials.

2. Why are procedures necessary to deal with hazardous materials in a disaster?

3. Why shouldn't the disaster recovery planning team try to interpret scientific data or government regulations for hazardous materials?

4. What types of items can be classified as art, antiques, and collectibles?

5. If art, antiques, and collectibles are destroyed or damaged beyond repair, what information might insurance companies require to settle a claim?

6. When art, antiques, and collectibles have not been appraised, what steps may be necessary to complete an insurance claim?

7. What should an organization do to support the value of historic documents?

8. What are perishable foods and materials?

9. When developing procedures to deal with perishable foods and materials during a disaster, what issues should the disaster recovery planning team consider?

10. Why should the disaster recovery planning team seek expert help when developing procedures for dealing with controlled substances?

11. Why is it important to have procedures to protect trade secrets and proprietary processes in a disaster?

12. Procedures for dealing with life forms often require what types of actions in a disaster?

13. Why is it important to secure precision equipment, electronics, and optics?

14. Why are procedures necessary for handling rare materials in a disaster?

15. Which issues often dictate the need for special procedures during disaster recovery?

16. List unusual circumstances that might require special procedures in a disaster.

17. Describe trade secrets and proprietary processes.

18. What issues should an organization address in procedures for dealing with hazardous materials during a disaster?

19. What issues should an organization cover in procedures to protect trade secrets in a disaster?

20. Why shouldn't the disaster recovery planning team stop developing procedures once a basic recovery plan is in place?

HANDS-ON PROJECTS

In this chapter, you studied the possible need to develop disaster recovery procedures for special circumstances and materials. In the following projects, you will demonstrate what you learned by creating evaluations and procedures on behalf of the organization for which you are developing a disaster recovery plan.

In Project 8-1, you will evaluate the need for specialized procedures to protect any unique capital in the organization. In Projects 8-2 to 8-10, you will develop procedures to protect this capital in a disaster. When you finish the evaluation and procedures, submit them to your instructor for review.

Project 8-1

Evaluate the need for specialized disaster recovery procedures in the organization for which you are developing a recovery plan. The evaluation should determine whether procedures are needed to deal with hazardous materials, art, antiques, collectibles, historic documents, perishable foods and materials, controlled substances, trade secrets, life forms, and rare materials.

Project 8-2

If required, develop procedures for dealing with the organization's hazardous materials after a disaster. The procedures should include the items listed in Table 8-2.

Project 8-3

If required, develop procedures for protecting an organization's art, antiques, and collectibles after a disaster. The procedures should include the items listed in Table 8-3.

Project 8-4

If required, develop procedures for dealing with an organization's historic documents in a disaster. Your procedures should include the items shown in Table 8-4.

Project 8-5

If necessary, develop procedures for preserving perishable foods and materials in the organization. For assistance, consult Table 8-5.

Project 8-6

If required, develop procedures for dealing with any controlled substances in the organization after a disaster. The procedures should include the items listed in Table 8-6.

Project 8-7

If necessary, develop procedures for protecting the organization's trade secrets in a disaster. For assistance, consult Table 8-7.

Project 8-8

If required, develop procedures for preserving animals and other life forms in the organization during a disaster. Your procedures should include the items shown in Table 8-8.

Project 8-9

If necessary, develop procedures for dealing with the organization's precision equipment in a disaster. The procedures should include the items shown in Table 8-9.

Project 8-10

If required, develop procedures for dealing with any rare materials in the organization during a disaster. For assistance, consult Table 8-10.

CASE PROJECTS

Case Project: Harris and Heartfield Manufacturing

Harris and Heartfield Manufacturing is a family-owned business that fabricates specialized metal parts for its North American clients. Most of its revenue comes from defense contracts and from producing parts for heavy-equipment manufacturers. The company has an excellent reputation for quality and prompt deliveries.

The company has 200 employees at its only location, in California. All 20 administrative employees have desktop PCs connected to the company's LAN. The 15 research and design engineers use Sun workstations that are also on the LAN. Three servers support administrative functions and six servers support design and manufacturing. About half the machining equipment on the shop floor is computerized.

Management is concerned about the company's future competitiveness, and about its ability to fulfill orders if a disaster hindered its operations. The board of directors is relatively business-savvy, but does not invest money unless it yields a positive return. As a result, the company hired you as a consultant to create a list of 10 key points that conveyed the importance of disaster recovery planning to the board. You also prepared 10 points for managers to discuss with employees about organizing and preparing to develop a plan.

You worked with company managers to develop a business process threat analysis for their product manufacturing, developed a list of questions for Harris and Heartfield to answer about insurance coverage, advised the company how to develop and staff a disaster response team, developed a list of organizations that the company should work with in a disaster, and developed guidelines for determining when the company should report computer hacking incidents to law enforcement agencies.

Your next assignment is to show Harris and Heartfield how to evaluate the need for specialized disaster recovery procedures. Develop a questionnaire to help department managers determine whether procedures are needed to deal with hazardous materials and other special materials discussed in this chapter.

OPTIONAL TEAM CASE PROJECTS

8

Team Case One

Your boss has asked you to identify contractors in your area that could assist the organization in handling hazardous materials during a disaster. Your assignment is to research and identify these contractors, and then write a one-page description of each. Your descriptions should include the contractor's location, contact information, a description of the contractor's service, and how to integrate the services into your disaster recovery plan.

Team Case Two

Next, your boss wants you to identify contractors in your area that could assist the organization in preserving perishable foods and materials during a disaster. Your assignment is to research and identify these contractors, and then write a one-page description of each. Your descriptions should include the same types of information you provided in Team Case One.

ENDNOTES

1. *www.fema.gov.*

2. *www.epa.gov/tri/tri_program_fact_sheet.htm.*

3. *www.epa.gov/tri/tridata/tri00/press/execsummary_final.pdf.*

4. 2000 Toxics Release Inventory (TRI), Public Data Release Report Executive Summary. The United States Environmental Protection Agency, Office of Environmental Information. Washington, DC. EPA-260-S-02-001. May 2002.

5. *art.progressive.com.*

6. *www.smh.com.au/articles/2002/11/17/1037490053883.html.*

7. *www.saralee.com/citizenship.*

8. *www.microsoft.com/mscorp/artcollection/why.htm.*

9. *www.safeco.com/safeco/about/collections.asp.*

10. *www.christies.com/corporate_collections/overview.asp.*

11. *www.arch.umd.edu/programs/preservation/intro.html.*

12. *www.aaslh.org.*

13. *www.cybercrime.gov/ipmanual/08ipma.htm#VIII.B.1.*

14. *www.fas.org/irp/congress/1996_hr/h960509f.htm.*

15. *www.hsus.org/ace/11366.*

16. *www.avma.org/disaster/responseguide.asp.*

9

IMPLEMENTING DISASTER RECOVERY PLANS

After reading this chapter, you will be able to:

♦ Develop an implementation plan

♦ Assign responsibilities for implementation

♦ Establish an implementation schedule

♦ Distribute the disaster recovery documentation

♦ Assess the value and effectiveness of mitigation steps

♦ Manage internal and external awareness campaigns

♦ Launch a training program for disaster recovery

In many ways, developing a disaster recovery plan and the necessary recovery procedures is only the first phase of disaster preparedness. After an organization develops a plan, it must implement the plan.

This chapter explains how an organization develops an implementation plan, assesses the value of mitigation steps, and assigns responsibilities and schedules for implementation. In addition, the organization must distribute recovery plan documents to all affected parties, and launch a disaster recovery training program. It is also a good idea to launch internal and external awareness programs.

A disaster recovery plan is only as good as the training that employees receive. An organization could be thrown into chaos unless employees know how to respond with recovery efforts. Proper training helps to ensure a synchronized and integrated recovery.

DEVELOPING AN IMPLEMENTATION PLAN

Once the organization develops a disaster recovery plan, the planning team can begin to implement it. The **implementation plan** affects all the departments in an organization; the plan must be managed step by step, and progress must be evaluated on a scheduled basis. The implementation plan requires training for all employees, and might require new equipment and procedures. Several other events occur during implementation:

- Responsibilities for implementation are assigned to members of the disaster recovery planning team and departmental groups.

- An implementation schedule is developed, with timelines and planned progress evaluations.

- Disaster recovery documentation is distributed to everyone who needs copies, or online access is provided.

- The value and effectiveness of mitigation steps are assessed. New mitigation steps could be put into place, and existing steps may be modified.

- The organization plans and launches internal and external awareness campaigns.

- The organization develops and launches employee training programs for disaster recovery procedures.

Some implementation activities require organization-wide action, including raising awareness and training. Other activities, such as the deployment of new equipment, require action at the facility level. If procedures must be changed or added to ease disaster recovery, the affected departments and work groups must make these changes and additions. Table 9-1 summarizes these activities.

Table 9-1 Organizational levels for implementing parts of the plan

Organizational level	Activities
Organization-wide	Training, raising awareness of plan
Facility level	Equipment purchases and deployment
Department level	Changing procedures and implementing new procedures that affect specific departments
Work group level	Changing procedures and implementing new procedures that affect specific work groups

Assigning Responsibilities for Implementation

The activities required to implement a disaster recovery plan range from directing management to establishing liaisons with local law enforcement and emergency services. The disaster recovery planning coordinator and the planning team assign responsibilities for implementing the plan. The coordinator takes the lead role in monitoring and evaluating the progress of implementation. Table 9-2 shows activities that occur over several months while the disaster recovery plan is being implemented.

Table 9-2 Implementation activities

Activity	Responsible party
Directing plan activity	Disaster recovery planning coordinator, functional department managers, and business unit managers
Changing existing procedures	Staff in affected departments
Purchasing equipment	Purchasing manager, with support from disaster recovery team and functional departments
Deploying equipment	Staff in affected departments
Contracting for services	Purchasing manager, with support from disaster recovery team and functional departments
Establishing liaisons	Disaster recovery coordinator, functional department managers
Raising awareness	Disaster recovery coordinator, functional department managers, Public Relations Department

Managers of functional departments and business units need to assign activities to their employees. Departmental planning groups work to implement aspects of the disaster recovery plan that affect their own departments. These activities include changing existing procedures and evaluating mitigation steps, as well as developing new mitigation procedures to support recovery priorities in the plan.

The Purchasing Department takes the lead in processing all the bids and paperwork to acquire new equipment needed to implement the plan or disaster mitigation steps. Managers of facilities or other functional departments deploy this equipment. If only one department uses the new equipment, staff from that department may be responsible for installing it. If new contracts are needed for disaster response and recovery, the affected facility or department develops them with the help of the Purchasing Department, and pays any necessary fees or retainers.

The organization must also establish solid liaisons with emergency service organizations, law enforcement agencies, and contractors. The disaster recovery coordinator, facility managers, and disaster response team work to establish these liaisons, as well as maintain the relationships over the long term.

Many planning activities can be broken down into more specific tasks. Not all members of the planning team need to be involved in such day-to-day tasks as developing awareness material or conducting training. Table 9-3 shows examples of implementation tasks that can be assigned to specific departments or employees.

Table 9-3 Implementation tasks

Task	Responsible party
Developing awareness material	Disaster recovery coordinator, Public Relations Department
Managing disaster plan documentation	Disaster recovery coordinator
Creating training program	Human Resources Department and disaster recovery staff
Briefing business partners	Product managers and business unit managers
Working with regulatory agencies	Managers that work in areas affected by specific laws and regulations

ESTABLISHING AN IMPLEMENTATION SCHEDULE

Once responsibilities have been assigned for specific activities and tasks, the disaster recovery planning team needs to establish an **implementation schedule** for completing each activity in the recovery plan. Of course, the speed of implementation depends on available resources, geographic distribution of facilities and employees, the availability of time for training, and other factors. Table 9-4 shows a sample implementation schedule.

Table 9-4 Sample implementation schedule

Time frame	Expected progress
Month 1	Purchase required equipment, initiate negotiations with contractors, establish liaisons with emergency service organizations and law enforcement agencies, design training program, create awareness material
Month 2	Deploy new equipment, sign contracts, launch training program, and initiate awareness campaign
Month 3	Finish deploying equipment, complete training for 50% of employees, distribute awareness materials to all employees
Month 4	Complete training for 75% of employees
Month 5	Complete training for all employees
Month 6	Move to testing and rehearsal step

The disaster recovery coordinator and the planning team should monitor the progress of implementation. The coordinator should compile a monthly report of all accomplishments and any activities that are behind schedule. The planning team can modify the schedule if conditions warrant, or it can make recommendations to various departments about accelerating implementation.

If the planning team discovers a lack of resources or some other obstacle, it should make a request to the highest ranking executive responsible for disaster recovery planning. The executive can then use his or her influence to gain more resources or eliminate obstacles.

DISTRIBUTING THE DISASTER RECOVERY DOCUMENTATION

The disaster recovery plan must be distributed and made available during implementation, test and rehearsal steps, and thereafter. The **disaster recovery plan documents** include all the written analyses, policies, and procedures that employees and contractors should follow when responding to a disaster. There are several ways to distribute documents, including company intranets and paper versions. Organizations should not rely on just one method to make documents available to response teams.

Distributing documents on an intranet is acceptable as long as the intranet is working. Similarly, placing the documents on a secure Web server is fine, as long as the Web server is up and running, and response teams have access to Internet connections. Table 9-5 shows other distribution alternatives for the disaster recovery plan. Each method has advantages and disadvantages, which is why documents should be distributed in more than one manner.

9

Table 9-5 Distribution alternatives

Distribution method	Advantages	Disadvantages
Intranet	Ease of deployment, low costs, accessible by all employees and business partners	Not available if the intranet is down, remote connectivity is lost, or the server is down
Hosted Web server	Broader possible access than an intranet; server is maintained off site	Not available if Web server or hosting company is down; requires remote connectivity
CD-ROM copies	Does not rely on network connectivity; can be deployed on a laptop or notebook	CD-ROMs must be continually replaced with updated versions
Paper copies	Does not rely on network connectivity or computer availability	Paper copies must be continually replaced with updated versions

ASSESSING THE VALUE AND EFFECTIVENESS OF MITIGATION STEPS

Most organizations implement **mitigation steps** to reduce the impact of system failure or disruption of operations. Many of these steps are common practices for managing assets or business processes. Backing up computer files, for example, is a common approach to avoiding the consequences of system failure or disk crashes.

During the exposure inventory and risk assessments, the disaster recovery planning team collected information about how to mitigate and avoid business disruptions. As the team developed recovery procedures, it determined more methods of avoiding disruption.

More mitigation steps are needed when the organization implements the disaster recovery plan. These steps usually include more rigid backup procedures, redundant systems, or off-site duplication of resources. To determine whether a mitigation step is needed, the planning team evaluates the outcomes of the risk assessments, and then seeks technologies or design processes that are more resistant to failure.

All mitigation steps must have sound economic value. For example, uninterruptible power supplies (UPS), redundant computer systems, and fault-tolerant computers are all logical approaches that can prevent system downtime. However, such systems can be very expensive to deploy, and they might not be effective during a catastrophic disaster.

Using a UPS to protect servers from sudden power outages can be a cost-effective mitigation step. For example, Table 9-6 illustrates that if power is lost nine times per year, the **return on investment (ROI)** for using a UPS to protect the server is about 15 months. The formula for calculating the ROI is shown in the table. Note, however, that productivity is still lost because the server systematically shuts down using UPS power.

The loss of productivity can be more difficult to determine. If power is out for a building or a neighborhood, then employees cannot use their desktop computers. The server, however, is easy to restore once power is restored.

Table 9-6 Analysis of the value of UPS

Factor	Sample data
A. Times per year that power for servers is lost	9
B. Number of hours needed to restore server with no UPS installed	1.5
C. Minimum hours per year of nonavailability (A X B)	13.5
D. Labor cost to restore server per incident (B X labor cost for IT staff @ $35/hour)	$52.50
E. Cost per year (D X C)	$708.75
F. Cost to deploy a UPS	$900.00
G. Number of years for ROI (F/E)	1.27 years (15 months)

Because so many things can go wrong when a disaster strikes, the planning team needs to carefully determine how many scenarios it should analyze and what types of mitigation steps it should take to avoid disruption. The team must perform this analysis within the context of management policies and organizational practices.

Determining what kind of data back-up systems an organization should use is more difficult than analyzing the benefits of a UPS. System backups are certainly necessary to preserve computer files and databases, but the selection of particular back-up systems depends on a number of factors. Table 9-7 shows one approach for analyzing the value of data back-up systems.

Table 9-7   Analysis of the value of data backup systems

Factor	Sample data
A. Times per year that an incident results in data loss	2
B. Number of hours needed to restore data without a backup system (per incident)	25
C. Labor cost to restore server per incident (B X labor cost for IT staff @ $35/hour)	$875.00
D. Annual direct cost to restore data (A X C)	$1750.00
E. Number of staff hours lost per incident because the database is not available during restoration	300
F. Indirect costs per incident for lost productivity (E X labor cost for end users @ $25/hour)	$7,500.00
G. Annual indirect costs per year for lost productivity (A X F)	$15,000.00
H. Total direct and indirect costs per year (D + G)	$16,750.00

In the sample case presented in Table 9-7, the organization would suffer direct and indirect costs of $16,750 if a system crash occurred without a back-up system in place to restore data. This analysis provides an annual baseline for a cost that could be mitigated by a back-up system.

After determining how much money could be saved, the planning team can examine what types of data back-up systems to put in place, and how much the organization should spend for them. The answers are not as simple as they may first appear. The planning team should address several questions before selecting a back-up system, including:

- How resilient to failure is the back-up system?

- Can it be used for more than one system or application, thus improving ROI?

- What level of disaster does the back-up system help mitigate (e.g., catastrophic, major, or minor)?

- How much does it cost to deploy the back-up system?

- How much IT staff time is needed to maintain the back-up system?

Evaluating these mitigation steps is an ongoing process throughout recovery planning. The planning team should use ROI analyses like those in the preceding tables to evaluate mitigation steps that make economic sense.

MANAGING INTERNAL AND EXTERNAL AWARENESS CAMPAIGNS

As an organization develops and implements a disaster recovery plan, it needs to make employees highly aware of the plan. The better that employees, customers, and business partners understand disaster recovery, the easier recovery will be. During training, employees should learn the details of the plan and learn their roles and responsibilities during disaster response.

Human nature seems to dictate that employees do not take planning seriously if they are unconvinced it can benefit them personally. The goal of the awareness program is to indoctrinate employees about the importance of disaster response and recovery.

When disaster recovery planning began, the organization should have launched an awareness campaign to inform employees about planning efforts. Further awareness-building is needed as the disaster recovery plan is put into place. Depending on an organization's resources, there are several ways to increase awareness during plan implementation. The following sections explain some of these methods.

Using Existing Channels of Communication

An economic way of increasing awareness about disaster recovery is to use existing corporate communications. Organizations often have employee relations programs, customer relations management systems, and business partner communications that can help build awareness. Typical forms of communication include:

- Employee newsletters

- Bulletin boards

- Motivational posters

- Intranets with employee information sections

- E-mail announcement lists

- Customer relations e-mail newsletters and bulletins

- Business partner Web sites

- Corporate Web portals with sections for employees, customers, and business partners

Building Awareness Among Employees

In addition to using structured communication methods, organizations can use regularly scheduled department or work group meetings to call attention to disaster recovery planning efforts. The disaster recovery coordinator, in conjunction with the Human Resources or

Public Relations Department, should develop a series of announcements that department managers and supervisors can use in their meetings. These announcements should not be complex; each should have a primary focus, including:

- A basic description of disaster recovery planning

- The mission statement of the planning team

- The status of disaster recovery planning

- The status of implementing the recovery plan

- The schedule for disaster recovery training

- The schedule for testing recovery procedures

Building Awareness Among Customers and Business Partners

Managers of the Customer Relations Department can build awareness among customers through newsletter articles, e-mail bulletins, or announcements at meetings. Channel managers or product managers can build similar awareness among business partners.

The messages to deliver to employees, customers, and business partners are considerably different. However, bulletins and announcements to both customers and business partners should include the following materials:

- Basic description of disaster recovery planning

- How the organization works with customers or business partners to develop recovery procedures

- How the disaster recovery plan can benefit customers or business partners

- What customers or business partners can expect when a disaster strikes

- Basic steps for customers or business partners to follow in a disaster

LAUNCHING A TRAINING PROGRAM FOR DISASTER RECOVERY

A disaster recovery training plan is an essential element of being prepared for a disaster. The scope and depth of the training program depend on the size and type of the organization. Training must be developed for several levels of employee involvement. Training with local emergency organizations is also advisable.

Elements of a basic disaster recovery plan were presented in Chapter 5. Based on these elements, Table 9-8 shows a series of general training modules for executives, middle managers, supervisors, or all employees. Because these modules are more general in nature, they can be directed toward a broader audience.

Table 9-8 General disaster recovery training modules

General training module	Target audience
Overview of disaster recovery plan	Executives, middle managers, supervisors, and all employees
Executive and middle management responsibilities	Executives, middle managers
Procedures for working with emergency services and law enforcement organizations	Executives, middle managers, and supervisors
Disaster classification and procedures for direction, control, and administration, including organizing the response team and recovery team, establishing an emergency operations center, declaring and confirming disasters, issuing first alerts, and keeping activity logs	Executives, middle managers
Internal and external communications procedures, including organizing the communications team, as well as notifying emergency medical services, fire and rescue services, police, top management, insurance companies, employees and their families, customers, suppliers, and service providers	Executives, middle managers, and supervisors

Based on the disaster recovery elements presented in Chapter 5, Table 9-9 shows a series of more specific training modules directed toward middle managers, supervisors, and disaster response teams. These modules include training on how teams should be organized, along with activities that require managers and employees to be involved.

Table 9-9 Specialized training modules for managers, supervisors, and response teams

Safety and health procedures, including organizing the security team and rescue team, facility evacuation, reentry, movement of employees, and crisis counseling
Containment and property protection procedures, including organizing the insurance and damage assessment team, securing buildings, shutting off utilities, securing and retrieving assets, managing communications systems, and assessing damage
Resuming and recovering operations, including organizing the business continuation team, determining the duration of shutdowns, using back-up and alternate systems, activating hot or cold sites, moving records, moving equipment, moving supplies, and recovering systems and functions
Restoring facilities and normalizing operations, including organizing the restoration team, restoration estimates, temporary repairs, restoration work, and reoccupation of facilities

Several other special procedures may not be needed for all disaster recovery plans, but if they are included, the proper people must be trained in these procedures. Table 9-10 shows a series of special training modules directed toward middle managers, supervisors, and appropriate disaster response teams. These modules include training for working with other organizations, employees, families of employees, and the local community.

Table 9-10 Training modules for special disaster recovery procedures

Training module for special procedure	Target audience
Working with public utilities and Public Works departments	Middle managers, selected response teams
Working with insurance companies	Selected response teams
Working with disaster recovery service providers	Selected response teams
Working with telecommunications service providers	Selected response teams
Working with IT service providers	Selected response teams
Working with IT equipment providers and software companies	Selected response teams
Working with business partners	Middle managers, selected response teams
Working with suppliers and business service providers	Middle managers, selected response teams
Working with customers	Middle managers, selected response teams
Working with the media	Executives, selected response teams
Working with stockholders and investors	Executives, selected response teams
Communicating with employees and families of employees	Supervisors, selected response teams
Working with the local community	Selected response teams

9

Most of the material required to develop a training program should already be included in the disaster recovery plan. However, the plan documentation may not always be easy to convert to training material. To be effective, the training modules should contain several elements that are presented in different formats. Table 9-11 shows the elements that belong in all disaster recovery training modules.

Table 9-11 Elements of disaster recovery training modules

Training module element	Format
Presentation by trainer	Stand-up presentation accompanied by Microsoft PowerPoint slides
Overheads or slides that cover the disaster recovery plan and procedures	PowerPoint
Relevant sections of the disaster recovery plan	Workbook format or printed handouts
Supplemental material such as case studies to prompt discussion	Workbook format or printed handouts
Evaluation form for participants to grade the training and comment on it	Printed form

The disaster recovery planning team should watch and approve training presentations before they are given to the entire organization. The team should also require trainers to rehearse their presentations several times before teaching the modules in front of an audience. Trainers can use feedback from the evaluation forms to modify content and presentation styles as training progresses.

Overheads and slides used during disaster recovery training should look professional and be easy to read from all parts of the training rooms. The slides should be professionally edited, and should present an appropriate amount of information on each slide. Trainers can use feedback from the evaluation forms to modify the slides if necessary.

When trainers use sections of the disaster recovery plan in their training, they should organize the sections separately for each training module. If trainers use three-ring binders to hold their training material, they should use tabs to separate materials for each session. If trainers use handouts, then each should have a cover sheet that clearly identifies the module in which it is used. Supplemental material used to prompt discussion, such as case studies, should also be organized separately for each training module.

The evaluation form should inquire about the overall quality of the training, as well as the quality of materials used during training. All attendees should be required to complete an evaluation form.

The training modules described in the preceding tables should be designed for specific audiences within the organization, as described in the following sections. However, the overview of the recovery plan is designed for all employees, and should be included in all training modules. The overview should last about one hour; it should focus on what is expected from employees during a disaster, and how they should report to supervisors or middle managers.

Training for Executives

Training modules designed for executives should be tightly structured, and should include only as much detail as necessary to explain what is expected of them during a disaster. Table 9-12 shows a recommended training session for executives. The training is designed so that sessions can be held independently, grouped for the convenience of executives, or delivered in a single day. For more information on the procedures listed in the table, see Chapter 5.

Table 9-12 Disaster recovery training for executives

Training modules for executives	Recommended time
Overview of disaster recovery plan	1 hour
Executive and middle management responsibilities	1 hour
Procedures for working with emergency services and law enforcement organizations	1 hour
Procedures for classifying disasters, and for direction, control, and administration	2 hours
Internal and external communications procedures	1 hour
Working with the media	30 minutes
Working with stockholders and investors	30 minutes

Training for Middle Managers

Middle managers generally have far more extensive roles in disaster response and recovery than executives, so their recovery training needs to cover topics in greater depth. Table 9-13 shows a recommended training session for middle managers. Sessions can be held independently, grouped for the managers' convenience, or delivered in a three-day training session.

Table 9-13 Disaster recovery training for middle managers

Training modules for middle managers	Recommended time
Overview of disaster recovery plan	2 hours
Executive and middle management responsibilities	1 hour
Procedures for working with emergency services and law enforcement organizations	1 hour
Procedures for classifying disasters, and for direction, control, and administration	2 hours
Internal and external communications procedures	2 hours
Safety and health procedures	2 hours
Containment and property protection procedures	2 hours
Procedures for resuming and recovering operations	2 hours
Procedures for restoring facilities and normalizing operations	2 hours
Working with public utilities and Public Works departments	1 hour
Working with business partners	1 hour
Working with suppliers and business service providers	1 hour
Working with customers	1 hour

9

Training for Supervisors

Supervisors generally have more extensive roles in disaster response and recovery than executives, but they work under the direction of middle managers to implement procedures or support a specific response team. Thus, disaster recovery training for supervisors needs to cover the same topics as that for executives, but not in as much depth as the training for middle managers.

Table 9-14 shows a recommended training session for supervisors. Sessions can be held independently, grouped for the supervisors' convenience, or delivered in a one-day training session.

Table 9-14   Disaster recovery training for supervisors

Training modules for supervisors	Recommended time
Overview of disaster recovery plan	1 hour
Procedures for working with emergency services and law enforcement organizations	30 minutes
Internal and external communications procedures	30 minutes
Safety and health procedures	2 hours
Containment and property protection procedures	2 hours
Procedures for resuming and recovering operations	1 hour
Procedures for restoring facilities and normalizing operations	1 hour

Training for Disaster Response Teams

Training specific response teams is the most complicated aspect of disaster response and recovery training. Response teams must be trained on much of the same material as executives and middle managers, and they must be extremely well trained in their own roles to ensure that disaster response proceeds smoothly. Training modules for specific response teams should provide in-depth coverage of procedures, so that team members fully understand their responsibilities in a disaster. All response team members should attend disaster recovery training for middle managers, as well as specialized training designed for their team. Table 9-15 shows recommended training sessions for specific disaster response teams.

Table 9-15   Training sessions for specific response teams

Training modules	Response teams that require training in module	Recommended time
Direction, control, and administration procedures	Response team, recovery team	2 days
Safety and health procedures	Rescue team, security team	2 days
Internal and external communications procedures	Communications team	1 day
Containment and property protection procedures	Insurance and damage assessment team, security team	1 day
Resuming and recovering operations	Business continuation team	2 days
Restoring facilities and normalizing operations	Restoration team	1 day

Training for Employees

All employees should be required to attend training that is appropriate for their management level and participation on response teams. Disaster recovery coordinators should work with the Human Resources and Training departments to ensure that trainers receive a list of all employees who are scheduled to attend specific modules. Trainers should record attendance on a class roster and return it to the office that schedules training.

CHAPTER SUMMARY

◻ Once the organization develops a disaster recovery plan, the planning team can begin to implement it. The implementation plan affects all the departments in an organization; the plan must be managed step by step, and progress must be evaluated on a scheduled basis.

◻ The activities required to implement a disaster recovery plan range from directing management to establishing liaisons with local law enforcement and emergency services. The disaster recovery planning coordinator and the planning team assign responsibilities for implementing the plan. The coordinator takes the lead role in monitoring and evaluating the progress of implementation.

◻ Once responsibilities have been assigned for specific activities and tasks, the disaster recovery planning team needs to establish an implementation schedule for completing each activity in the recovery plan. Of course, the speed of implementation depends on available resources, geographic distribution of facilities and employees, the availability of time for training, and other factors.

◻ The disaster recovery plan must be distributed and made available during implementation, test and rehearsal steps, and thereafter. There are several ways to distribute documents, including company intranets and paper versions. Organizations should not rely on just one method to make documents available to response teams.

❑ During the exposure inventory and risk assessments, the disaster recovery planning team collected information about how to mitigate and avoid business disruptions. As the team developed recovery procedures, it determined more methods of avoiding disruption. All mitigation steps must have sound economic value. For example, uninterruptible power supplies (UPS), redundant computer systems, and fault-tolerant computers are all logical approaches that can prevent system downtime. However, such systems can be very expensive to deploy, and they might not be effective during a catastrophic disaster.

❑ As an organization develops and implements a disaster recovery plan, it needs to make employees highly aware of the plan. The better that employees, customers, and business partners understand disaster recovery, the easier recovery will be. During training, employees should learn the details of the plan and learn their roles and responsibilities during disaster response.

❑ The disaster recovery training plan is an essential element of being prepared for a disaster. The scope and depth of the training program depend on the size and type of the organization. Training must be developed for several levels of employee involvement. Training with local emergency organizations is also advisable.

KEY TERMS

disaster recovery plan documents — The written analyses, policies, and procedures that employees and contractors should follow when responding to a disaster.

implementation plan — The plan for implementing all the activities in the disaster recovery plan. The plan affects all departments in an organization; it must be managed step by step, and progress must be evaluated on a scheduled basis.

implementation schedule — A schedule for completing each required activity in the disaster recovery plan.

mitigation steps — Steps that organizations take to reduce the impact of system failure or disruption of operations. Many of these steps, such as backing up computer files, are commonly used to manage assets or business processes.

ROI — Return on investment.

REVIEW QUESTIONS

1. What activities occur when an organization implements its disaster recovery plan?

2. Disaster recovery training and awareness raising occur at what level of an organization?

   a. organization-wide

   b. facility level

   c. department level

   d. work group level

3. Modified and new procedures might be required to implement a disaster recovery plan. At what level of an organization are these procedures written? (Choose all that apply.)

   a. organization-wide

   b. facility level

   c. department level

   d. work group level

4. Equipment might have to be purchased and deployed to implement the disaster recovery plan. At what level of an organization is this equipment purchased?

   a. organization-wide

   b. facility level

   c. department level

   d. work group level

5. Who directs the activities required to implement the disaster recovery plan?

   a. the disaster recovery coordinator, functional department managers, and business unit managers

   b. staff in affected departments

   c. the purchasing manager, with support from the disaster recovery planning team and functional departments

   d. the purchasing manager, with support from the response team

6. Who is responsible for managing documentation for the disaster recovery plan?

   a. the disaster recovery coordinator and the Public Relations Department

   b. the disaster recovery coordinator

   c. the Human Resources Department and disaster recovery staff

   d. product managers and business unit managers

7. What are the advantages and disadvantages of distributing the disaster recovery plan on an intranet?

8. What are the advantages and disadvantages of distributing the disaster recovery plan on a hosted Web server?

9. What are the advantages and disadvantages of distributing the disaster recovery plan on a CD-ROM?

10. What questions should an organization ask before selecting a back-up system?

    a. How resilient to failure is the back-up system?

    b. Can the back-up system be used for more than one system or application, thus improving ROI?

    c. What level of disaster does the back-up system help mitigate (e.g., catastrophic, major, or minor)?

    d. all of the above

11. What is the advantage of using an ROI analysis to evaluate mitigation steps?

12. What types of communications are economic ways to increase awareness of the importance of the disaster recovery plan? (Choose all that apply.)

    a. employee newsletters

    b. bulletin boards

    c. intranets with employee information sections

    d. nationwide television spots

13. When managers and supervisors make announcements in their meetings about implementing the disaster recovery plan, what information should the announcements include? (Choose all that apply.)

    a. a basic description of disaster recovery planning

    b. the status of disaster recovery planning

    c. the status of plan implementation

    d. what other organizations in the community are saying about the plan

14. What are the five target audiences for disaster recovery training in an organization?

15. Which of the following groups should receive training on safety and health procedures? (Choose all that apply.)

a. executives

b. middle managers

c. supervisors

d. selected response teams

16. Which of the following groups should receive training in procedures for working with insurance companies?

a. executives

b. middle managers

c. supervisors

d. insurance and damage assessment team

17. Why should disaster recovery training for middle managers cover topics in greater depth than the training for executives?

18. Training specific response teams is the least complicated aspect of disaster response and recovery training. True or False?

19. Training for supervisors is designed so that sessions can be held independently, grouped for the convenience of supervisors, or delivered in a three-day training session. True or False?

20. The disaster recovery coordinator should work with the Human Resources or Training Department to ensure that trainers receive a list of all employees who are scheduled to attend specific training modules. True or False?

HANDS-ON PROJECTS

In the following projects, you will implement portions of the disaster recovery plan for the organization you have been assisting throughout this book. When you finish, submit the materials to your instructor for review.

HANDS-ON
PROJECTS

Project 9-1

Assign responsibilities for implementing the organization's disaster recovery plan. Include assignments for directing activities, changing existing procedures, purchasing equipment, deploying equipment, and contracting for services. Also include assignments for establishing liaisons, raising awareness, and developing and launching the training program. Assign other responsibilities if necessary.

Project 9-2

Develop an implementation schedule for the organization's disaster recovery plan. Activities should follow the sample schedule shown earlier in Table 9-4. Include other activities if necessary.

Project 9-3

Develop a disaster recovery distribution plan for the organization. You can choose several alternatives for distributing information, including the intranet, hosted Web servers, CD-ROM copies, and paper copies.

Project 9-4

Conduct an ROI analysis for deploying UPS devices on the organization's servers. You can use the formula shown earlier in Table 9-6 or another formula like it.

Project 9-5

Conduct an ROI analysis for deploying data back-up systems on the organization's servers. You can use the formula shown earlier in Table 9-7 or another formula like it.

Project 9-6

Develop an employee awareness campaign for the organization's disaster recovery plan. Show how you will use the following communications channels:

- Employee newsletters
- Bulletin boards
- Motivational posters
- Intranets with employee information sections
- E-mail announcement lists
- Corporate Web portals with sections for employees

Project 9-7

Write announcements for managers and supervisors to make at departmental and work group meetings about the organization's disaster recovery plan. Be sure that the announcements include a basic description of the planning process, the mission statement of the planning team, and the status of recovery planning and plan implementation. The announcements should also include schedules for disaster recovery training and for testing recovery procedures.

Project 9-8

Develop disaster recovery awareness campaigns for the organization's customers and business partners. Show how you will use any of the following communications channels:

- E-mail announcement lists
- E-mail newsletters and bulletins for customers and business partners
- Business partner Web sites
- Corporate Web portals with sections for customers and business partners

Project 9-9

Write announcements to use in disaster recovery awareness campaigns for the organization's customers and business partners. Although these two campaigns require different materials, be sure to cover the following areas in both:

- Basic description of disaster recovery planning
- How the organization works with customers and business partners to develop recovery procedures
- How the disaster recovery plan can benefit customers and business partners
- What customers and business partners can expect when a disaster strikes
- Basic steps for customers and business partners to follow in a disaster

Project 9-10

Develop general disaster recovery training modules for the organization. Be sure to cover the areas shown earlier in Table 9-8.

Project 9-11

Develop specialized disaster recovery training modules for the organization. Be sure to cover the areas shown earlier in Table 9-9.

Project 9-12

Develop training modules for special disaster recovery procedures in the organization. Cover the areas shown earlier in Table 9-10.

CASE PROJECTS

Case Project: Harris and Heartfield Manufacturing

Harris and Heartfield Manufacturing is a family-owned business that fabricates specialized metal parts for its North American clients. Most of its revenue comes from defense contracts and from producing parts for heavy-equipment manufacturers. The company has an excellent reputation for quality and prompt deliveries.

The company has 200 employees at its only location in California. All 20 administrative employees have desktop PCs connected to the company's LAN. The 15 research and design engineers use Sun workstations that are also on the LAN. Three servers support administrative functions and six servers support design and manufacturing. About half the machining equipment on the shop floor is computerized.

Management is concerned about the company's future competitiveness, and about its ability to fulfill orders if a disaster hindered its operations. The board of directors is relatively business-savvy, but does not invest money unless it yields a positive return. As a result, the company hired you as a consultant to create a list of 10 key points that conveyed the importance of disaster recovery planning to the board. You also prepared 10 points for managers to discuss with employees about organizing and preparing to develop a plan.

You worked with company managers to develop a business process threat analysis for their product manufacturing, developed a list of questions for Harris and Heartfield to answer about insurance coverage, and advised the company how to develop and staff a disaster response team. You also developed a list of organizations that the company should work with in a disaster, developed guidelines to determine when the company should report computer hacking incidents to law enforcement agencies, and developed a questionnaire to help department managers determine whether recovery procedures were needed for any special materials and circumstances.

Your next assignment is to outline a series of awareness campaigns for employees, customers, and business partners. Create a three-page memo that outlines the material to cover in each awareness campaign.

OPTIONAL TEAM CASE PROJECTS

Team Case One

Your boss has asked you to identify avenues of communication that your organization could use to implement an awareness campaign for employees. After you identify these avenues, write a description of each. Include contact information for the parties responsible for each avenue of communication, and describe how to best integrate their services into the disaster recovery awareness campaign.

Team Case Two

Next, your boss wants you to identify possible sources of general disaster recovery training for your organization. After you identify these training sources, write a description of each. Include the same types of contact information and integration tips you provided in the previous team case project.

9

CHAPTER

10

TESTING AND REHEARSAL

After reading this chapter, you will be able to:

◆ Test and rehearse disaster recovery plans and procedures

◆ Use a step-by-step testing process

◆ Develop test scenarios

◆ Rehearse the abilities of subunits to execute disaster recovery procedures

◆ Measure the effectiveness of disaster recovery plans and procedures, and fine-tune them

Short of working through an actual disaster, testing and rehearsing disaster recovery plans is the only way an organization can determine how well the plans and related procedures work. The planning team must develop testing scenarios and use a step-by-step testing process to evaluate the effectiveness of plans and procedures.

The process starts with tests of key parts of the disaster recovery plan. These tests focus on specific procedures, as well as groups of related procedures. Eventually, the organization should try to test the entire plan in a mock disaster atmosphere.

After each partial or full test, the disaster recovery planning team uses qualitative and quantitative data to fine-tune plans and procedures.

THE TESTING AND REHEARSAL PROCESS

An organization uses several types of tests to determine how well its disaster recovery plans and procedures work. In many ways, this testing is like a military exercise:

- Small groups may practice independently.

- Combinations of groups practice to see if they can properly coordinate their actions.

- Groups of organizations practice to see if they can properly coordinate their actions and achieve desired results.

In military settings, the combinations of groups keep growing until entire military forces practice together to see if they can respond effectively to a scenario.

Several types of tests are shown in Table 10-1, along with the results that each test can achieve. The tests start at the procedural level and expand to live tests of related procedures. Eventually, these tests grow to demonstrate whether work groups, departments, facilities, and even entire organizations can execute the disaster recovery plan.

Table 10-1 Types of tests for disaster recovery plans and procedures

Type of test	Type of results
In **procedure audits**, employees walk through the procedure to determine if the information is correct and if the procedure can actually be executed as written.	Shows whether information is current, resources are in the correct location, designated equipment is installed, necessary staff is available, and employees understand the procedures
In **live walk-throughs of procedures**, the procedures are actually implemented to determine their effectiveness.	Shows whether designated equipment is working properly, response time of staff is appropriate, and procedures actually result in designed outcomes
In **live walk-throughs of related procedures**, the related procedures are actually implemented to determine their effectiveness.	Shows whether procedures are properly coordinated and systems interact as designed
Scenario testing creates a mock disaster, such as severe weather or a fire, to determine how well procedures designed for these events work.	Shows whether procedures are designed well enough to handle specific situations
Work group-level tests create a mock disaster to which a specific group of people must respond.	Shows how well procedures work for a work group in a mock disaster
Department-level tests create a mock disaster to which an entire department must respond.	Shows how well procedures work for a department in a mock disaster
Facility-level tests create a mock disaster to which an entire facility must respond.	Shows how well procedures work for a facility in a mock disaster
Enterprise-level tests create a mock disaster to which an entire organization must respond.	Shows how well procedures work for the entire organization in a mock disaster

USING A STEP-BY-STEP TESTING PROCESS

Although drafts of disaster recovery procedures are reviewed by the planning team and an independent review group, the actual procedures should be tested using a step-by-step process. Procedures should be tested after they are developed, and then tested periodically to make sure that the disaster recovery plan and all procedure documents contain current information.

Procedures should be audited once a year. Employees who are responsible for executing the procedures should walk through them to determine if the information is correct, and if the procedure can still be executed as written.

It is best to conduct a procedure audit with a group of people, or to have several people audit the procedure independently and submit comments to the disaster recovery coordinator. Building evacuation procedures should be reviewed by security staff, building maintenance staff, and other employees who participate in the evacuation. Procedure auditors should complete a form and submit it to the disaster recovery coordinator. The form should indicate any necessary changes to the procedure or note that it is adequate as written. Table 10-2 shows a sample procedure audit report.

Organizations should conduct a live walk-through of all procedures on an annual basis, or any time a procedure or related procedures have changed. Live walk-throughs should be conducted for individual procedures and groups of related procedures. In live walk-throughs, procedures are actually implemented to determine their effectiveness. As with the procedure audit, several staff members should walk through the procedure, either as a group or independently, then complete a report and submit it to the disaster recovery coordinator. The report should indicate any changes that are needed to the procedures, based on the walk-through. Table 10-3 shows a sample procedure walk-through test report.

10

Table 10-2 Sample procedure audit report

Procedure review questions	Audit result (circle one)
Procedure audited:	Date the procedure was last updated: _____
Is the procedure written clearly enough to be executed? Review the clarity of language, use of terms, descriptions of locations, and descriptions of action steps.	Adequate as written Changes needed as indicated Not applicable Not auditable
Has anything occurred that makes the procedure outdated or inadequate? Review physical changes in building layout, location of equipment, and names of equipment.	Adequate as written Changes needed as indicated Not applicable Not auditable
Have the personnel involved in executing the procedure changed? Review the names and contact information of relevant staff and other organizations to ensure that they are current.	Adequate as written Changes needed as indicated Not applicable Not auditable
Have other procedures changed that affect the execution of this procedure?	Adequate as written Changes needed as indicated Not applicable Not auditable
Recommended changes in the procedure:	
Print procedure auditor's name: _____	Procedure auditor's title: _____
Procedure auditor's signature: _____	Phone number: _____ Date: _____

Table 10-3 Sample procedure walk-through test report

Walk-through test questions	Test result (circle one)
Procedure audited:	Date the procedure was last updated: _____
Are the steps in the procedure adequate to execute it?	Adequate as written Changes needed as indicated Not applicable Not testable
Did any specific instructions not work in the procedure?	Adequate as written Changes needed as indicated Not applicable Not testable
Did all of the appropriate personnel respond when executing the procedure?	Adequate as written Changes needed as indicated Not applicable Not testable
Have other procedures changed that affect the execution of this procedure?	Adequate as written Changes needed as indicated Not applicable Not testable
Recommended changes in the procedure:	
Print walk-through tester's name: _____	Walk-through tester's title: _____
Walk-through tester's signature: _____	Phone number: _____ Date: _____

In some cases, organizations can apply sophisticated testing processes to technology systems. These processes include vulnerability audits and intrusion testing for computer systems and networks. **Vulnerability audits** generally use automated procedures to compare the profiles of networked computer devices with those of more secure configurations and software settings. Reports are generated for each device, and include recommended changes for improving security.

Intrusion tests often use a combination of automated and hands–on methods to see how easily an intruder can break into computer systems or networks. The results of the intrusion test are combined with recommendations for improving security.

DEVELOPING TEST SCENARIOS

Once organizations have audited disaster recovery procedures and conducted walk-through tests, they should test procedures in a more complex and lifelike situation. Based on the risk assessments they conducted previously, organizations should develop scenarios to simulate the most likely threats they face. Scenario testing uses mock disasters such as severe weather or a fire to determine how well any related procedures will work during real events.

Scenarios can take the form of relatively simple but realistic circumstances, such as a building fire, a tornado hitting a facility, a mock bank robbery, a hazardous waste spill, or a power outage. Many organizations find such tests useful in determining the effectiveness of their disaster recovery procedures.

However, there is also considerable resistance to such testing, because of its impact on productivity. The resources of entire work groups, departments, facilities, or organizations can be consumed for hours or days during a test of complex scenarios. Such resource consumption and unproven return on investment make many managers skeptical of the value of scenario testing.

Evacuation and Safety Exercises

The need to test disaster scenarios may vary among organizations, but some procedures virtually demand testing by all organizations. In some political jurisdictions, for example, there are minimum requirements for conducting evacuation tests.

The age-old fire drill should not be underrated as a valuable exercise. When terrorists attacked the World Trade Center in September 2001, one of the biggest challenges was evacuating the building and accounting for personnel. All organizations face the threat of fire, regardless of the cause, so they should test their fire drills or building evacuation procedures on a regular basis.

Depending on a facility's geographical location, other evacuation and safety exercises might be necessary. In the U.S. Midwest and South, tornados are real threats for many months of the year. Therefore, organizations in these regions should test the safety procedures they have designed to deal with such events. In the Western United States, organizations should test their procedures for dealing with earthquakes, mudslides, and wildfires.

Bear in mind that evacuation procedures in many organizations involve far more than people running from a building and assembling in the parking lot for a head count. If an organization has procedures to deal with special capital such as hazardous materials, controlled substances, valuable items, or rare materials, it must implement these procedures during evacuation. Also, the evacuation of a work environment that employs continuous manufacturing may require equipment to be shut down and systems to be secured in standby mode.

Thorough evacuation procedures can create a safer corporate environment and avoid problems that may occur in an actual fire or other disaster. Some of the elements of an evacuation test are shown in Table 10-4.

Table 10-4 Elements of an evacuation test

Test element
The time and date of the evacuation test
Descriptions of activities in the facility at the time of the test
How the evacuation test is monitored, and who the monitors are
What related procedures are tested
How the monitors record their observations
How the monitors' notes are analyzed

Testing for Special Circumstances

Organizations should develop test scenarios for any special circumstances and materials they have to deal with during a disaster. The following list shows several special circumstances that may require scenario testing. The same test elements shown in Table 10-4 apply to these tests.

- Hazardous materials include explosives, flammable and combustible substances, poisons, and radioactive materials.

- Art, antiques, and collectibles are rare and expensive items that may not be replaceable.

- Historic documents include rare items such as photos, letters, books, and music that may not be replaceable.

- Perishable foods and materials are items that need to be stored at certain temperatures to prevent spoilage.

- Controlled substances include drugs and the materials used to manufacture drugs.

- Trade secrets and proprietary processes are ideas, patents, plans, and manufacturing processes on which an organization depends.

- Life forms include animals, plants, lab specimens, and experimental organisms.

- Precision equipment includes electronics, test devices, and optical devices.

- Rare materials include precious metals, gemstones, chemicals, and solvents.

Organizations that have hazardous materials must test their procedures for dealing with such materials. Not only can hazardous materials be a source of disasters, they can compound problems caused by unrelated disasters. Table 10-5 shows some important issues that organizations need to evaluate when testing their procedures for dealing with hazardous materials.

10

Table 10-5   Testing procedures for dealing with hazardous materials

Questions to ask during testing
Did the procedures include correct contact information for employees who are responsible for hazardous materials?
Did the procedures include correct contact information and locations for emergency service organizations that specialize in hazardous materials?
Did the procedures correctly describe conditions that require these emergency service organizations to be contacted?
Were events and circumstances appropriately described to the dispatchers for these organizations?
Were the facilities and locations appropriately identified for these organizations?
Were proper instructions for entering the facility given to responders?
Were the proper documents available to responders upon their arrival, such as copies of building plans, and locations and types of hazardous materials?
Were the proper employees present to assist responders upon arrival?

Organizations that have historic documents, antiques, art, and collectibles must test their procedures for protecting these items in a disaster—they are valuable and difficult to replace. Table 10-6 shows some important issues that organizations need to evaluate when testing these procedures.

Table 10-6   Testing procedures to protect historic documents, art, antiques, and collectibles

Questions to ask during testing
Did the procedures include correct contact information for employees who are responsible for historic documents, art, antiques, and collectibles?
Did the procedures include correct contact information and locations for contractors who remove and restore historic documents, art, antiques, and collectibles?
Did the procedures correctly describe conditions that require these contractors to be contacted?
Were events and circumstances appropriately described to the dispatchers for these contractors?
Were the facilities and locations properly identified for responders?
Were responders given proper instructions for entering the facility?
Were the proper documents available to responders upon arrival, such as copies of building plans, and locations and types of art and collectibles?
Were the proper employees available to assist responders upon their arrival?
Was proper documentation available to describe the acquisition and value of art and collectibles? Did the procedure correctly indicate where these documents were stored?

Organizations that use perishable foods, controlled substances, or related materials must test their procedures for dealing with these materials during a disaster. These procedures must comply with a variety of complex laws and regulations, including those from the U.S. Food and Drug Administration, state agencies, and local health agencies. Table 10-7 shows some important issues that organizations need to evaluate when testing their procedures for preserving perishable foods and controlled substances.

Table 10-7   Testing procedures to protect perishable foods and controlled substances

Questions to ask during testing
Did the procedures include correct contact information for employees who are responsible for perishable foods, controlled substances, or related materials?
Did the procedures include correct contact information and locations for contractors who specialize in perishable foods or controlled substances?
Did the procedures correctly describe conditions that require these contractors to be contacted?
Were events and circumstances appropriately described to the dispatchers for these contractors?
Were facilities and locations properly identified for responders?
Were responders given proper instructions for entering the facility?
Were proper documents available to responders upon arrival, such as copies of building plans, and locations and types of perishable foods or controlled substances?
Were the proper employees available to assist responders upon their arrival?

Trade secrets and proprietary processes are some of an organization's most valuable assets. When disaster strikes, procedures must be in place to ensure that trade secrets and proprietary processes are preserved and kept confidential. Table 10-8 shows some important issues that organizations need to evaluate when testing these procedures.

10

Table 10-8   Testing procedures to protect trade secrets during a disaster

Questions to ask during testing
Did the procedures include correct contact information for employees who are responsible for the confidentiality of trade secrets?
Did the procedures clearly describe conditions that require a lockdown of trade secrets and other confidential materials?
Was there a confidential building plan that indicates where trade secrets are kept?
Were the procedures for locking down trade secrets clearly written? Could employees execute the procedures?
Were the procedures for relocating trade secrets clearly written? Could employees execute the procedures?
Did the procedures designate an off-site, secure location where trade secrets could be stored?
Did the procedures include clear instructions for returning trade secrets after disaster recovery efforts have ended? Could employees execute the procedures?

Organizations that use test animals or organisms in their research and development must test their procedures for protecting these life forms in a disaster. In many cases, the life forms must be moved to another part of a facility or completely removed to ensure their safety and preservation. Table 10-9 shows some important issues that organizations need to evaluate when testing their procedures to protect life forms.

Table 10-9 Testing procedures to protect life forms in a disaster

Questions to ask during testing
Did the procedures include correct contact information for employees who are responsible for protecting life forms?
Did the procedures include correct contact information and locations for contractors who specialize in moving animals or organisms?
Did the procedures correctly describe conditions that require these contractors to be contacted? Were the procedures clearly written, and could employees execute them?
Were events and circumstances appropriately described to the dispatchers for these contractors?
Were facilities and locations properly identified for responders?
Were responders given proper instructions for entering the facility?
Were proper documents available to responders upon arrival, such as copies of building plans, and locations and types of life forms?
Were the proper employees available to assist responders upon their arrival?

Organizations that have expensive precision equipment or rare materials must test their procedures for protecting these items during a disaster. In many cases, precision equipment must be cleaned or restored after a disaster.

Rare materials are often used in manufacturing processes or test environments. These materials can include precious metals, gemstones, chemicals, solvents, or paints. Such items could be stolen during a chaotic situation, lost during cleanup procedures, or misplaced during remodeling or renovation. Procedures must ensure that these materials are quickly secured or removed to a safe location during a disaster.

Table 10-10 shows some important issues that organizations need to evaluate when testing their procedures for protecting precision equipment or rare materials.

Table 10-10 Testing procedures to protect precision equipment or rare materials

Questions to ask during testing
Did the procedures include correct contact information for employees who are responsible for precision equipment or rare materials?
Did the procedures include correct contact information and locations for contractors who specialize in moving precision equipment or rare materials?
Were the procedures for locking down precision equipment or rare materials clearly written? Could employees execute the procedures?
Did the procedures clearly designate conditions that require contractors to be contacted?
Were the events properly described to the dispatchers for these contractors?
Were facilities and locations properly identified for these contractors?
Were responders given proper instructions for entering the facility?
Were the proper documents available to responders upon their arrival, such as copies of building plans, and locations and types of precision equipment or rare materials?
Were the proper employees present to assist responders upon their arrival?

Testing Shutdown and Lockdown Procedures

Many of the special circumstances discussed in the preceding sections require shutdown or lockdown procedures. Also, work environments that employ continuous or discrete manufacturing may require equipment to be shut down in an emergency. These shutdown procedures must be well documented, and supervisors and employees who work with the equipment must be able to implement the procedures. Any scenario that tests disaster response must include a test of shutdown procedures, and should take the questions in Table 10-11 into consideration. Monitors should observe the shutdown tests and record their impressions of all aspects of testing.

Table 10-11 Testing shutdown procedures

Questions to ask during testing
How quickly did supervisors and employees respond to the shutdown alarm?
Were the shutdowns implemented according to procedures?
If shutdowns were not implemented according to procedures, where and when did human errors occur?
If shutdown procedures failed, but not because of human error, what went wrong?
If a shutdown procedure requires several pieces of equipment to be shut down in sequence, was the sequence properly executed? Was the procedure effective?
If the preceding procedure was not effective, was there a human error?
If there was no human error, what was wrong with the procedure?
Was the shutdown procedure fast enough for employees to shut down equipment and evacuate their work area or building?

Organizations must also test lockdown and security procedures for valuable items, rare materials, and life forms. Any scenario that tests disaster response must include a test of lockdown procedures, and should take the questions in Table 10-12 into consideration. Monitors should observe the lockdown tests and record their impressions of all aspects of testing.

Table 10-12 Testing lockdown procedures

Questions to ask during testing
How quickly did supervisors and employees respond to the lockdown alarm?
Were the lockdowns implemented according to procedures?
If lockdowns were not implemented according to procedures, where and when did human errors occur?
If lockdown procedures failed, but not because of human error, what went wrong?
Was the lockdown procedure fast enough for employees to lock down equipment and evacuate their work area or building?

10

Testing Emergency Service Response Procedures

Most organizations depend on local emergency agencies for fire, medical, and police services. Firefighters and other emergency service responders sometimes tour buildings in their vicinity to become familiar with facilities. In addition, many emergency service organizations can provide speakers for training sessions.

Disaster recovery planners must establish strong working relationships with local emergency service providers. These relationships can include joint drills and rehearsals of disaster response procedures. The better that emergency service responders know a facility, the better they can respond when they arrive. Thus, organizations should include local emergency service agencies in rehearsals of their disaster recovery plans. They should take the questions in Table 10-13 into consideration.

Monitors from the organization and emergency service agencies should observe joint rehearsals. Both groups of monitors can evaluate the effectiveness of the procedures and provide each other feedback.

Table 10-13 Testing emergency response procedures

Questions to ask during testing
Did the procedures for contacting emergency service providers contain correct contact information?
How quickly did supervisors and employees respond to an incident and contact emergency service providers?
How quickly did emergency service providers respond once they were contacted?
Were the circumstances that prompted the call adequately described?
Were the facilities and locations adequately identified for emergency responders?
Were emergency responders given adequate instructions for entering the facility?
Were the proper items available to emergency responders upon their arrival?
Were the correct employees present to assist emergency responders upon arrival?

REHEARSING THE ABILITIES OF SUBUNITS

Procedure audits, live walk-throughs of procedures, and testing procedures for shutdowns, lockdowns, and special circumstances are only the beginning of the testing process. Next, an organization should test the ability of all its subunits to execute disaster recovery procedures. **Subunits of an organization** can include work groups, departments, or facilities.

Developing scenarios to test and evaluate the ability of subunits can be relatively easy. However, organizations that have no experience with such testing should start on a small scale. Creating scenarios to test work groups or small facilities is the best way to start.

Bear in mind that scenarios need to be realistic. Hurricanes do not occur in Minnesota, and few tornados strike Southern California. The scenario should depict a disaster that all employees can accept as something that could really happen.

The key to getting the best test results is to have a well-planned test. To achieve good results, the disaster recovery coordinator must develop a sufficient level of detail for the test, and managers and supervisors must understand the test scenario. Table 10-14 shows several important elements that the coordinator must incorporate into the test scenario.

The scope and parameters of the scenario should not only test an employee's ability to respond, they should improve employee response. Thus, the first run of a test scenario should not be so complicated that it frustrates employees. Subsequent test scenarios can become progressively more difficult as employee response improves.

Table 10-14   Test scenario elements

The date and time of the test
The duration of the test, in hours or days
The scope of the test, including all participating work groups, departments, or facilities
Whether outside contractors or emergency services are involved in the test
The nature of the test, such as for a natural disaster, a human error, or an accident
How the response is monitored
How the notes of the monitors are analyzed
How feedback is given to employees

Severe Weather Test Scenario

Severe weather test scenarios are relatively easy to execute, and should include an entire facility. The disaster recovery coordinator, in conjunction with department managers, should choose a date and time for the test. Managers, supervisors, and monitors should then be briefed on the test parameters.

In the severe weather test scenario shown in Table 10-15, the test begins at 9:30 a.m. and runs for three hours. The facility has no electricity, computer networks, or telephones during the scenario. Employees do not have access to one-third of the facility, which was destroyed by a tornado; this area can be locked down or blocked off. Employees in the destroyed third of the facility are not available to provide assistance or fulfill their assigned roles in management or disaster response. (These employees can function as monitors, however.)

Monitors should make notes about the behavior and response of managers and employees. These employees should execute the procedures in the disaster recovery plan and handle disaster response.

Table 10-15 Severe weather test scenario

Test element	Description
Date and time	Tuesday, March 12, 9:30 a.m.
Duration of the test	Three hours
Location of the test	West Valley facility
Scope of the test	Entire facility
Parameters of the test	A tornado hits the west side of town, causing extensive damage
	One-third of the facility is destroyed
	Electric utilities and telephones are out
	Computer networks are down
	Emergency service responders will not arrive for 30 minutes

MEASURING EFFECTIVENESS AND FINE-TUNING PROCEDURES

Measuring the effectiveness of disaster recovery plans and procedures goes hand in hand with measuring an organization's ability to respond to a disaster. Testing and rehearsal provide an opportunity to conduct detailed evaluations of the disaster recovery plan and procedures, as well as the abilities of employees, contractors, and emergency response organizations to respond.

The disaster recovery team can sometimes quantify evaluation results, but the results usually take the form of qualitative data. The team should use the results of evaluations to modify and improve the disaster recovery plan, and to determine where additional training is needed.

Activities that the team can quantify include response time and completion of containment, lockdown, and shutdown tasks. Response time is related to the need to save lives, reduce exposure, and minimize damage. Areas that require qualitative assessments include the effectiveness of recovery procedures, employee performance during scenarios, employee response to unanticipated situations, and employees' abilities to solve problems during disaster response.

The disaster recovery coordinator should compile an evaluation report after every test or rehearsal, and include input from monitors and participants. The organization should conduct debriefing sessions with employees and emergency responders after each test. These sessions should offer evaluation forms for employees and open-ended discussions about the experience. Table 10-16 shows an outline for a scenario test evaluation report.

Table 10-16 Outline of scenario test evaluation report

Contents	Sources of data
Title page and table of contents	
Executive summary	Contents of the report
Test scenario description	Documents and plans outlining the scenario
Chronology of events	Disaster response activity logs, reports and forms completed by the disaster response team
Synthesized evaluation results	Reports from monitors, completed evaluation forms, results of debriefing sessions
Recommended changes in plans or procedures	Synthesized evaluation results
Recommendations for further training or changes in training content or process	Synthesized evaluation results
Exhibits and attachments	Disaster response activity logs, reports and forms completed by the disaster response team, reports from monitors, completed evaluation forms, results of debriefing sessions

Organizations should not overlook feedback from employees and other participants in the evaluation process. In fact, feedback can be an integral part of the scenario test evaluation report. Employees and participants should have the opportunity to openly discuss their experiences and give their impressions. The supervisors can record this information, as can a specified employee who attends debriefing sessions. Organizations should also use a structured data collection form in the debriefing sessions. Table 10-17 shows the types of questions to include on the employee evaluation form, along with the structure for responses.

10

Table 10-17 Scenario test employee survey

Types of questions	Response structure
Effectiveness of the plan or procedures	Rating scale of 1 to 5
Clarity of instructions that employees received from supervisors or response teams during the test	Rating scale of 1 to 5, and open-ended answers for comments and feedback
Effectiveness of response teams	Rating scale of 1 to 5, and open-ended answers for comments and feedback
Effectiveness of outside contractors	Rating scale of 1 to 5, and open-ended answers for comments and feedback
Major concerns that employees had during the test	Open-ended answers for comments and feedback
How the employee felt physically during the test	List of descriptive terms, such as tired, exhausted, tense
How the employee felt emotionally during the test	List of descriptive terms, such as anxious, nervous, scared
Assessment of the test as a learning experience	Rating scale of 1 to 5, and open-ended answers for comments and feedback

Once the evaluation report is complete, the disaster recovery planning team should review the report, make necessary changes in the recovery plan, and modify specific procedures as needed. All plan revisions and procedure modifications should pass through the full review process, just as they did during development. The planning team and independent reviewers need to check and approve the procedures before placing the final versions in the recovery plan.

CHAPTER SUMMARY

- An organization uses several types of tests to determine how well its disaster recovery plans and procedures work. In many ways, this testing is like a military exercise.

- Although drafts of disaster recovery procedures are reviewed by the planning team and an independent review group, the actual procedures should be tested using a step-by-step process. Procedures should be tested after they are developed, and then tested periodically to make sure that the disaster recovery plan and all procedure documents contain current information. Procedures should be audited once a year. Employees who are responsible for executing the procedures should walk through them to determine if the information is correct, and if the procedure can still be executed as written.

- Once organizations have audited disaster recovery procedures and conducted walk-through tests, they should test procedures in a more complex and lifelike situation. Based on the risk assessments they conducted previously, organizations should develop scenarios to simulate the most likely threats they face. Scenario testing uses mock disasters such as severe weather or a fire to determine how well any related procedures will work during real events.

- Procedure audits, live walk-throughs of procedures, and testing procedures for shutdowns, lockdowns, and special circumstances are only the beginning of the testing process. An organization should also test the ability of all its subunits to execute disaster recovery procedures. Subunits of an organization can include work groups, departments, or facilities.

- Measuring the effectiveness of disaster recovery plans and procedures goes hand in hand with measuring an organization's ability to respond to a disaster. Testing and rehearsal provide an opportunity to conduct detailed evaluations of the disaster recovery plan and procedures, as well as the abilities of employees, contractors, and emergency response organizations to respond.

KEY TERMS

department-level tests — Tests that create a mock disaster to which an entire department must respond.

enterprise-level tests — Tests that create a mock disaster to which an entire organization must respond.

facility-level tests — Tests that create a mock disaster to which an entire facility must respond.

intrusion tests — Tests that often use a combination of automated and hands-on methods to see how easily an intruder can break into computer systems or networks. The results of the intrusion test are combined with recommendations for improving security.

live walk-throughs of procedures — Tests in which procedures are actually implemented to determine their effectiveness.

live walk-throughs of related procedures — Tests in which related procedures are actually implemented to determine their effectiveness.

procedure audits — Tests in which employees walk through procedures to determine if the information in them is correct, and if they can actually be executed as written.

scenario testing — Testing that creates a mock disaster, such as severe weather or a fire, to determine how well procedures designed for these events work.

subunits of an organization — Subunits can include work groups, departments, or facilities.

vulnerability audits — Audits that generally use automated procedures to compare the profiles of networked computer devices with those of more secure configurations and software settings. Reports are generated for each device, and include recommended changes for improving security.

work group-level test — Tests that create a mock disaster to which a specific group of employees must respond.

10

REVIEW QUESTIONS

1. What is the purpose of a procedure audit?

2. How does an organization perform a live walk-through of procedures?

3. What is the purpose of a live walk-through of related procedures?

4. How does an organization perform scenario testing?

5. How does an organization perform facility-level tests?

6. When auditing disaster recovery procedures, what questions must the auditors address?

7. When conducting walk-through tests for disaster recovery procedures, what questions must the testers address?

8. How does an organization generally conduct audits of computer system and network vulnerability?

9. How does an organization conduct intrusion tests of computer systems and networks?

10. Why is there resistance to large-scale scenario tests of disaster recovery plans and procedures?

11. When staging a test of evacuation procedures, which of the following points should an organization note and consider? (Choose all that apply.)

    a. descriptions of activities in the facility at the time of the test

    b. how the evacuation test is monitored, and who the monitors are

    c. the methods the monitors use to record their observations

    d. the number of people in the building

12. When staging a test of shutdown procedures, which of the following questions should an organization note and consider?

    a. How quickly did supervisors and employees respond to the shutdown alarm?

    b. Were the shutdowns implemented according to procedures?

    c. If the shutdowns were not implemented according to procedures, where and when did the human error occur?

    d. all of the above

13. When staging a test of lockdown procedures, what should an organization test for?

14. What issues should organizations evaluate when testing their procedures for dealing with hazardous materials in a disaster?

15. What issues should organizations evaluate when testing their procedures for protecting art, antiques, and collectibles in a disaster?

16. What issues should organizations evaluate when testing their procedures for protecting trade secrets in a disaster?

17. What elements make up a test scenario?

18. During a scenario test, what types of activities can be measured using quantitative data?

19. During a scenario test, what types of activities can be measured using qualitative data?

20. What information should be included in the scenario test evaluation report?

21. In the scenario test evaluation report, what data sources are used to create the chronology of events?

22. In the scenario test evaluation report, what data sources are used to create synthesized evaluation results?

HANDS-ON PROJECTS

In the following projects, you will test and evaluate portions of the disaster recovery plan for the organization you have been assisting throughout this book. When you finish, submit the materials to your instructor for review.

Project 10-1

Conduct a procedure audit of any three recovery procedures you developed for the organization. Use the sample procedure audit form in Table 10-2 or create your own. The procedure audit should at least address the following questions:

- Is the procedure written clearly enough to be executed? Review the clarity of language, use of terms, descriptions of locations, and descriptions of action steps.

- Has anything occurred that makes the procedure outdated or inadequate? Review physical changes in building layout, location of equipment, and names of equipment.

- Have the personnel involved in executing the procedure changed? Review the names and contact information of relevant staff and other organizations to ensure that they are current.

- Have other procedures changed that affect the execution of this procedure?

10

Project 10-2

Conduct a walk-through test of any three recovery procedures you developed for the organization. Use the sample procedure walk-through form in Table 10-3 or create your own. The walk-through test should at least address the following questions:

- Are the steps in the procedures adequate to execute them?

- Did any specific instructions not work in the procedure?

- Did all of the appropriate personnel respond when executing the procedure?

- Have other procedures changed that affect the execution of this procedure?

Project 10-3

Develop a scenario to test and evaluate evacuation procedures for the organization. The test scenario should include the elements listed in Table 10-4.

Project 10-4

Develop a scenario to test and evaluate shutdown procedures for equipment in the organization. The test scenario should include the items listed in Table 10-11.

Project 10-5

Develop a scenario to test and evaluate lockdown procedures for valuable items in the organization. The test scenario should include the items listed in Table 10-12.

Project 10-6

If applicable, develop a scenario to test and evaluate hazardous material procedures in the organization. The test scenario should include the items listed in Table 10-5.

Project 10-7

If applicable, develop a scenario to test and evaluate procedures for securing antiques, art, collectibles, and historic documents in the organization. The test scenario should include the items listed in Table 10-6.

Project 10-8

If applicable, develop a scenario to test and evaluate procedures for perishable foods, controlled substances, or related materials in the organization. The test scenario should include the items listed in Table 10-7.

Project 10-9

If applicable, develop a scenario to test and evaluate procedures that protect trade secrets in the organization. The test scenario should include the items listed in Table 10-8.

Project 10-10

If applicable, develop a scenario to test and evaluate procedures that protect life forms in the organization. The test scenario should include the items listed in Table 10-9.

Project 10-11

If applicable, develop a scenario to test and evaluate procedures that protect precision equipment and rare materials in the organization. The test scenario should include the items listed in Table 10-10.

Project 10-12

Develop a severe weather test scenario for the organization. The test scenario should include the items listed in Table 10-14.

Project 10-13

From the severe weather test scenario you developed in Project 10-12, develop an evaluation survey to collect data from employees who participated in the test. The survey should cover at least the following topics:

- Effectiveness of the plan or procedures

- Clarity of instructions that employees received from supervisors or response teams during the test

- Effectiveness of response teams and outside contractors

- Major concerns that employees had during the test

- How the employees felt during the test, both physically and emotionally

- Assessment of the test as a learning experience

10

CASE PROJECTS

Case Project: Harris and Heartfield Manufacturing

Harris and Heartfield Manufacturing is a family-owned business that fabricates specialized metal parts for its North American clients. Most of its revenue comes from defense contracts and from producing parts for heavy-equipment manufacturers. The company has an excellent reputation for quality and prompt deliveries.

The company has 200 employees at its only location in California. All 20 administrative employees have desktop PCs connected to the company's LAN. The 15 research and design engineers use Sun workstations that are also on the LAN. Three servers support administrative functions and six servers support design and manufacturing. About half the machining equipment on the shop floor is computerized.

Management is concerned about the company's future competitiveness, and about its ability to fulfill orders if a disaster hindered its operations. The board of directors is relatively business-savvy, but does not invest money unless it yields a positive return. As a result, the company hired you as a consultant to create a list of 10 key points that conveyed the importance of disaster recovery planning to the board. You also prepared 10 points for managers to discuss with employees about organizing and preparing to develop a plan.

You worked with company managers to analyze business process threats to product manufacturing, developed a list of questions about insurance coverage, and advised the company how to develop a disaster response team. You also developed a list of organizations that the company should work with in a disaster, developed guidelines for reporting computer hacking incidents to law enforcement agencies, developed a questionnaire to help determine whether recovery procedures were needed for special circumstances, and outlined awareness campaigns for employees, customers, and business partners.

Your assignment now is to develop a list of possible scenarios to test Harris and Heartfield's disaster recovery plan and procedures. Develop five scenarios and briefly explain the value of each.

OPTIONAL TEAM CASE PROJECTS

Team Case One

Your boss has asked you to identify possible scenarios to test your organization's disaster recovery plan and procedures. Your assignment is to research and identify the most likely events that threaten your organization, and then write a scenario to test the response to those threats.

Team Case Two

Next, your boss wants you to develop checklists for monitors to use when testing your organization's disaster recovery plan and procedures. Your assignment is to develop the checklist for the test and a brief description of how the monitors should record information.

11

CONTINUED ASSESSMENT OF NEEDS, THREATS, AND SOLUTIONS

After reading this chapter, you will be able to:

♦ Organize for long-term disaster recovery management

♦ Establish a monitoring process

♦ Monitor compliance with procedures

♦ Evaluate new technologies

♦ Accommodate changes in relationships between organizations

♦ Schedule regular reviews of plans and procedures

♦ Update documentation in disaster recovery plans

♦ Keep training programs current

The process of developing, implementing, and testing disaster recovery plans and procedures is a long one. Once the disaster recovery planning team has finished this process, it should make the transition into a maintenance mode for recovery planning.

The planning team should develop methods to manage the planning process over a long period of time. The team must also establish a monitoring process to determine when and if changes are needed to the plans and procedures.

Team members should continually evaluate new technologies to determine whether they can make the recovery process easier and more economical. But, just as technology changes, so do an organization's business conditions and partnerships. Changes in organizational structures and business relationships may dictate the need for changes to the disaster recovery plan and procedures.

To ensure that these changes are accommodated, the disaster recovery planning team must establish a regularly scheduled review of all plans and procedures. Documentation must be updated and training programs must be kept current.

ORGANIZING FOR LONG-TERM DISASTER RECOVERY MANAGEMENT

After the disaster recovery planning team has developed, implemented, and tested an organization's recovery plans and procedures, the team enters a new phase of operation. In **maintenance mode** , the team monitors, tests, and modifies the disaster recovery plan to keep it current with changes in organizational structure, business operations, and new technologies.

In the maintenance mode, the work is not as intense and time consuming; nevertheless, it is important. Organizations tend not to maintain the same structure over long periods of time. New management, new staff, new laws and regulations, and new business practices frequently affect most organizations. The disaster recovery planning team must ensure that such changes do not make the disaster recovery plan and procedures obsolete.

Many organizations grapple with how the disaster recovery task force should work after developing, implementing, and testing the recovery plan. There is no absolute solution to the problem. If the existing disaster recovery planning team stays in place, there is little to decide. However, there are several logical choices other than leaving the existing planning team in place. Table 11-1 shows several organizational approaches for maintaining a disaster recovery plan.

Table 11-1 Organizational options for maintaining a disaster recovery plan

Options for maintenance management
The existing disaster recovery planning team stays in place.
Some members of the planning team remain in place, while others are called upon as necessary to maintain the plan.
No one on the planning team remains in place; the team is replaced by other middle managers and technical experts in the organization.
A full-time or part-time disaster recovery planning coordinator is appointed, and calls upon departments to help when necessary.
The operations director or chief operating officer takes over the maintenance of the disaster recovery plan.

There are several advantages to leaving some members of the planning team in place, while calling upon others as necessary to help maintain the plan. Members of the planning team have skills, knowledge, and institutional memory that were established during the original planning process, which can make it easier to maintain the plan over the long term. New members of the team may not possess the same skills and knowledge.

Table 11-2 shows the advantages of retaining members of the original disaster recovery planning team.

Table 11-2 Retaining members of the original disaster recovery planning team

Team member	Advantages
Corporate security representative(s)	Corporate security staff always play a key role on many disaster response teams.
Building maintenance representative(s)	Building maintenance staff have ongoing exposure to changes in the facility layout and how the facility is used.
Administrative division representative(s)	Administrative divisions execute many critical functions for an organization, such as payables, receivables, and order management.
Human resources representative(s)	The Human Resources Department can play a key role in training new employees and tracking previous training.
Public relations representative(s)	Staff from the Public Relations Department play a key role in dealing with outside entities during disaster response.
IT department representative(s)	The IT Department maintains critical infrastructure that is often evolving and changing.
Network management representative(s)	The Network Management Department maintains critical infrastructure that is often evolving and changing.
Business unit representative(s)	Business units are usually aware of changes in business practices and business relationships.
Production department representative(s)	Production departments are usually aware of changes in manufacturing processes, materials used, and facilities involved in manufacturing.

11

Organizations have several options if they want to retain some members of the disaster recovery planning team while calling upon others as necessary to maintain the recovery plan. For example, a core team could be established to operate on an ongoing basis. Each department would sustain its membership on the disaster recovery planning team, but would not necessarily be involved in all activities.

In the core team option for disaster recovery planning, team members who have the greatest recovery responsibilities or work with the most critical systems stay on the team full-time. Table 11-3 shows the core team option and the status of membership for departmental representatives. Team members who do not have substantial responsibilities for disaster response or critical infrastructures should work with the team on a part-time, as-needed basis.

Table 11-3 The core team option

Team member	Membership status
Corporate security representative(s)	Full-time members who participate in all activities
Building maintenance representative(s)	Part-time members who participate in activities related to facility changes
Administrative division representative(s)	Full-time members who participate in all activities
Human resources representative(s)	Part-time members who participate in training activities
Public relations representative(s)	Part-time members who participate in activities related to communications
IT department representative(s)	Full-time members who participate in all activities
Network management representative(s)	Full-time members who participate in all activities
Business unit representative(s)	Part-time members who participate in activities related to unit operations
Production department representative(s)	Part-time members who participate in activities related to production and manufacturing

Regardless of the organizational approach or how the disaster recovery planning team is restructured, one person in the organization must have primary responsibility for maintaining the disaster recovery plan. Organizations must have a full-time or part-time disaster recovery coordinator in place, or appoint a middle to high-level manager from an administrative department to lead the effort. Deciding who to keep as a lead person for disaster recovery planning will probably depend on available resources.

ESTABLISHING A MONITORING PROCESS

A major difficulty in maintaining a disaster recovery plan is determining when changes are needed to the plan or procedures. Many changes may be needed as a result of renovations, new construction, or the acquisition of new buildings or new equipment. Table 11-4 shows U.S. capital expenditures during 1999 and 2000. Each expenditure may have resulted in alterations or additions that required disaster recovery procedures to be updated.

Table 11-4 U.S. capital expenditures, 1999 and 2000

Capital items	2000 (Millions of U.S. $)	1999 (Millions of U.S. $)
Structures		
New	$327,870	$296,496
Used	$39,723	$23,583
Total structures	$367,593	$320,079
Equipment		
New	$758,043	$689,553
Used	$45,989	$37,321
Total equipment	$804,032	$726,874
Total capital expenditures	$1,171,625	$1,046,953

Source: U.S. Census Bureau[1]

To develop the disaster recovery plan, the planning team processed information from dozens, if not hundreds, of relevant laws, social conditions, exposures, and risks. After the plan is put into effect, the team must establish a **disaster recovery plan monitoring process** to keep information coming from all of these sources.

When new information becomes available that requires changes to plans and procedures, the disaster recovery plan maintenance team needs to modify existing procedures or add new ones. New procedures must be developed in the same manner as original procedures. Modifying existing procedures is less complex, but the modified procedures still require reviews and testing.

To monitor internal changes that require revisions to disaster recovery plans and procedures, the managers and employees who are most directly involved in affected areas should be the primary source of information about needed changes. Table 11-5 shows several internal sources of information to update procedures. These sources should be assigned the responsibility of keeping the disaster recovery coordinator and team updated with information that requires changes to plans and procedures.

11

Table 11-5 Internal sources of information to update procedures

Type of information	Source of information
Changes in staff that require changes in contact persons, team composition, and notification lists	Human Resources Department, business unit managers, department managers
Changes in facilities that require revisions to evacuation procedures, building plans for use by responders, and maps that show the location of dangerous or valuable materials	Property managers, building maintenance staff, plant engineers, department managers
Changes in the manufacturing process that introduce new materials or eliminate existing materials that may be hazardous	Manufacturing managers, product designers, research and development staff
Changes in computer systems or networks that require new procedures	IT and Network Management departments
Changes or additions to art, antique, or collectible inventories that require new documentation to be compiled about their value and location	Department managers, collection curators, collection managers
Changes or additions to the historic documents inventory, which require new documentation to be compiled about their value and location	Department managers, collection curators, collection managers
Changes in business relationships that require contact lists to be modified or updated	Business unit managers, department managers
Changes in the use of life forms that require procedures to be modified	Manufacturing managers, product designers, research and development staff
Changes in the types of perishable foods and materials or controlled substances that require modifications of procedures	Manufacturing managers, product designers, research and development staff
Changes in the manufacturing process that introduce new precision equipment or rare materials, and require changes in procedures	Manufacturing managers, product designers, research and development staff
New trade secrets and proprietary processes, or changes to where information is stored	Manufacturing managers, department managers, research and development staff
Changes in any laws or regulations that govern any activity of the organization, and may affect disaster recovery plans and procedures	Legal counsel, manufacturing managers, department managers, research and development staff

An organization has many sources of information for monitoring external changes that require revisions to disaster recovery plans and procedures. However, unlike internal sources of information, an organization has little control over external sources. These organizations can be contacted on a regular basis to determine if changes are necessary. Active participation in local and regional disaster response organizations, industry organizations, and business organizations is an excellent way to develop relationships that can facilitate the flow of information.

Table 11-6 shows several external sources of information that can help determine whether updates to procedures are necessary. The organizations listed as sources of information should be contacted frequently to keep the disaster recovery coordinator and team apprised of information that requires changes to plans and procedures.

Table 11-6   External sources of information to update procedures

Type of information	Source of information
Additional or reduced emergency services for local response organizations	Emergency service organizations, local and regional disaster response organizations
Changes in roads, exits, access, and public construction projects	Local and state Public Works departments
Additions or changes to regional manufacturing facilities that may eliminate threats or introduce new threats	Local and state Public Works departments, chambers of commerce, local or regional business organizations
Changes in public utility infrastructures that may eliminate threats or introduce new threats	Local and state Public Works departments, public utilities
Changes in flood plain management, waterway management, land use, or environmental management practices that may eliminate threats or introduce new threats	Local, state, and federal Public Works departments, regional planning commissions
Changes in laws or regulations that may affect an organization directly or indirectly	Local, state, and federal Public Works departments, industry organizations, professional organizations

11

Depending on an organization's activities and locations, it may also need to monitor changes in political and social conditions that could constitute threats. In an age of terrorism, such monitoring is essential for multinational organizations, defense and security organizations, and organizations that have high profiles because of economic, political, or social policies.

Table 11-7 shows several sources of information that can help determine whether political or social conditions require updates to procedures. The organizations listed as sources of information should be contacted frequently to keep the disaster recovery coordinator and team apprised of information that requires changes to plans and procedures.

Table 11-7 Sources of information for political and social conditions

Type of information	Source of information
Internal and cross-border terrorist threats in specific countries or locations	National law enforcement agencies such as the FBI and counterparts in other countries
General security conditions and alerts for specific regions or countries	The U.S. Department of State and counterparts in other countries
Shifts in political, economic, and social conditions in specific countries	The U.S. Department of State and counterparts in other countries; international organizations such as the World Bank and the United Nations
Specific threats against a facility, organization, or management staff	National law enforcement agencies such as the FBI and counterparts in other countries; private security contractors
Security conditions and alerts for specific industry groups	Industry associations, business organizations

Because information can come from so many sources, as shown in Tables 11-5 through 11-7, systematic processes must be implemented to maintain an orderly flow of information to the disaster recovery coordinator and planning team. Planners should distribute a standardized **disaster planning monitoring report** to all employees within an organization, and to all people who act as liaisons or contact points for external sources of information, to report actions or changes that may require a review of disaster recovery procedures.

Table 11-8 shows a sample disaster planning monitoring report. This report can be submitted on paper or electronically through a Web site or an intranet. The disaster planning coordinator should routinely review these reports and place them on the agenda of the disaster recovery planning team for action.

Table 11-8 Sample disaster planning monitoring report

<table>
<tr><td colspan="2" align="center">**Disaster Planning Monitoring Report**
Date submitted: _____</td></tr>
<tr>
<td>Report submitted by:
Name:_____
Title:_____
Address: _____
_____
_____
Telephone: _____
E-mail:_____</td>
<td>How should this report be handled?
(Please circle one)

Urgent—Must be addressed immediately

Important—Must be addressed in less
than two weeks

Routine—Can be addressed at
next meeting</td>
</tr>
<tr>
<td colspan="2">Briefly describe the circumstance, and explain why the disaster recovery planning team should deal with this issue. (Please attach supporting documentation.)</td>
</tr>
<tr>
<td colspan="2">Please list the source(s) of information used to support this report:</td>
</tr>
<tr>
<td colspan="2">Which specific procedure(s) should be modified as a result of this information? (Please list procedure number and name, or describe procedure.)</td>
</tr>
</table>

11

MONITORING COMPLIANCE WITH PROCEDURES

In addition to monitoring changes in the organization or external environment that may require modified disaster recovery plans and procedures, the planning team must monitor compliance with procedures. Because organizations change quickly and facilities are often remodeled or renovated, some recovery procedures could be affected inadvertently.

In addition, the implementation and testing of the disaster recovery plan may have required changes in shutdown or lockdown procedures, the storage and handling of materials, or the design of labs or manufacturing areas. These changes may have been necessary to improve evacuation response time or the speed with which systems or processes could be shut down in dangerous conditions or situations.

The disaster recovery coordinator and planning team can conduct monitoring on a random basis, or they can systematize the process with regularly scheduled reviews of important egress paths, as well as important procedures for shutdowns or evacuations. In addition, programs can be implemented to allow employees to report violations of required procedures.

In such reviews, it is more convenient to inspect specific areas of a building for all possible violations. This approach requires a list of procedures or configuration requirements to be maintained to ease the monitoring process. Each department, in conjunction with the disaster recovery coordinator and planning team, should maintain a list of procedures and requirements that directly affect the immediate work area and processes used in it. Table 11-9 shows a sample **disaster recovery procedure inventory sheet** ; it has spaces for the procedure number, the purpose of the procedure, and the compliance status.

All monitoring reports should be submitted to the disaster recovery coordinator's office for review and action by the planning team. Of course, there may be some logical reason why a specific work area does not comply with a specific procedure. New technology may have been added, or new government regulations may have required the work group to perform tasks in a certain manner. If so, then the work group should file the appropriate report or request to modify or eliminate the procedure.

Table 11-9 Sample disaster recovery procedure inventory sheet

Procedure number	Procedure purpose	Compliance status (circle one)
Lab0101	Monitoring lab conditions	In compliance Not in compliance Not auditable
Lab0201 to 0234	Evacuating lab areas	In compliance Not in compliance Not auditable
Lab0301 to 0321	Securing rare material	In compliance Not in compliance Not auditable
Lab0401 to 0414	Securing hazardous material and disposing of hazardous material	In compliance Not in compliance Not auditable
Lab0501 to 0527	Protecting life forms	In compliance Not in compliance Not auditable
Lab0551 to 0559	Moving lab specimens	In compliance Not in compliance Not auditable
Lab0571 to 0574	Daytime storage of lab specimens	In compliance Not in compliance Not auditable
Lab0581 to 0589	Overnight storage of lab specimens	In compliance Not in compliance Not auditable

11

EVALUATING NEW TECHNOLOGIES

Technologies are constantly evolving, which means that some of the technology an organization deploys can become obsolete. In addition, a relatively constant stream of new technologies can be deployed, either to reduce costs or improve operations. In general, each new wave of technology has design features that eliminate or reduce problems with previous models. Table 11-10 shows a model of technology design and marketing cycles devised by the author while teaching Technology Forecasting at the University of Denver.

Table 11-10 Technology design and marketing cycles

Technology is designed and marketed to meet perceived needs

↓

Customer accepts or rejects products	Competition drives changes through a race for functionality and reliability
↓	↓
Vendors monitor customer response	Vendors assess competitive products
↓	↓

Vendors develop and market new models based on customer response and competitive products

All manufacturers want to expand market share, increase product use, increase revenue, and increase profit. When manufacturers introduce new products, a variety of market research and sales activities often accompany the introduction. These activities include interviews with customers, market penetration and unit sales reports by market research firms, and advertising and sales efforts.

All of these activities provide an input cycle and feedback for product developers. The feedback is used to enhance a product's competitive position by improving its functionality and cost effectiveness, or at least creating an image of improvement.

Customers then respond by evaluating how well the new technology fits with their product mix or how well it can replace existing products. The purchasing decision for most organizations with complex technology infrastructures and architectures is very sophisticated. Table 11-11 shows a typical technology acquisition and evaluation process for a large organization.

Table 11-11 Technology acquisition and evaluation

Technology is designed and marketed to meet perceived needs		
↓		
Customer evaluates technology		
Does the vendor have a good reputation for this type of technology and the support required to deploy it?		
Yes ↓	No →	Alternative products are evaluated
Does the technology fit well in the customer's environment?		
Yes ↓	No →	Alternative products are evaluated
Is the cost of ownership acceptable?		
Yes ↓	No →	Alternative products are evaluated
Does the technology introduce new problems or weaknesses?		
No ↓	Yes →	Alternative products are evaluated
Technology is acquired and deployed		
Does the technology meet the expectations of the customer, and is the technology reliable and cost effective?		
Yes ↓	No →	Alternative products are evaluated
Additional units are purchased and older units are upgraded		

As technology evolves and customer expectations of technology become more sophisticated, the demands of the customer increase. The downtime of computer systems and peripherals, for example, was a major issue in the late 1980s and early 1990s. Customers started comparing the mean time between failure of the products they were considering for purchase. Technology manufacturers responded by improving the reliability of products.

11

Computers, for example, were equipped with dual power supplies, redundant processors, and redundant internal disk drives. The operating-system software was designed to detect failure, route activities to working components, and even place a service call for repairs to be made. Various types of reliable storage products were brought to market, including RAID architectures and networked storage devices for backup.

In the late 1990s, many organizations became more concerned about computer and network security. As a result, manufacturers introduced a wave of more secure products, as well as an array of add-on products to improve computer and network security.

The technology design and marketing process will continue with the same marketing and feedback cycles. As technology becomes more reliable and more resilient to failure, organizations will have new opportunities to acquire and deploy technologies that can reduce downtime and ease the process of disaster recovery.

ACCOMMODATING CHANGES BETWEEN ORGANIZATIONS

To maintain operations at the highest possible level, disaster recovery plans and procedures are designed to deal with relationships between organizations, including relationships with business partners, suppliers, service providers, and customers. All employees who are familiar with an organization's business relationships should use the disaster planning monitoring report.

A major item to keep current in the disaster recovery plan is the contact list. This list helps the communications team to quickly and efficiently contact business partners, suppliers, service providers, and customers. If contact lists are outdated, the communications team cannot respond as quickly, and all of the organizations involved may suffer greater disruption and inconvenience. Table 11-12 is a checklist of typical procedures and information that affect business relationships. The disaster recovery coordinator, as well as departments involved with business partners, can use this list to guide their audits of procedures and information that relate to business partners.

Table 11-12 Checklist for auditing procedures that affect business relationships

Information to keep updated
Names and contact information for liaisons in business-partner organizations that must be contacted in a disaster
Account numbers used to purchase or sell products or services to or from business partners
Procedures related to processing orders with business partners during a disaster
Procedures related to handling incoming material or supplies from business partners during a disaster
Procedures related to handling outgoing material or supplies from business partners during a disaster
Procedures for halting or postponing services from business partners during a disaster
Procedures for initiating emergency and disaster recovery services from contractors
Procedures for rerouting telecommunications, data communications, and network access from service providers
Procedures for activating hot-site or cold-site services with providers
Procedures to account for personnel from business partners that may be on site at a facility when a disaster strikes

A variety of changes can occur in relationships between organizations. For example, your organization might merge with business partners or acquire them. Both circumstances can pose considerable challenges for disaster recovery planners. Table 11-13 shows several possible changes in organizational relationships that disaster recovery planners might need to address.

Table 11-13 Possible changes in relationships between organizations

Type of change
Business partner is acquired by your organization or merges with it
Two business partners merge with each other
Business partner is acquired by another organization with which there was no prior relationship, or merges with the organization
Business partner goes out of business
Your organization is acquired by another organization, or merges with it

If an organization acquires another organization that was a business partner in the past, the disaster recovery planning team needs to bring the acquired organization fully into the planning process. This may require developing a new disaster recovery plan for the acquired facilities and operations. If the acquired organization already has a recovery plan in place, then it must be evaluated to ensure its consistency with management goals for disaster recovery.

If an organization acquires an organization with which there was no previous relationship, the acquired organization must be assimilated into the disaster recovery plan. This process is slightly different than that for an organization with a past relationship, because there was no prior work on disaster planning.

If a business partner is acquired by another organization, then disaster recovery planners need to develop new relationships with the acquiring organization and update contact lists. Existing procedures need to be evaluated in conjunction with the new ownership to ensure that procedures are still workable, or to ensure that needed changes are recommended. If your organization is acquired by another organization or merges with it, then the disaster recovery plans also need to be integrated.

Establishing Regularly Scheduled Reviews

Maintaining disaster recovery plans requires discipline and appropriate resource allocation. The disaster recovery planning team, with the support of management, should establish a structured review process that prevents the recovery plan from becoming outdated. The monitoring process described earlier in this chapter provides a steady stream of input and a means of keeping the plan up to date. However, without the discipline of regularly scheduled comprehensive reviews, the plan could become outdated without anyone in the organization realizing it.

Some departments are more disciplined than others in monitoring themselves and submitting monitoring reports to the disaster recovery coordinator for action by the planning team. Managers and employees usually balance numerous priorities; when they do not see an immediate return on investment for an activity, they give the activity lower priority.

The disaster recovery coordinator can take several approaches to ensure that regular reviews take place. Table 11-14 shows several approaches that can encourage more reviews of the disaster recovery plan and procedures. The table also shows the advantages and disadvantages of each approach.

Table 11-14 Approaches to scheduling reviews

Approaches to scheduling reviews	Advantages	Disadvantages
Set dates for comprehensive review of the entire disaster recovery plan	Ensures complete reviews of all plans and procedures	Time consuming, and requires considerable resources
Allow departments or facilities to schedule their own reviews and monitor themselves	Requires fewer resources than comprehensive review, and allows unit independence and autonomy	Time consuming, and requires considerable resources
Schedule reviews in departments and facilities that have not submitted monitoring reports during the last six months	Focuses on units or facilities that have put forth the least effort	Does not cover the entire organization
Conduct spot checks of compliance with procedures in all units and facilities, and then require comprehensive reviews in areas with the most problems	Covers the entire organization and identifies the weakest areas	Spot checks are not comprehensive in coverage

Disaster recovery planners should bear in mind that many departments and employees may embrace the planning process at first. However, the attention and fascination with disaster recovery planning may falter a bit after so much work is put into a plan. The terrorist attacks of September 11, 2001, did raise the consciousness of many people about the necessity for disaster recovery planning. However, these jolts often fade as quickly as they occur.

Even in the most favorable circumstances, some employees or departments resent how much time is dedicated to disaster recovery planning. In such cases, resistance can build, and some managers may even complain to upper management about the resources that recovery planning requires.

The disaster recovery planning team needs to anticipate such resistance, and develop methods to prevent it from hindering plan maintenance efforts. Table 11-15 shows several methods that can help counter resistance to maintaining the disaster recovery plan and procedures.

Table 11-15 Methods to counter resistance to disaster recovery planning

Give recognition to departments and facilities that help to keep disaster recovery plans and procedures updated
Give recognition to employees who do outstanding work to keep disaster recovery plans and procedures updated
Schedule regular motivational presentations about the importance of maintaining the plan
Include plan maintenance in the duties of department managers
Include efforts to maintain the plan in the performance evaluations of department managers
Reiterate the importance of maintaining the plan when there is national or local news about disasters

11

UPDATING DOCUMENTATION FOR DISASTER RECOVERY PLANS

As changes are made to the disaster recovery plan and procedures, the disaster planning document manager must revise all existing copies of the recovery plan. In addition, all parties who have copies of the plan must be notified of the changes, and instructed to review the changes.

Changes should be made to each documentation method and then edited to ensure correctness. All hyperlinks should also be tested to ensure that the document is working properly. Table 11-16 is a checklist for managing updates to intranet and Web server documents. The steps in the checklist help to maintain quality control.

Table 11-16 Checklist for managing updates to intranet and Web server documents

Quality-control steps for updates
Verify that the source documents used to make updates are the correct versions
Transfer documentation into the proper format for the intranet or Web server
Make sure all information has been transferred from source documents
Use spell-checking software, if available
If necessary, create graphics, tables, and charts
Have an editor read the intranet and Web server versions to ensure accuracy
Have an editor review the graphics, tables, and charts in the intranet and Web server versions to ensure accuracy
If applicable, check all hyperlinks from a remote station to ensure that they work properly
Post change notices on the intranet and Web server
Notify all users that changes have been made

Updating paper or CD-ROM versions of disaster recovery documents requires several more steps than updating intranet or Web server versions of the documents. If paper documents are used, employees must receive instructions for removing and inserting material from older binders or books. If CD-ROM or paper versions are used, employees must receive instructions for returning or disposing of previous versions. Table 11–17 is a checklist for managing updates to paper and CD-ROM documents. The steps in the checklist help to maintain quality control.

Table 11-17 Checklist for managing updates to paper and CD-ROM documents

Quality-control steps for updates
Verify that the source documents used to make updates are the correct versions
Transfer documentation into the proper format for paper or CD-ROM documents
Make sure all information has been transferred from source documents
Use spell-checking software, if available
If necessary, create graphics, tables, and charts
Have an editor read paper or CD-ROM versions to ensure accuracy
Have an editor review the graphics, tables, and charts in paper or CD-ROM versions to ensure accuracy
If applicable, check all hyperlinks on the CD-ROM to ensure that they work properly
For paper versions, write update instructions to show which old sections should be removed and which sections should be added; instructions should also be given for returning or destroying older paper documents
For CD-ROM versions, include instructions for returning or destroying older versions
Notify all users that changes have been made

Updating Training Programs

A major challenge in maintaining a high level of disaster preparedness is to make sure that training materials are updated and that employees are trained on current procedures. This challenge includes ensuring that new employees are appropriately trained on the disaster recovery plan in general, and on specific plans and procedures in their department, work area, or facility.

Establishing a process to train new employees is critical to the success of disaster preparedness. As shown in Table 11-18, an average organization can expect a turnover rate of three to four percent per year. In some professional fields, turnover rates can be even higher.

Thus, the Human Resources Department, disaster recovery coordinator, Training Department, and department managers throughout the organization need to cooperate to ensure that new employees receive training. New employees must be scheduled for training; when training is complete, the employees' personnel files must be updated to indicate their participation. Department managers must be willing to schedule time for new employees to attend training and reinforce its importance.

Table 11-18 Turnover and new hire rates for an average organization

Changes in employees	May 2002	May 2001
New hire rate (number of hires during the month, divided by employment)	3.7%	4.3%
Separation rate (number of separations during the month, divided by employment)	3.1%	3.7%

Source: U.S. Bureau of Labor Statistics[2]

Just as disaster recovery documentation must be updated when changes are made, the training material and training status of employees must also be updated. Updating training material requires quality control steps similar to those for distributed disaster recovery documents. When new procedures are added, new training materials are also needed to cover the new procedures. Table 11-19 is a checklist for maintaining quality control when updating training materials.

11

Table 11-19 Checklist for updating training materials

Quality-control steps for updating training materials
Verify that the source documents used to make updates are the correct versions
Transfer documentation into the proper format for training materials, including training manuals and PowerPoint presentations
If necessary, create graphics, tables, and charts
Use spell-checking software, if available
Have an editor read the training material for accuracy and correctness
Have the disaster recovery coordinator review the revised or new training material
Rehearse the revised or new training modules
If necessary, modify the revised or new training modules
Conduct pilot tests of revised or new training modules with employees
Have employees complete evaluation forms for the training sessions
If necessary, modify the revised or new training modules based on employee evaluations

After the organization updates training materials to reflect changes in the disaster recovery plan and procedures, it must review the training status of all employees to determine who should be retrained. Organizations should review training records to find the last time each employee completed training modules that have since been modified. An organization should schedule an adequate number of training sessions to ensure that all employees are kept current in their training.

CHAPTER SUMMARY

- After the disaster recovery planning team has developed, implemented, and tested an organization's recovery plans and procedures, the team enters a new phase of operation. In maintenance mode, the team monitors, tests, and modifies the disaster recovery plan to keep it current with changes in organizational structure, business operations, and new technologies.

- A major difficulty in maintaining a disaster recovery plan is determining when changes are needed to the plan or procedures. To develop the disaster recovery plan, the planning team processed information from dozens, if not hundreds, of relevant laws, social conditions, exposures, and risks. After the plan is put into effect, the team must establish a disaster recovery plan monitoring process to keep information coming from all of these sources.

- In addition to monitoring changes in the organization or external environment that may require modified disaster recovery plans and procedures, the planning team must monitor compliance with procedures. Because organizations change quickly and facilities are often remodeled or renovated, some recovery procedures could be affected inadvertently.

- Technologies are constantly evolving, which means that some of the technology an organization deploys can become obsolete. In addition, a relatively constant stream of new technologies can be deployed, either to reduce costs or improve operations. In general, each new wave of technology has design features that eliminate or reduce problems with previous models. The technology design and marketing process will continue with the same marketing and feedback cycles. As technology becomes more reliable and more resilient to failure, organizations will have new opportunities to acquire and deploy technologies that can reduce downtime and ease the process of disaster recovery.

◻ To maintain operations at the highest possible level, disaster recovery plans and procedures are designed to deal with relationships between organizations, including those with business partners, suppliers, service providers, and customers. All employees who are familiar with an organization's business relationships should use the disaster planning monitoring report.

◻ Maintaining disaster recovery plans requires discipline and appropriate resource allocation. The disaster recovery planning team, with the support of management, should establish a structured review process that prevents the recovery plan from becoming outdated. The monitoring process described in this chapter provides a steady stream of input and a means of keeping the plan up to date. However, without the discipline of regularly scheduled comprehensive reviews, the plan could become outdated without anyone in the organization realizing it.

◻ As changes are made to the disaster recovery plan and procedures, the disaster planning document manager must revise all existing copies of the recovery plan. In addition, all parties who have copies of the plan must be notified of the changes, and instructed to review the changes.

◻ Just as disaster recovery documentation must be updated when changes are made, the training material and training status of employees must also be updated. Updating training material requires quality control steps similar to those for distributed disaster recovery documents. When new procedures are added, new training materials are also needed to cover the new procedures.

KEY TERMS

disaster planning monitoring report — A standardized report of actions or changes that may require a review of disaster recovery procedures. This report can be filed by employees or by liaisons and contacts outside the organization.

disaster recovery plan monitoring process — A process for monitoring changes in laws, social conditions, exposures, and risks to determine if revisions are needed in the disaster recovery plan.

disaster recovery procedure inventory sheet — A form that shows the compliance status of departments with disaster recovery procedures.

maintenance mode — The next step after the disaster recovery plan is developed, implemented, and tested. The purpose of the maintenance mode is to monitor, test, and modify the recovery plan to keep it current with changes in organizational structure, business operations, and new technologies.

REVIEW QUESTIONS

1. Explain the meaning of the maintenance mode in disaster recovery planning.

2. What are the advantages of keeping corporate security representatives as full-time members of the disaster recovery planning team during the maintenance mode?

3. What are the advantages of keeping representatives of the IT and Network Management departments as full-time members of the disaster recovery planning team during the maintenance mode?

4. What are the major options for keeping a person in the organization who has primary responsibilities for maintaining the disaster recovery plan?

5. What internal sources can provide information to update contact persons, team composition, and notification lists in the disaster recovery plan?

6. What internal sources can provide information to revise procedures that become outdated because of changes to evacuation procedures, building plans for use by responders, and maps that show the location of dangerous or valuable materials?

7. What internal sources can provide information to revise procedures because of changes in the manufacturing process that introduce new materials or eliminate existing materials that may be hazardous?

8. What external sources can provide information to update procedures because of additional or reduced emergency services for local response organizations?

9. What external sources can provide information to update procedures because of changes in roads, exits, access, and public construction projects?

10. What external sources can provide information to update procedures because of changes in laws or regulations that may affect an organization directly or indirectly?

11. What organizations can provide information to update procedures because of internal and cross-border terrorist threats in specific countries or locations?

12. What organizations can provide information to update procedures because of shifts in political, economic, and social conditions in specific countries?

13. What organizations can provide information to update procedures because of changes in security conditions and alerts for specific industry groups?

14. Explain the handling instructions of "urgent," "important," and "routine" on the disaster planning monitoring report, and how the planning team should respond to these instructions.

15. Explain three approaches to monitoring compliance with procedures that are designed to ease disaster recovery.

16. Why should organizations monitor new technologies in consideration of their disaster recovery needs?

17. What possible changes in organizational relationships might disaster recovery planners need to address?

18. What are the advantages and disadvantages of setting dates for a comprehensive review of the entire disaster recovery plan?

19. What are the advantages and disadvantages of allowing departments or facilities to set their own schedules and monitor themselves when reviewing the disaster recovery plan to support maintenance efforts?

20. What methods can you use to overcome resistance to ongoing maintenance of the disaster recovery plan?

21. What steps should you take to ensure quality control when updating intranet or Web server versions of the disaster recovery plan?

22. What steps should you take to ensure quality control when updating training modules for the disaster recovery plan?

HANDS-ON PROJECTS

In the following projects, you will assess portions of the disaster recovery plan for the organization you have been assisting throughout this book. When you finish, submit the materials to your instructor for review.

Project 11-1

Evaluate options for moving the organization's disaster recovery planning team into maintenance mode. Analyze the advantages and disadvantages of each option and make a recommendation. Consider at least the options shown in Table 11-1.

Project 11-2

Identify internal sources of information to update recovery procedures for the organization. Identify the sources by title and name, and provide contact information for them. At minimum, identify sources for making changes to the types of information shown in Table 11-5.

Project 11-3

Identify external sources of information to update recovery procedures for the organization. Identify the sources by title and name, and provide contact information for them. At minimum, identify sources for making changes to the types of information shown in Table 11-6.

Project 11-4

Identify sources of information for political and social conditions that you can use to update the organization's disaster recovery procedures. Identify the sources by title and name, and provide contact information for them. At minimum, identify sources for the following types of information:

- Internal and cross-border terrorist threats in specific countries or locations
- General security conditions and alerts for specific regions or countries
- Shifts in political, economic, and social conditions in specific countries
- Specific threats against a facility, organization, or management staff
- Security conditions and alerts for specific industry groups

Project 11-5

Devise a system to monitor compliance with procedures designed to ease the organization's disaster recovery process. The procedure can use one or more of the following approaches:

- Random monitoring by the disaster recovery planning coordinator
- Regularly scheduled checks by department managers
- A system for employees to report violations

Project 11-6

Determine an approach for scheduling reviews of the organization's disaster recovery plan. Evaluate each of the following approaches, then select one or more that work best for the organization.

- Set dates for comprehensive review of the entire disaster recovery plan.
- Allow departments or facilities to schedule their own reviews and monitor themselves.
- Schedule reviews in departments and facilities that have not submitted monitoring reports during the last six months.
- Conduct spot checks of compliance with procedures in all units and facilities, and then require comprehensive reviews in the areas where you discover the most problems.

Project 11-7

Select a method to counter resistance to allocating resources for maintaining the organization's disaster recovery plan. Evaluate each of the approaches shown in Table 11-15, then select one or more that work best for the organization.

CASE PROJECTS

CASE PROJECTS

Case Project: Harris and Heartfield Manufacturing

Harris and Heartfield Manufacturing is a family-owned business that fabricates specialized metal parts for its North American clients. Most of its revenue comes from defense contracts and from producing parts for heavy-equipment manufacturers. The company has an excellent reputation for quality and prompt deliveries.

The company has 200 employees at its only location in California. All 20 administrative employees have desktop PCs connected to the company's LAN. The 15 research and design engineers use Sun workstations that are also on the LAN. Three servers support administrative functions and six servers support design and manufacturing. About half the machining equipment on the shop floor is computerized.

Management is concerned about the company's future competitiveness, and about its ability to fulfill orders if a disaster hindered its operations. The board of directors is relatively business-savvy, but does not invest money unless it yields a positive return. As a result, the company hired you as a consultant to create a list of 10 key points that conveyed the importance of disaster recovery planning to the board. You also prepared 10 points for managers to discuss with employees about organizing and preparing to develop a plan.

You worked with company managers to analyze business process threats to product manufacturing, developed a list of questions about insurance coverage, and advised the company how to develop a disaster response team. You also developed a list of organizations that the company should work with in a disaster, developed guidelines for reporting computer hacking incidents to law enforcement agencies, created a questionnaire to help determine whether recovery procedures were needed for special circumstances, and outlined awareness campaigns for employees, customers, and business partners. In the previous chapter, you developed a list of possible scenarios to test the company's disaster recovery plan and procedures.

Your assignment now is to prepare a briefing session for company managers to discuss how they should enter the maintenance mode for their disaster recovery plan. Based on the material in this chapter, prepare 10 discussion points for the management team. Next, create a PowerPoint presentation that covers the 10 points, why the points are important, and the action steps that Harris and Heartfield should take to enter the maintenance mode.

11

OPTIONAL TEAM CASE PROJECTS

OPTIONAL CASE PROJECTS

Team Case One

Your boss has asked you to determine how outside organizations can help ensure that your organization maintains its disaster recovery plan and keeps it up to date. Your assignment is to research and identify organizations that can provide motivational speakers to visit your organization and make presentations on the importance of maintaining disaster recovery plans. Write a one-page summary of each organization, what services it can provide, appropriate contacts in the organizations, and how and where you obtained the information.

OPTIONAL
CASE
PROJECTS

Team Case Two

Your boss has asked you to work with the Human Resources and Training departments to establish a process to ensure that new employees receive training on the disaster recovery plan. Your assignment is to work with the departments to develop appropriate policies and a process to ensure that training occurs. After consultation with the departments, write a summary of how the organization should ensure that employees are trained.

ENDNOTES

1. U.S. Census Bureau (*www.census.gov*).

2. U.S. Bureau of Labor Statistics (*www.bls.gov*).

12

LIVING THROUGH A DISASTER

After reading this chapter, you will be able to:
◆ Develop tactics to deal with human dynamics during a disaster
◆ Deal with increasing complexity during a disaster
◆ Conduct post-event debriefings
◆ Conduct post-event evaluations of response
◆ Review and modify plans after a disaster
◆ Understand the residual effects of a disaster

Organizations face many challenges when a disaster strikes. Among the most difficult challenges is managing staff during a disaster. Human behavior changes during an emergency, sometimes for the better and sometimes for the worse. Disaster recovery response teams must deal with the stress that disasters cause employees, families, and business partners.

It is also important to learn from disasters. The knowledge and experience gained by living through a disaster needs to be captured and used to modify disaster recovery plans and procedures. This requires a series of debriefings and evaluations that can generate actions to improve plans, procedures, and day-to-day operations.

Managers and planners must also recognize that disasters can have long-term residual effects on individual employees and entire organizations. In the case of the September 11, 2001, terrorist attacks, political processes and social perceptions were altered in the United States and much of the world. A balanced perspective is needed to transform such events into a constructive learning process.

MANAGING HUMAN DYNAMICS DURING A DISASTER

The dynamics of human behavior during disasters are almost impossible to predict. Organizations face fluctuating emotions of employees, as well as those of the communities, social environments, and political arenas in which the organization exists. The breadth of a disaster's impact usually becomes apparent only through personal experience or the news coverage an event receives.

There are many disasters around the world, details of which seldom reach the local television news or newspapers. To explore the human dynamic during a disaster, it is helpful to look at disasters from a global perspective.

For the last 30 years, the Munich Re Group has conducted research on the effects of disaster for the insurance industry and loss prevention.[1] Munich Re reported that in 2002, about 11,000 people around the world were killed in approximately 700 natural catastrophes. The economic losses for 2002 reached U.S. $55 billion, with insured losses calculated at $11.5 billion. In 2001, at least 25,000 people lost their lives in disasters; economic losses reached U.S. $36 billion, and insured losses were $11.5 billion.

Disaster recovery planners must conduct mitigation assessments and determine what can be done to prevent disasters, as discussed in preceding chapters. Natural disasters can seldom be prevented, but well-designed safety programs can reduce the number of industrial accidents. Table 12-1 shows the number of industrial accidents by year from 1975 to 2001, along with the total numbers of people killed and affected.

Table 12-1 Industrial accidents by year from 1975 to 2001

Year	Total events	Total killed	Total affected
2001	54	1148	18,804
2000	48	1613	16,618
1999	36	742	3192
1998	43	1942	62,881
1997	35	1033	163,356
1996	35	674	15,912
1995	39	513	27,069
1994	34	779	19,273
1993	36	1244	7790
1992	24	1385	18,263
1991	52	1700	78,925
1990	27	905	8653
1989	24	2209	1007
1988	20	684	42,085
1987	21	626	45,085
1986	10	322	141,045
1985	16	254	106,258
1984	22	4046	352,307
1983	14	358	29,375
1982	12	326	65,147
1981	9	701	30,004
1980	13	377	57,826
1979	17	549	435,853
1978	11	370	16,662
1977	5	373	12,165
1976	5	85	193,423
1975	11	470	20,650

Source: EM-DAT: The OFDA/CRED International Disaster Database, Université catholique de Louvain, Brussels, Belgium[2]

The American Red Cross provides insight into the breadth of several specific disasters:

Taiwan — Powerful aftershocks rumbled across Taiwan on Wednesday, sending shelter residents and rescue teams alike scrambling for the safety of open spaces. There were no reports of additional injuries or damage from the strong tremors, one of which measured 6.8 on the Richter scale, but they hampered search and rescue operations and further strained already frayed nerves on the island nation. The death toll topped 2000 earlier in the day, and Taiwanese officials said perhaps as many as 3000 people still are believed trapped beneath collapsed buildings. More than 4400 people were injured in Tuesday's magnitude-7.6 temblor, and at least 100,000 were left homeless. Rescue and relief operations have been seriously hampered by Taiwan's shattered transportation and communication infrastructures. The earthquake and more than 2000 aftershocks have crippled bridges and highways alike, knocked out electricity and phone service to more than six million people, and shattered water and sanitation systems. [3]

Central America — Honduras, Nicaragua, and other Central American nations on Wednesday found themselves on the brink of a humanitarian nightmare one week after Hurricane Mitch killed at least 9000 people and left one million people homeless. Honduran President Carlos Flores said preliminary damage assessments indicate that Mitch destroyed 70 percent of the country's bridges, 60 percent of its water systems, and 70 percent of its agriculture. The devastated infrastructure is compounding efforts to reach rural areas where many residents have gone more than a week without food or clean water. [4]

China — Waters on the Nen and Songhua rivers reached record heights this week, and more than a million soldiers and civilians have been engaged in a round-the-clock battle to keep the floods at bay. Authorities said 1000 of the [Daqing] field's 20,000 oil wells were closed as a result of the breach and incessant rains, and a massive campaign is under way to create an inland barrier to protect the other wells. The Daqing field produces about half of all of China's oil. The closure of so many wells will only serve to exacerbate the growing economic toll the floods are having on China. Official estimates suggest the floods already have cost $24 billion and will reduce by at least one-half point China's gross domestic product this year. [5]

Nigeria and Colombia — At least 700 people were killed in Nigeria and another 43 killed in Colombia over the weekend when massive explosions ripped through fuel pipelines and sent flames racing through unsuspecting villages. Authorities blamed the inferno in southern Nigeria on thieves who periodically siphon fuel from the myriad above-ground pipelines that link an oil refinery in the town of Warri with the capital city of Lagos. Officials with Nigeria's state-owned oil corporation said the thieves probably sparked the explosion with the tools they used to break into the pipe. On the other side of the globe in Colombia, rebels were blamed for a weekend gas-line blast that killed at least 43 people and injured 100 others. The explosion occurred in a rural village about 180 miles north of Bogota. [6]

In addition to the terrorist attacks of September 11, 2001, the preceding examples show how far-reaching disasters can be in terms of death toll and economic impact. These descriptions provide a context for exploring human behavior during a disaster.

Table 12-2 shows various types of social dynamics that can occur during and after a disaster. These issues affect how disaster recovery planners should prepare for dealing with human dynamics.

Table 12-2 Social dynamics during a disaster

Social groups	Positive dynamics	Negative dynamics
Employees	Contribute to the overall recovery effort and humanitarian efforts	Become self-serving and territorial in protecting their self-interests that may be affected by events
Families of employees	Provide mutual support and participate in recovery activities	Become impatient and thwart efforts of employees to participate in recovery efforts
Members of local communities	Assist with recovery effort and provide resources and support	Factions take positions about blame and responsibilities when recovery efforts are under way
Elected officials	Provide positive support and help eliminate obstacles to recovery efforts	Use events as a political platform to leverage power base or media exposure
Special interest groups	Provide expert assistance to deal with specific recovery efforts	Use events to promote their own social or political agenda
Suppliers	Assist in smooth recovery by holding or modifying orders on short notice	Exploit opportunities to add service charges, increase prices, or immediately claim contract violations
Business partners	Assist in smooth recovery by adjusting business activities and plans	Exploit opportunities to leverage business favors, modify contracts, or prematurely disrupt long-term relationships
Customers	Assist in smooth recovery by waiting for orders and maintaining proper contact and inquiry procedures	Exploit opportunities to leverage discounts, threaten cancellations, and react impatiently when receiving information on order status

12

During a disaster, an organization's various response teams are standing in the middle of a storm. The pressure to succeed, to save lives, and to restore operations is immense. People are simultaneously concerned about dozens of problems, and can easily become overly stressed. One of the goals of creating a well-designed response team, and a structure that establishes a clear division of labor, is to enable responders to focus on specific tasks.

When the efforts of the various teams are coordinated, disaster response and recovery can move forward in a more orderly manner. An important aspect of the team structure is that distributed responsibilities allow teams to interact with the various constituencies an organization must deal with during disaster response.

Each social group with which the response teams interact has its own agenda, fears, and goals related to the disaster. The shock of events often reduces these agendas, fears, and goals down to a more immediate concern of how the disaster may affect them personally.

In the case of employees and their families, a foremost concern is the safety of family and friends. Some people respond calmly in a disaster, but others may panic. Therefore, it is critical to address the mental health of employees and their families during and after a disaster. When dealing with employees and their families, the best way to shape a potential negative dynamic into a positive one is to start crisis-counseling efforts quickly. Proper planning is essential in initiating rapid crisis counseling; organizations need to know who to contact and who provides the services.

The next closest constituency of an organization is usually the community in which facilities are located. In that community, an organization is likely to have friends and foes, both of which are more than willing to participate in the human dynamics of the disaster. Friends will be helpful and supportive. However, foes often prey on the opportunity to dispense criticism of the organization and bring a negative tone to the aftermath of a disaster.

Elected officials are part of the community or country in which a facility is located. Although some officials might try to exploit the misfortune of others for their own political gain, many of them can contribute to positive dynamics during response and recovery. Some elected officials work to mobilize the resources of local, state, and federal governments to assist in disaster recovery efforts.

Special interest groups, especially those that are opposed to an organization's policies, practices, or activities, may very well take the opportunity to say "I told you so" after a disaster. Such statements can generate press coverage for these groups, and motivate their members and believers to contribute money.

When skilled public relations staff are part of the disaster recovery team, they can help to formulate responses to situations in which community members, elected officials, and special interest groups attempt to exploit promotional opportunities. It is best, however, not to focus on fighting with such groups during a disaster. Public relations professionals interviewed for this chapter advise organizations to take the high ground and focus on efforts to care for employees and families, and to restore operations as quickly as possible for the good of everyone affected.

Suppliers, business partners, and customers can also be a source of support or a source of difficulty during a disaster. History will be played out when dealing with these groups. If relationships have been positive in the past, suppliers, business partners, and customers will probably be supportive. However, if an organization's ethics toward these groups have been less than favorable, even the best customer relations staff and channel managers face a challenge in keeping them satisfied, regardless of the events affecting the organization.

All things considered, a history of negative dynamics and poor relationships can haunt a disaster recovery effort. It is a natural human response to help good citizens, just as it is to show little mercy on those who have inflicted harm in the past. An organization's citizenship record can help determine how social groups respond to the organization.

DEALING WITH INCREASING COMPLEXITY DURING A DISASTER

When things go wrong, there is often a domino effect. The complexities of relationships between organizations, the integration of computer and manufacturing systems, and the overload of emergency response systems intersect during a disaster. This can easily result in unforeseen consequences that compound damages, as this section illustrates.

One area that has just started to attract the attention of disaster planners is how to deal with disabled people during a disaster. As a society, we have worked to make facilities handicapped-accessible, and to make job opportunities available to people with disabilities. Disaster recovery planning requires the same advances.

Imagine yourself on the sixtieth floor of a burning office building. The elevators are not working, and people are running for their lives. If you are in a wheelchair, or blind, or even if you have a broken leg in a cast, you might need special assistance in escaping. Since the terrorist attacks of September 11, 2001, many organizations have started evaluating how to ensure that all people can be evacuated from a building.[7] In many ways, such situations can add to the complexity of disaster recovery efforts and even the aftermath of a disaster.[8]

- First and foremost, people can die or sustain injuries because they cannot get out of a burning building without assistance.

- Attempting to rescue disabled people as an afterthought, without rehearsal or training, and without systems in place can endanger rescuers and slow down the overall response.

- The organization looks unprepared and even foolish. Hiring the physically challenged is good policy, but the disaster recovery plan needs to make provisions for their safety.

- If an organization does not prepare to protect the safety of physically challenged employees during a disaster, it could face a multiyear, multimillion dollar lawsuit.

12

Rest assured, the complexity of a disaster can rapidly increase. The procedures for developing, implementing, and testing a disaster recovery plan are designed to help reduce this complexity.

Timothy P. Cullen, CISSP, CCSA, a senior network security consultant, was one of many participants in the survey that was conducted for this book. He provided some excellent insight:

Disaster recovery processes have become an integral part of any and all businesses. They are living entities and should be treated as such. Recently, our company tested parts of our disaster recovery plan. We failed miserably. It was like the old saying, looks good on paper! But the paper was more tissue than paper. We conducted a debriefing and highlighted all the successes and failures. We assigned timelines for repairs and will test again soon. We made the mistake of treating the disaster recovery [plan] like a finished project, when in actuality it is an ongoing, never-ending, and ever-changing process.

Lance Revo, CISSP, a business continuity expert, also responded to the survey for this book. He also provided excellent insight into human dynamics during disaster response:

The human dynamics are truly dynamic. I remember working at a Nuclear Energy research facility located in an isolated high-plain desert. A maintenance worker changing out a chlorine bottle on the water purification system cross-threaded the connection. Deadly gas quickly spread throughout the building. As the wind moved the gas throughout the site, literally hundreds of employees were evacuated to an area downwind from the source. Over 20 ambulances were requested from a number of small communities approximately 30 miles away.

As the incident unfolded, scores of victims were laid down on the lawn outside the security fence. The collateral effect—those not really in contact with the chlorine but displaying the same symptoms—instantly resulted in additional scores of casualties. We were treating twice the number of victims for shock, unconsciousness, and nausea. It was impossible to determine who was in direct contact with the chlorine gas and those suffering from hysteria. Operations came to a standstill. Those on the disaster recovery team were victims as well; buildings containing disaster recovery plans were inaccessible. Only resourcefulness and on-the-spot decision-making brought order to the chaos. Critical nuclear operations were on autopilot. Fortunately, safety procedures and controls averted an even more serious event.

To help the disaster recovery team plan for events where complexity rapidly increases, it should designate one or more silent observers at the emergency operations center and the facilities that were affected by the disaster. The role of the **silent observer** is to monitor activities and make notes about the disaster response. The observer should monitor all activities, including what went wrong and what went smoothly. The monitoring reports are used in the post-event evaluation.

CONDUCTING POST-EVENT DEBRIEFINGS

Some people say that life is the best teacher. Therefore, organizations need to make sure they evaluate their experiences after surviving a disaster. The **post–event debriefing process** is designed to bring together as many perspectives as possible and capture the lessons people learned during the disaster. This process needs to take place with several groups over a period of time. Table 12-3 shows some of the important groups to debrief after a disaster.

The debriefing process should have both formal and informal aspects. Informal discussion is helpful to encourage people to provide input. The informal approach can be used with employees, their families, and representatives from the local community. There should be at least two leaders in each debriefing session; both should prepare separate notes after each session. Table 12-4 shows some important general topics to cover in the informal post-event debriefings.

Table 12-3 Post-event debriefing groups

Groups to be debriefed
Primary response team members
Emergency operations center staff
Communications team members
Security team members
Rescue team members
Recovery team members
Members of the insurance and damage assessment team
Business continuation team members
Restoration team members
Department managers who are not on any teams
Selected employees from departments throughout the organization
Sample groups of customers, suppliers, and business partners
Sample groups of employees' family members
Representatives from the local community
Members of emergency service organizations and contract disaster recovery firms that responded

Table 12-4 General post-event debriefing topics

Topics for discussion
Overall impressions of individuals or groups about response and recovery
How well the evacuation was executed (if applicable)
How effective the communications team was (if applicable)
The quality of the response by emergency service organizations (if applicable)
The quality of work done by special-purpose contractors (if applicable)
How the news media depicted the event and the response (if applicable)
The quality of leadership during response and recovery (if applicable)
The nature of support from the local community during response and recovery (if applicable)

12

All the members of all disaster response teams should participate in informal discussions. However, because these team members have considerable knowledge and experience to share, they should also participate in very structured debriefings after the disaster. Table 12-5 shows several important, specialized debriefing topics to discuss in sessions with team members.

Table 12-5 Specialized post-event debriefing topics

Specialized topics
What was the best thing that happened during response and recovery?
What was the worst thing that happened during response and recovery?
Which, if any, procedures worked extremely well?
Which, if any, procedures worked very poorly?
Were there any personnel problems during response or recovery?
Were there problems with any of the response teams?
Did problems grow in complexity? If so, why?
Was the speed of response adequate?
Did events happen for which there was no procedure?
What were the strengths and weaknesses of leadership, management, and supervisors?
Is there any expected residual fallout, such as litigation?
Did the IT, computer network, and telecommunications backup systems work as expected?

CONDUCTING POST-EVENT EVALUATIONS OF RESPONSE

A **post-event evaluation** is a structured process used after a disaster to determine what should be changed in the disaster recovery plan and procedures. The disaster recovery team uses several sources of data and information to conduct the evaluation. The basic rule of compiling this data is to use as many sources as possible, and to evaluate circumstances from all perspectives. Table 12-6 shows many important sources of data and information that can be helpful for post-event evaluations.

Table 12-6 Sources of data and information for post-event evaluations

Data or information source
Results of post-event debriefings for all groups for which debriefings were held
Disaster response activity logs that were maintained by the response team
All forms completed during disaster response and recovery
Notes from the various teams that responded, including the primary response team, emergency operations center staff, communications team, security team, rescue team, recovery team, insurance and damage assessment team, business continuation team, and restoration team
Reports completed by any emergency service responders, including ambulance and emergency medical services, fire departments, police departments, hazardous material response teams, regional and local disaster service agencies, vehicle removal services, debris removal services, and building maintenance and construction contractors
Reports completed by any electric power utilities, water and sewer utilities, telecommunications providers, steam service providers, waste removal contractors, road and highway maintenance and repair departments, forestry services, recycling services, environmental protection services, flood control services, animal control and protection agencies, and building inspection agencies

Data or information source
Videotapes and photographs taken during response and recovery efforts
The monitoring reports of the designated silent observers
Correspondence from business partners, suppliers, customers, and organizations in the local community
Reports and response from the insurance companies
If a computer system is involved, then various computer logs and intrusion detection system reports can be used

Post-event evaluations should encompass all activities, plans, and procedures that were affected or used during disaster response. The basic rule of post-event evaluations is to study as many areas as possible, and to consider the perspectives of all people and organizations that were involved or affected. Table 12-7 shows many important areas to review during post-event evaluations.

Table 12-7 Areas to evaluate after a disaster

Area to be evaluated
First alert and disaster declaration procedures
Direction, control, and administration procedures
Internal and external communications procedures
Safety and health procedures
Containment and property protection procedures
Procedures for resuming and recovering operations
Procedures for restoring facilities and normalizing operations
Procedures for special circumstances such as hazardous materials, controlled substances, art, antiques, collectibles, historic documents, perishable foods and materials, trade secrets, life forms, precision equipment, and rare materials
IT, computer network, and telecommunications backup systems
The effectiveness of shutdown and lockdown procedures
Accessibility of the disaster recovery plan and procedures
Performance of response teams and employees
Performance of emergency service responders
Performance of contractors

12

The disaster recovery coordinator should compile the evaluation report with input from the monitors, the response teams, and other applicable sources. Table 12-8 shows an outline of a post-event evaluation report. All involved parties should review a draft copy of the report and submit comments on it to the disaster recovery coordinator. The comments should be used to help compile a final report. All involved parties should receive copies of the final report, and then prepare to modify plans and procedures based on the outcome of the post-event evaluation.

Table 12-8 Outline for post-event evaluation report

Contents
Title page
Table of contents
Executive summary
Event description
Chronology of events
Synthesized results of the debriefing sessions
Synthesized results of reports completed by external responders and in-house response teams
Plans or procedures that should be modified
Recommendations for further training or changes in training content or process
Exhibits and attachments

REVIEWING AND MODIFYING PLANS AFTER A DISASTER

Once the evaluation report is complete, the disaster recovery planning team should review the report, make necessary changes in the recovery plan, and modify specific procedures as needed. All plan revisions and procedure modifications should pass through the full review process, just as they did during development. The planning team and independent reviewers need to check and approve the procedures before placing the final versions in the recovery plan (Table 12-9).

Table 12-9 Checklist for updating disaster plan documents

Quality-control steps for updates
Verify that the source documents being used to make updates are the correct versions
Transfer documentation into the proper format for the intranet, Web server, CD-ROM, or paper copies
Make sure all information has been transferred from source documents
Use spell-checking software, if available
If necessary, create graphics, tables, and charts
Have an editor read the updates to ensure accuracy
Have an editor review the graphics, tables, and charts to ensure accuracy
If applicable, check all hyperlinks from a remote station to ensure that they work properly
Post change notices on the intranet and Web server
Notify all users that changes have been made
Distribute new documents as applicable

Just as disaster recovery documentation must be updated when changes are made, the training materials and training status of employees must also be updated. Updating training materials requires quality–control steps such as those for distributed disaster recovery documents. When new procedures are added, new training materials must also be developed to cover the procedures. Table 12-10 is a checklist for maintaining quality control when updating training materials.

Table 12-10 Checklist for updating training materials

Quality-control steps for updates
Verify that the source documents used to make updates are the correct versions
Transfer documentation into the proper format for training materials, including training manuals and PowerPoint presentations
If necessary, create graphics, tables, and charts
Use spell-checking software, if available
Have an editor read the training material for accuracy and correctness
Have the disaster recovery coordinator review the revised or new training material
Rehearse the revised or new training modules
If necessary, modify the revised or new training modules
Conduct pilot tests of revised or new training modules with employees
Have employees complete evaluation forms for the training sessions
If necessary, modify the revised or new training modules based on employee evaluations

After updating training materials to reflect changes in the disaster recovery plan and procedures, the organization must review the training status of all employees to determine who should be retrained. Organizations should review training records to find the last time each employee completed training modules that have since been modified. An organization should schedule an adequate number of training sessions to ensure that all employees are kept current in their training.

12

UNDERSTANDING THE RESIDUAL EFFECTS OF A DISASTER

The residual effects of disasters can last for several years. One of the more dramatic examples of events with such effects occurred on December 3, 1984, when gas leaked from a tank of methyl isocyanate (MIC) at a plant in Bhopal, India, owned and operated by Union Carbide India Limited (UCIL). The Madhya Pradesh state government of India reported that approximately 3800 people died and 2680 people suffered permanent partial disabilities.[9]

Union Carbide Corporation's (UCC) actions to deal with the disaster and relief for the victims started immediately after the event, when UCC offered more than $20 million in aid that was unrelated to eventual settlements or damages. In April 1985, UCC provided a $2.2 million grant to Arizona State University to establish a vocational–technical training center in Bhopal.

At the request of the Indian Supreme Court, UCC and UCIL agreed in October 1991 to pay about $17 million for a hospital to be built in Bhopal. They later increased the commitment to about $20 million. UCC also gave the hospital and local clinics an additional $54 million from the sale of UCC shares in UCIL. The Bhopal government started construction of the new hospital in October 1995. Beginning with the days immediately following the accident, UCC's aid efforts have continued for the last 18 years. Table 12-11 shows a timeline of UCC's aid and relief efforts. A detailed chronology of events is shown in Table 12-12.

The final settlement of $470 million was significantly more than the $350 million settlement accepted by U.S. attorneys representing the Indian victims in U.S. courts. Attorneys sued in American courts for more than $50 billion, but eventually accepted the final settlement. According to a Press Trust of India report, the government of India submitted proof to the Supreme Court of India that the $470 million settlement would eventually provide $3.1 billion, if invested funds yielded 10 percent interest compounded over a 20-year period. This period equaled the amount of time the Attorney General in India projected that lawsuits would take to be settled.

Table 12-11 UCC aid efforts to Bhopal, India

Year	Aid efforts
1984	Days after the December 3 event, UCC and UCIL offer about $2 million in immediate aid to the Prime Minister's Relief Fund. UCC underwrites expenses for equipment and world-recognized medical experts to go to Bhopal to assist the local medical community.
1985	In February and May, UCC sends more medical equipment to Bhopal.
	Union Carbide employees and retirees donate $120,000.
	In April, UCC agrees with a U.S. Federal judge's suggestion to contribute another $5 million in immediate aid. Also, UCC announces a $2.2 million grant for Arizona State University to establish a vocational-technical center in Bhopal.
	In June, UCC contributes funds for Indian medical experts to attend special meetings on research and treatment of victims.
1986	In January, UCC offers $10 million to fund a hospital for Bhopal victims. The Indian government declines.
	Arizona State University's vocational-technical center begins operations.
1987	In March, the Indian government closes and levels Bhopal Technical and Vocational Training Center, set up by Arizona State.
	In August, UCC offers $4.6 million in interim humanitarian relief to Bhopal victims.
1989	In February, as directed by India's Supreme Court, UCC and UCIL pay $470 million in settlement to the Indian government for Bhopal victims.
1992	In April, UCC establishes and commits about $20 million to an independent charitable trust for a Bhopal hospital, and announces plans to sell its interest in UCIL.
	A local Bhopal court orders attachment of UCC's shares in UCIL, effectively delaying the sale and funding plans for the hospital.
1994	In February, the India Supreme Court says it will allow UCC to sell its shares in UCIL so the assets can be used to build the Bhopal hospital. By December, UCC and UCIL fulfill their commitment for the Bhopal hospital, with about $20 million turned over to the charitable trust.
1995	Groundbreaking for the hospital begins in mid October.
1997	The hospital charitable trust has $100 million, including an additional $54 million from the sale of Union Carbide's shares in UC India Ltd.
1999	According to Indian press reports, the hospital is expected to open in early 2000. The building is completed, equipment is being installed, and physicians and medical staff are being selected, but they have not yet assumed their duties. The hospital has facilities planned for the treatment of eye, lung, and heart problems.

12

Source: www.bhopal.com/anr.htm (Courtesy of Union Carbide Corp.)[10]

Table 12-12   Chronology of the Bhopal disaster

Date	Occurrence
December 3, 1984	Gas leaks from a tank of MIC at a plant in Bhopal, India, owned and operated by UCIL.
December 4, 1984	As word of the disaster reaches UCC's headquarters in Danbury, Connecticut, Chairman and CEO Warren Anderson announces that he and a technical team will go to Bhopal to assist the government in dealing with the incident. Upon his arrival, Anderson is placed under house arrest, returned to the airport in Delhi, and urged to leave India within 24 hours. UCC underwrites expenses for world-recognized medical experts and medical equipment to assist the local medical community.
December 10, 1984	Anderson returns from India and holds a news conference at UCC headquarters. He describes his arrest and emphasizes that he was treated with "courtesy and consideration."
December 14, 1984	Anderson testifies before two subcommittees of the House Commerce and Energy Committee; he emphasizes safety and stresses UCC's determination "to make sure that what happened at Bhopal cannot happen again."
December 18, 1984	Remaining MIC at Bhopal plant is converted into finished product.
February 14, 1985	UCC Employees' Bhopal Relief Fund collects more than $100,000 for victims. UCC sends more medical equipment to Bhopal.
March 15, 1985	UCC establishes in-depth programs to study the effects of overexposure to MIC.
March 20, 1985	A UCC scientific team reports that a large volume of water triggered the reaction that resulted in the emission of MIC. An Indian government scientific study issued in December 1985 reaches the same conclusion.
April 18, 1985	UCC announces before U.S. District Court Judge John Keenan that it will pay an additional $5 million toward Bhopal disaster relief, bringing company contributions to more than $7 million.
April 24, 1985	Anderson, at a Danbury press briefing, reports that the government of India (GOI) rejected "out of hand" a fair and comprehensive proposal to aid the Bhopal victims. UCC also announces a $2.2 million grant for Arizona State University to establish a vocational-technical center in Bhopal.
June 1, 1985	UCC contributes funds for Indian medical experts to attend meetings on research and treatment of victims.
July 2, 1985	Additional core samples confirm UCC's finding that a large volume of water caused the reaction in the MIC tank at Bhopal.
Jan. 6, 1986	UCC and UCIL offer $10 million to build a hospital to aid the victims in Bhopal.

Date	Occurrence
March 12, 1986	UCC scientists report results of MIC studies at a National Institute of Environmental Health Sciences meeting at Research Triangle Park, N.C. Studies suggest that MIC injures respiratory tissues, which subsequently blocks air passages.
March 24, 1986	UCC says that a proposed settlement of $350 million could produce a fund of between $500 million and $600 million for Bhopal victims. The tentative agreement receives the overwhelming support of plaintiffs' U.S. attorneys.
May 12, 1986	Judge Keenan announces a decision to transfer the Bhopal litigation to India.
November 25, 1986	UCC files a brief in the U.S. Court of Appeals in Manhattan that "reaffirms our position that the proper forum for the case is in India."
January 14, 1987	U.S. Court of Appeals upholds Judge Keenan's decision to send the Bhopal case to India and states that UCIL is a separate and independent legal entity, managed and operated exclusively by Indian citizens in India.
February 4, 1987	UCC files a motion to restrain GOI and its Central Bureau of Investigation from further harassment of a key witness (S. Sunderajan).
March 11, 1987	The Indian government closes and levels Arizona State University's Bhopal Technical and Vocational Training Center.
August 17, 1987	UCC announces an offer of an additional $4.6 million in humanitarian interim relief for immediate rehabilitation of Bhopal victims.
September 14, 1987	UCC and GOI express optimism about reaching a settlement.
December 5, 1987	The Jabalpur High Court rejects charges that UCC sought to delay proceedings of Bhopal litigation, and directs parties to cooperate in early disposal of claims from the Bhopal tragedy.
December 17, 1987	UCC charges that a Bhopal District Court order to pay $270 million in interim compensation amounts to awarding damages without a trial, a practice that runs counter to the laws of India and other democracies.
January 18, 1988	UCC files an appeal in the High Court of State of Madhya Pradesh to have the interim compensation order set aside.
April 4, 1988	Judge Seth in the Madhya Pradesh High Court upholds the interim relief order and reduces the amount to $192 million. UCC says that holding the corporation liable before a trial will not serve the needs of the Bhopal victims.
May 10, 1988	Independent investigation by Arthur D. Little, Inc. shows "with virtual certainty" that the Bhopal incident was caused by a disgruntled employee who introduced a large volume of water to the tank by connecting a water hose directly to it.

12

Date	Occurrence
June 3, 1988	UCC says it will appeal to the Supreme Court of India the April 4 ruling by the State High Court.
July 26, 1988	Explaining its appeal to the Indian Supreme Court of the ruling on interim compensation, UCC says that India's use of untested legal theories made it necessary to launch the appeal. "No court that we know of in India or elsewhere in the world has previously ordered interim compensation where there is no proof of damages or where liability is strongly contested."
September 8, 1988	The Indian Supreme Court agrees to hear UCC's appeal of the order for interim compensation.
October 14, 1988	The Madhya Pradesh High Court directs that the case be taken away from Bhopal District Court Judge Deo, on grounds of bias, and given to a senior judge of the same court.
November 2, 1988	India's Supreme Court asks GOI and UCC to make an effort to reach a settlement in the case. Chief Justice R.S. Pathak tells both sides: "You can start with a clean slate."
February 14, 1989	The Supreme Court of India directs a final settlement of $470 million for all Bhopal litigation, to be paid by March 31, 1989. Both GOI and UCC accept the court's direction.
February 15, 1989	The Supreme Court of India directs that UCIL be made a party to the litigation, with UCC paying $420 million of the settlement and UCIL paying the rupee equivalent of $45 million. The $5 million payment made by UCC before Judge Keenan is credited toward the settlement.
February 24, 1989	UCC reports that it and UCIL have made full payment of the $470 million Bhopal settlement directed by the Supreme Court of India.
May 4, 1989	The Supreme Court, in a long opinion, explains the rationale for the settlement. The Court emphasizes that the compensation levels provided in the settlement are well in excess of those that would ordinarily be payable under Indian law.
December 22, 1989	The Supreme Court upholds the validity of the Bhopal Gas Leak Act, which authorized the government of India to act in behalf of the victims of the tragedy.
January 12, 1990	The new government of India announces that it will support review petitions seeking to overturn the Bhopal settlement.
January 23, 1990	Legal experts doubt that the government of India will succeed in getting more money than Union Carbide has already paid in the Bhopal settlement, according to a *Wall Street Journal* article.

Date	Occurrence
November 16, 1990	The State Government of Madhya Pradesh submits to the Supreme Court of India the completed categorization of the claims of all victims. The state determines that there were 3828 deaths, 40 victims with permanent total disabilities, 2680 people with permanent partial disabilities, 1313 people with temporary disabilities from permanent injuries, 7172 people with temporary disabilities from temporary injuries, 18,922 people with permanent injuries but no disability, 173,382 people with temporary injuries but no disability, and 155,203 people who came in for medical examination but had no injury.
December 18, 1990	Review petition hearings end before the Supreme Court.
October 3, 1991	The Supreme Court of India upholds the civil settlement of $470 million in its entirety; sets aside the portion of the settlement that quashed the criminal prosecutions that were pending at the time of the settlement; requires the GOI to purchase, out of the settlement fund, a group medical insurance policy to cover 100,000 asymptomatic people who may later develop symptoms; requires the GOI to make up any shortfall, however unlikely, in the settlement fund; gives directions concerning the administration of the settlement fund; dismisses all outstanding petitions seeking review of the settlement; and requests UCC and UCIL to voluntarily fund the capital and operating costs of a hospital in Bhopal that the Court estimates would require "around Rs. 50 crores" (approximately $17 million at the time), with the land to be provided free by the State of Madhya Pradesh.
October 16, 1991	UCC and UCIL agree to fund the hospital in Bhopal as requested by the Supreme Court.
April 15, 1992	UCC announces plans to sell its 50.9 percent interest in UCIL. UCC also establishes a charitable trust to ensure its share of the funding of a hospital in Bhopal, and operations for up to eight years.
October 4, 1993	The U.S. Supreme Court declines to review a U.S. Appeals Court ruling, which reaffirmed that victims of the Bhopal tragedy lacked legal standing to seek damages in the U.S. courts.
February 14, 1994	The Supreme Court of India says it will allow UCC to sell its shares in UCIL, so that assets can be used to build the Bhopal hospital.
September 9, 1994	UCC contracts with McLeod Russel (India) Ltd. of Calcutta for sale of its 50.9 percent interest in UCIL.
November 23, 1994	UCC announces completion of the sale of its 50.9 percent interest in UCIL to McLeod Russel.
December 1994	UCC fulfills its commitment for the Bhopal hospital, with about $20 million turned over to the charitable trust.
October 16, 1995	Groundbreaking for the hospital begins.

12

Date	Occurrence
January 16, 1997	The hospital charitable trust has $100 million, including an additional $54 million from the sale of Union Carbide's shares in UCIL.
November 1999	According to Indian press reports, the hospital is expected to open in 2000 (see Table 12-11).
August 28, 2000	Judge Keenan dismisses a lawsuit brought in federal court in Manhattan, which sought to reopen the Bhopal litigation, on the grounds that plaintiffs lacked standing to sue and the claims for compensation have been settled. He finds that UCC has fully complied with his earlier decision and the orders of the Supreme Court of India.
2001	The Bhopal Memorial Hospital and Research Centre, set up with the proceeds from Union Carbide's sale of its shares in Union Carbide India Ltd., begins treating patients.
February 6, 2001	Union Carbide merges with a subsidiary of The Dow Chemical Company and becomes a wholly-owned subsidiary. Following the merger transaction, Dow owns all the shares of stock of Union Carbide, which remains a separate legal entity.
August 6, 2001	The Indian Attorney General, Soli Sorabjee, issues his opinion that "proceedings in the United States for extradition of Mr. Warren Anderson are not likely to succeed and therefore, the same may not be pursued."
November 15, 2001	The 2nd Circuit Court of Appeals affirms Judge Keenan's dismissal of the lawsuit, with one exception. The Court's opinion remands the case to Judge Keenan for further explanation regarding his dismissal of the "environmental claims," which are based on plaintiffs' allegations of contamination that occurred after the accident.
May 24, 2002	The Central Bureau of Investigation (CBI) in India asks that charges against Anderson be reduced from culpable homicide to a negligent act.
August 28, 2002	A Bhopal court rejects the application made by the CBI, and directs the CBI to pursue the extradition of Anderson.

Source: www.bhopal.com/chrono.htm (Courtesy of Union Carbide Corp.)[11]

Organizations need to realistically prepare for the possibility that some events might have a residual impact of several years, and perhaps even decades. The Bhopal event and subsequent actions on the part of numerous organizations clearly show that a disaster is not over after the cleanup. As this textbook was being written, residual activity from the Bhopal event had entered its eighteenth year, and it could continue for several more years.

After the bombing of the Oklahoma City federal office building, cleanup took several years; the bombing's total impact on Oklahoma City will probably never be mitigated fully. Residual activity from the World Trade Center attacks of 2001 will also last for several years.

CHAPTER SUMMARY

- The dynamics of human behavior during disasters are almost impossible to predict. Organizations face fluctuating emotions of employees, as well as those of communities, social environments, and political arenas in which the organization exists. The breadth of a disaster's impact usually becomes apparent only through personal experience or the news coverage an event receives.

- When things go wrong, there is often a domino effect. The complexities of relationships between organizations, the integration of computer and manufacturing systems, and the overload of emergency response systems intersect during a disaster. This can easily result in unforeseen consequences that compound damages.

- Some people say that life is the best teacher. Therefore, organizations need to make sure they evaluate their experiences after surviving a disaster. The post-event debriefing process is designed to bring together as many perspectives as possible and capture the lessons people learned during the disaster. This process needs to take place with several groups over a period of time.

- A post-event evaluation is a structured process used after a disaster to determine what should be changed in the disaster recovery plan and procedures. The disaster recovery team uses several sources of data and information to conduct the evaluation. The basic rule of compiling this data is to use as many sources as possible, and to evaluate circumstances from all perspectives.

- Once the evaluation report is complete, the disaster recovery planning team should review the report, make necessary changes in the recovery plan, and modify specific procedures as needed. All plan revisions and procedure modifications should pass through the full review process, just as they did during development. The planning team and independent reviewers need to check and approve the procedures before placing the final versions in the recovery plan.

- The residual effects of disasters can last for several years. One of the more dramatic examples of events with such effects occurred on December 3, 1984, when gas leaked from a tank of methyl isocyanate at a plant in Bhopal, India, owned and operated by Union Carbide India Limited. The Madhya Pradesh state government of India reported that approximately 3800 people died and 2680 people suffered permanent partial disabilities.

12

KEY TERMS

post-event debriefing process — A process designed to bring together as many perspectives as possible and capture the lessons that all people learned during a disaster.

post-event evaluation — A structured evaluation process used after a disaster to determine what should be changed in the disaster recovery plan and procedures.

silent observer — A person who monitors activities and makes notes about disaster response. The observer should monitor all activities, including what went wrong and what went smoothly. The monitoring reports are used in the post-event evaluation.

Review Questions

1. Describe the positive and negative social dynamics that can result from experiences of employees during a disaster.

2. Describe the positive and negative social dynamics that can result from experiences of employees' families during a disaster.

3. Describe the positive and negative social dynamics that can result from experiences of members of local communities during a disaster.

4. Describe the positive and negative social dynamics that elected officials can create during a disaster.

5. Describe the positive and negative social dynamics that special interest groups can create during a disaster.

6. Describe the positive and negative social dynamics that business partners can create during a disaster.

7. Describe the positive and negative social dynamics that suppliers can create during a disaster.

8. Describe the positive and negative social dynamics that customers can create during a disaster.

9. Explain the role of the silent observer during a disaster.

10. What is the purpose of the post-event debriefing process?

11. Describe and explain the purpose of the post-event evaluation process.

12. What should be evaluated during a post-event evaluation?

13. Which groups of people should be debriefed during the post-event evaluation process?

14. What topics should be covered in a general post-event debriefing session?

15. What topics should be covered in a specialized post-event debriefing session?

16. What sources of data and information should be used to conduct post-event evaluations?

17. What elements should be included in a post-event evaluation report?

18. Who should review a draft of the post-event evaluation report?

19. How should an organization handle revisions of the disaster recovery plan and procedures after the post-event evaluation process?

20. After updating training materials to reflect changes in the disaster recovery plan and procedures as a result of the post–event evaluation, what should the training staff do?

HANDS-ON PROJECTS

In the following projects, you will continue to assist the organization for which you developed a disaster recovery plan. Because this section contains a large number of projects, your instructor might want to assign only a subset of these projects, rather than all of them. When you finish, submit your work to the instructor for review.

Project 12-1

Develop three methods to neutralize negative dynamics on the part of employees during a disaster. Write a one-page overview of each method.

Project 12-2

Develop three methods to neutralize negative dynamics on the part of employees' families during a disaster. Write a one-page overview of each method.

Project 12-3

Develop three methods to neutralize negative dynamics on the part of members of local communities during a disaster. Write a one-page overview of each method.

Project 12-4

Develop three methods to neutralize negative dynamics on the part of elected officials during a disaster. Write a one-page overview of each method.

Project 12-5

Develop three methods to neutralize negative dynamics on the part of special interest groups during a disaster. Write a one-page overview of each method.

Project 12-6

Develop three methods to neutralize negative dynamics on the part of suppliers during a disaster. Write a one-page overview of each method.

Project 12-7

Develop three methods to neutralize negative dynamics on the part of business partners during a disaster. Write a one-page overview of each method.

Project 12-8

Develop three methods to neutralize negative dynamics on the part of customers during a disaster. Write a one-page overview of each method.

Project 12-9

Develop an outline for a general post-event debriefing session in the organization for which you developed a disaster recovery plan. When you finish, submit your work to the instructor for review.

Project 12-10

Develop an outline for a specialized post-event debriefing session of the security team in the organization for which you developed a disaster recovery plan.

Project 12-11

Develop an outline for a specialized post-event debriefing session of the organization's rescue team.

Project 12-12

Develop an outline for a specialized post-event debriefing session of the organization's insurance and damage assessment team.

Project 12-13

Develop an outline for a specialized post-event debriefing session of the organization's business continuation team.

Project 12-14

Develop an outline for a specialized post-event debriefing session of the organization's restoration team.

Project 12-15

Develop an outline for a specialized post-event debriefing session of members of emergency service organizations and contract disaster recovery firms that would respond in a disaster.

CASE PROJECTS

Case Project: Harris and Heartfield Manufacturing

Harris and Heartfield Manufacturing is a family-owned business that fabricates specialized metal parts for its North American clients. Most of its revenue comes from defense contracts and from producing parts for heavy-equipment manufacturers. The company has an excellent reputation for quality and prompt deliveries.

The company has 200 employees at its only location in California. All 20 administrative employees have desktop PCs connected to the company's LAN. The 15 research and design engineers use Sun workstations that are also on the LAN. Three servers support administrative functions and six servers support design and manufacturing. About half the machining equipment on the shop floor is computerized.

Management is concerned about the company's future competitiveness, and about its ability to fulfill orders if a disaster hindered its operations. The board of directors is relatively business-savvy, but does not invest money unless it yields a positive return. As a result, the company hired you as a consultant to create a list of 10 key points that conveyed the importance of disaster recovery planning to the board. You also prepared 10 points for managers to discuss with employees about organizing and preparing to develop a plan.

You worked with company managers to analyze business process threats to product manufacturing, developed a list of questions about insurance coverage, and advised the company how to develop a disaster response team. You also developed a list of organizations with which the company should work in a disaster, developed guidelines for reporting computer hacking incidents to law enforcement agencies, created a questionnaire to help determine whether recovery procedures were needed for special circumstances, and outlined awareness campaigns for employees, customers, and business partners. You developed a list of possible scenarios to test the company's disaster recovery plan and procedures, and you developed a briefing session for company managers to discuss how they should enter the maintenance mode for their disaster recovery plan.

Your assignment now is to develop a checklist of everything Harris and Heartfield should do after a disaster.

12

Optional Team Case Projects

Team Case One

Your boss has asked you to determine if any organizations in your area can assist in conducting a post-disaster evaluation. Your assignment is to research and identify these organizations. Write a one-page summary of each organization, what assistance it can provide, the appropriate contact people in each organization, and how and where you obtained the information.

Team Case Two

Your boss has asked you to determine if any organizations in your area can assist in mitigating or reducing negative human dynamics during a disaster. Your assignment is to research and identify these organizations. Write a one-page summary of each organization, what assistance it can provide, the appropriate contact people in each organization, and how and where you obtained the information.

Endnotes

1. *www.munichre.com.*

2. EM-DAT: The OFDA/CRED International Disaster Database, Universit catholique de Louvain, Brussels, Belgium.

3. Death Toll from Taiwan Earthquake Tops 2,000 — Thousands Still Trapped, October 22, 1999, Doug Rekenthaler Jr., Managing Editor, *www.disasterrelief.org* (Courtesy of the American Red Cross).

4. Hurricane Mitch Death Toll Nears 9,000; Volcano Poses Added Threat in Nicaragua, November 5, 1998, Doug Rekenthaler, Managing Editor, *www.disasterrelief.org* (Courtesy of the American Red Cross).

5. China Floods Worsen, Wreaking Havoc on Nation's Health, Bottom Line, August 14, 1998, *www.disasterrelief.org* (Courtesy of the American Red Cross).

6. Death Toll Surpasses 700 in Nigerian and Colombian Pipeline Explosions, October 21, 1998, Doug Rekenthaler, Managing Editor, *www.disasterrelief.org* (Courtesy of the American Red Cross).

7. Employers should plan for workers' safety, iCan News Service, October 3, 2001. *www.ican.com/news/fullpage.cfm?articleid=4E2614ED-227E-4F75-AEE7B5EC2323E86D&cx=news.special_reports.*

8. The Access Board Web site (*www.access-board.gov*), which helps protect the safety of people with handicaps and disabilities.

9. *www.bhopal.com/review.htm* (Courtesy of Union Carbide Corp.).

10. *www.bhopal.com/anr.htm* (Courtesy of Union Carbide Corp.).

11. *www.bhopal.com/chrono.htm* (Courtesy of Union Carbide Corp.).

12

A

DISASTER RECOVERY SURVEY RESULTS

The survey for this book was conducted during November 2002. Disaster recovery professionals, information technology professionals, and managers from a wide variety of organizations were invited to complete the survey. During four weeks of data collection, 255 people responded to the survey. The backgrounds of these respondents are shown in the following tables:

- Table A-1 shows the job titles of the respondents.

- Table A-2 shows the industry sectors of the organizations in which the respondents are employed.

- Table A-3 shows the number of employees and networked computers for the organizations that had representatives respond to the survey.

- Table A-4 shows the annual budget for disaster recovery planning efforts.

The remaining tables in this appendix show the respondents' answers to the survey questions. For ease of interpretation by students, data was reported in terms of every 10 respondents.

Table A-1   Job titles of survey respondents

Job title	Percentage of respondents
CEO	2.7%
COO	0.0%
CFO	0.0%
CIO	7.1%
CSO	4.3%
Disaster recovery/planning director	3.5%
Disaster recovery/planning staff	4.3%
MIS director	7.5%
IT security director	8.6%
IT security staff	17.3%
IT staff	12.5%
Corporate security director	2.7%
Corporate security staff	2.7%
Department manager	7.5%
Department staff	1.2%
Other	18.0%

Table A-2   Industry sectors of survey respondents organizations

Industry sector	Percentage of organizations
Banking/finance	10.2%
Education	5.5%
Government	16.9%
Insurance	5.9%
Manufacturing	13.3%
Military	1.6%
Professional services	16.9%
Retail/wholesale distribution	3.5%
Trade services	1.6%
Transportation	2.4%
Utilities	3.5%
Other	18.8%

Table A-3 Number of employees and networked computers per organization

	Number of employees	Number of users on network[1]
10th percentile	20	35
25th percentile	150	150
Median	1,400	1,600
75th percentile	9,000	10,000
90th percentile	36,000	42,000

1. Includes nonemployees.

Table A-4 Annual budget for disaster recovery planning efforts

Under $100,000	24.02%
$100,001 to $500,000	6.69%
$500,001 to $1,000,000	2.36%
$1,000,001 to $3,000,000	2.36%
$3,000,001 to $5,000,000	0.79%
Over $5,000,000	0.79%
Not applicable	14.17%
Cannot reveal this information	19.69%
Respondent did not know	29.13%

Table A-5 Does your organization have a disaster recovery plan in place?

Organizations that do not have a plan in place	
Organizations with plans in development	
Organizations that have had plans in place for less than one year	
Organizations that have had plans in place for two to five years	
Organizations that have had plans in place for six to 10 years	
Organizations that have had plans in place for more than 10 years	

A

Table A-6 Has your organization increased its spending for disaster recovery planning since September 2001?

Organizations that say their spending for disaster recovery planning has stayed the same	
Organizations that say their spending for disaster recovery planning has increased slightly	
Organizations that report spending dramatically more for disaster recovery planning	
Organizations that report spending dramatically less for disaster recovery planning	
Organizations that would not answer this question	

Table A-7 Does your organization have a centralized office of disaster recovery planning?

Have established some type of centralized disaster recovery planning	
Do not have centralized disaster recovery planning	

Table A-8 Does your organization have a disaster recovery planning director or coordinator?

Coordinator does not work full-time on disaster recovery planning	
Coordinator works full-time on disaster recovery planning	
Organizations that do not have a disaster recovery planning coordinator	
Organizations with more than one full-time position for disaster recovery planning	

Table A-9 How many people work in the disaster recovery function in your organization?

Organizations that have only one person assigned to disaster recovery planning	
Organizations with more than one person assigned to disaster recovery planning	
Organizations with no staff assigned to disaster recovery planning	

Table A-10 Does your organization test or rehearse parts or all of your disaster recovery plan on a regular basis?

Surveyed organizations that do not test or rehearse disaster recovery plans	
Surveyed organizations that only test or rehearse parts of their plan	
Surveyed organizations that rehearse their entire plan	
Not applicable	

Table A-11 Do you think that tests or rehearsals are beneficial to your organization?

Managers who said "Yes"	
Managers who said "No"	

Table A-12 Has your organization ever been through a disaster?

Surveyed organizations that have suffered disasters	
Surveyed organizations that have not suffered disasters	

A

Table A-13 If your organization has been through a disaster, how well did the disaster recovery plan work?

The plan was not in place at the time of the disaster	
Respondents who said the plan worked fairly well	
Respondents who said the plan worked extremely well	
Not applicable	

Table A-14 How many people in your organization receive disaster recovery training?

Respondents who said no one in their organization receives disaster recovery training	👤 👤 👤 👤 👤 👤 👤 👤 👤 👤
Respondents who said only managers in their organization receive disaster recovery training	👤 👤 👤 👤 👤 👤 👤 👤 👤 👤
Respondents who said some departments in their organization receive disaster recovery training	👤 👤 👤 👤 👤 👤 👤 👤 👤 👤
Not applicable	👤 👤 👤 👤 👤 👤 👤 👤 👤 👤

Table A-15 Do you think enough people in your organization receive disaster recovery training?

Managers who think enough people in their organization receive disaster recovery training	👤 👤 👤 👤 👤 👤 👤 👤 👤 👤
Managers who do not think enough employees receive disaster recovery training	👤 👤 👤 👤 👤 👤 👤 👤 👤 👤
Managers who were undecided on the question	👤 👤 👤 👤 👤 👤 👤 👤 👤 👤
Not applicable	👤 👤 👤 👤 👤 👤 👤 👤 👤 👤

Table A-16 What does your organization perceive as the most severe type of disaster that could affect operations?

The worst disaster would affect national infrastructure	👤 👤 👤 👤 👤 👤 👤 👤 👤 👤
The worst disaster would involve fire	👤 👤 👤 👤 👤 👤 👤 👤 👤 👤
The worst disaster would involve outages of IT services and loss of customer data	👤 👤 👤 👤 👤 👤 👤 👤 👤 👤
The worst disaster would be regional, including earthquakes, floods, and windstorms	👤 👤 👤 👤 👤 👤 👤 👤 👤 👤
The worst disaster would destroy buildings and facilities	👤 👤 👤 👤 👤 👤 👤 👤 👤 👤

Table A-17 Does your organization have business continuity insurance?

Surveyed organizations that reported having business continuity coverage	
Surveyed organizations that did not have business continuity coverage	
Respondents who were not sure whether their organization had business continuity insurance	
Respondents who said they could not reveal such information	

Table A-18 If your organization has business continuity insurance, do you think the insurance is adequate to cover potential losses?

Respondents who believed their company's insurance would cover potential losses	

Table A-19 If your organization has business continuity insurance, does the insurance company require minimum standards in disaster recovery planning?

Respondents who said the insurance company requires minimum standards for disaster recovery planning	
Respondents who said the insurance company does not require minimum standards for disaster recovery planning	
Respondents who did not know this information	
Respondents who said they could not reveal this information	
Not applicable	

Table A-20 How often does your organization update its disaster recovery plan?

Organizations that update their disaster recovery plans quarterly	
Organizations that update their plans annually	
Organizations that update their plans as needed	
Not applicable, or respondent was unsure of the update schedule	

Table A-21 Do you think upper management in your organization takes disaster recovery planning seriously enough?

Upper-level managers do not take disaster recovery planning seriously enough	
Upper-level managers take disaster recovery planning seriously enough	

Table A-22 Do you think that employees in your organization take disaster recovery planning seriously enough?

Surveyed managers who think employees do not take disaster recovery planning seriously enough	
Surveyed managers who think employees take disaster recovery planning seriously enough	

Table A-23 Do you think that disaster recovery procedures in your organization are adequately documented?

Managers who think disaster recovery procedures in their organization are not adequately documented	
Managers who think disaster recovery procedures in their organization are adequately documented	
Managers who are undecided on the question	

Table A-24 Do you think that disaster recovery procedures in your organization are easy to read and understandable by the employees responsible for implementing the procedures?

Respondents who answered "Yes"	
Respondents who answered "No"	
Respondents who were undecided	
Not applicable	

Table A-25 Has your organization used the services of a disaster recovery planning consultant in the last year?

| Surveyed organizations that have hired an outside disaster recovery planning consultant | |
| Surveyed organizations that have not hired an outside disaster recovery planning consultant | |

A

B

SELECTED DISASTER RESOURCES ON THE WORLD WIDE WEB

- CBS News disaster links — *www.cbsnews.com/digitaldan/disaster/disasters.shtml*

- Disaster News Network — *www.disasternews.net*

- Disaster Relief — *www.disasterrelief.org*

- Emergency Preparedness Information Exchange — *http://epix.hazard.net/internet_sites.html*

- Federal Emergency Management Agency (FEMA) — *www.fema.gov*

- FireNET — *www.fire-net.org*

- Homeland Security — *www.whitehouse.gov/homeland*

- Incident.com — *www.incident.com*

- Munich Re Group — *www.munichre.com*

- National Earthquake Information Center, World Data Center for Seismology, Denver, CO — *www.neic.cr.usgs.gov*

- Office of Response and Restoration, National Ocean Service, National Oceanic and Atmospheric Administration — *http://response.restoration.noaa.gov*

- Relief Web — *www.reliefweb.int/w/rwb.nsf*

- The American Red Cross — *www.redcross.org*

- The Centre for Research on the Epidemiology of Disasters (CRED) — *www.cred.be*

- The Disaster Center — *www.disastercenter.com*

- U.S. Environmental Protection Agency (EPA) — *www.epa.gov*

- U.S. Fire Administration — *www.usfa.fema.gov*

Index